Luke

INTERPRETATION
A Bible Commentary for Teaching and Preaching

INTERPRETATION
A BIBLE COMMENTARY FOR TEACHING AND PREACHING

James Luther Mays, *Editor*
Patrick D. Miller, Jr., *Old Testament Editor*
Paul J. Achtemeier, *New Testament Editor*

FRED B. CRADDOCK

Luke

INTERPRETATION

*A Bible Commentary
for Teaching and Preaching*

John Knox Press
LOUISVILLE

Library of Congress Cataloging-in-Publication Data

Craddock, Fred B.
　　Luke / Fred B. Craddock.
　　　　p.　　cm. — (Interpretation, a Bible commentary for teaching and preaching)
　　ISBN 0-8042-3123-0

　　1. Bible. N.T. Luke—Commentaries. 2. Bible. N.T. Luke—Homiletical use. I. Title. II. Series.
BS2595.3.C73 1990
226.4'07—dc20　　　　　　　　　　　　　　　　　　90-32985
　　　　　　　　　　　　　　　　　　　　　　　　　　　　CIP

© copyright John Knox Press 1990
10　9　8　7　6　5　4　3　2　1
Printed in the United States of America
John Knox Press
Louisville, Kentucky 40202-1396

SERIES PREFACE

This series of commentaries offers an interpretation of the books of the Bible. It is designed to meet the need of students, teachers, ministers, and priests for a contemporary expository commentary. These volumes will not replace the historical critical commentary or homiletical aids to preaching. The purpose of this series is rather to provide a third kind of resource, a commentary which presents the integrated result of historical and theological work with the biblical text.

An interpretation in the full sense of the term involves a text, an interpreter, and someone for whom the interpretation is made. Here, the text is what stands written in the Bible in its full identity as literature from the time of "the prophets and apostles," the literature which is read to inform, inspire, and guide the life of faith. The interpreters are scholars who seek to create an interpretation which is both faithful to the text and useful to the church. The series is written for those who teach, preach, and study the Bible in the community of faith.

The comment generally takes the form of expository essays. It is planned and written in the light of the needs and questions which arise in the use of the Bible as Holy Scripture. The insights and results of contemporary scholarly research are used for the sake of the exposition. The commentators write as exegetes and theologians. The task which they undertake is both to deal with what the texts say and to discern their meaning for faith and life. The exposition is the unified work of one interpreter.

The text on which the comment is based is the Revised Standard Version of the Bible and, since its appearance, the New Revised Standard Version. The general availability of these translations makes the printing of a text in the commentary unnecessary. The commentators have also had other current versions in view as they worked and refer to their readings where it is helpful. The text is divided into sections appropriate to the particular book; comment deals with passages as a whole, rather than proceeding word by word, or verse by verse.

Writers have planned their volumes in light of the requirements set by the exposition of the book assigned to them. Biblical books differ in character, content, and arrangement. They also differ in the way they have been and are used in the liturgy, thought, and devotion of the church. The distinctiveness and use of particular books have been taken into account in decisions about the approach, emphasis, and use of space in the commentaries. The goal has been to allow writers to develop the format which provides for the best presentation of their interpretation.

The result, writers and editors hope, is a commentary which both explains and applies, an interpretation which deals with both the meaning and the significance of biblical texts. Each commentary reflects, of course, the writer's own approach and perception of the church and world. It could and should not be otherwise. Every interpretation of any kind is individual in that sense; it is one reading of the text. But all who work at the interpretation of Scripture in the church need the help and stimulation of a colleague's reading and understanding of the text. If these volumes serve and encourage interpretation in that way, their preparation and publication will realize their purpose.

The Editors

PREFACE

In preparing this volume I have tried to keep before me those persons whose ministry it is to preach and to teach in the churches. That attempt has been filled with delight, calling up the names and faces of so many ministers I have come to know through the years, not to mention my own present and former students. But the effort has also been filled with difficulty. The phrase "for those who preach and teach" covers a multitude of needs, abilities, and expectations. To write for one is not to write for all, and to write for all is not to write for one. The task, then, was to steer a course that lay somewhere between disappointment and insult: disappointment if the comments did not struggle with the text with its frequent complexities, and insult if the comments rushed too soon and too easily to pulpit and lectern, spaces belonging to the reader, not to the writer. In an article in the October 1982 issue of the journal *Interpretation*, I classified resources for preaching according to days of the week, Monday being farthest from the pulpit, Saturday being closest. The technically and critically heavy books and articles are called Monday books; those less so, Tuesday books. Wednesday books refer to those which are biblically and theologically substantive but which have preachers in mind. Thursday books make suggestions about how to preach their contents, Friday books contain sermon outlines, and Saturday books are collections of full sermons. I have attempted to make this a Wednesday book, gathering up a great deal of research and study and offering it in the direction of pulpit and lectern.

It has been rewarding to walk again through Luke's Gospel, this time talking about what I have seen and heard with persons taking the same walk. That reward will be multiplied if now and then someone reports that the volume has been helpful.

I wish now to thank publicly those whose contributions to this book have been essential to its completion: Nettie, my wife, who has provided the support, seclusion, and comfort necessary for writing; Jim Waits, Dean of Candler School of Theology, who granted me leave from teaching duties; Janet Gary, my secretary, who again has converted my scribblings into copy acceptable to an editor; and Russell Faulk, proofreader, who placed her corrections gently on my pride. But for all their efforts, for which I am most grateful, I must insist on claiming the faults for myself.

F. B. C.

CONTENTS

Introduction

Until fairly recent times it has been customary for commentaries to offer at the outset discussions of such matters as authorship, date, destination, provenance, purpose, and distinctive features of the work being investigated. Many of the comments were speculative, of course, but they were based on such information as the biblical text itself provided, along with any supportive evidence from writings of the period, presented in conversation with other scholars on the subject. Many commentaries continue the practice, but some others, and quite good ones at that, no longer do so. Commentaries that have dropped these traditional introductions have explained that such opening comments are not introductory at all but rather are conclusive, informing the reader what is to be discovered in the text. Were these matters to be reserved to a closing summary, they have argued, the reader of the text would be more respected as a colleague, searching his or her own conclusions, thus able to enter more informedly into conversation with the commentator. Others have abandoned the practice in the conviction that such introductions actually offered little help in understanding the text. In fact, many users of commentaries have acknowledged that they never read the introductory section. They move directly to the comments on the particular passage with which they are seeking help. Even so, it must be admitted that an introduction, suggestive rather than conclusive, and not too extended, can be very helpful as an overview, enabling the student of the biblical text to have some sense of the forest before the tree-by-tree analysis.

Fortunately, in the case of the Third Gospel those on all sides of the question of introduction can feel some satisfaction. An introduction is provided, but not one contrived by the commentator. Rather, it is Luke himself who prefaces his Gospel

1

with a brief statement touching upon matters that he regards as important to know before one reads his narrative. This preface (1:1–4), unique among New Testament writings, will serve as our introduction to Luke's Gospel.

What the reader needs to know at this point, then, has to do only with this commentary, its perspective, scope, and format.

Perspective: Luke as a Preacher

It is not uncommon for preachers and teachers to approach the Scriptures as though they were a mass of raw material, or in a more homely analogy, as a large lump of dough from which suitable portions are to be taken and shaped into sermons and lessons. The overlooked fact is that the texts have already been shaped, by the writer, by the tradition to which the writer is heir, or by the uses of the material in the believing community. The text comes to us as songs, parables, proverbs, farewell speeches, proclamations, catechisms, conversations, and so forth. The writer has put the materials together in such a way as to make it appropriate to ask not only what the author is saying but also what the author is doing. What is being done for, with, and to those who are reading or hearing the text? What response is desired? In other words, the writer is a communicator with purpose. The perspective of this commentary will be to observe Luke at work as well as to listen to his message, to note how he selects, arranges, and presents the parts of the narrative as well as to be attentive to what he is saying. All this is to say that Luke will be viewed as a preacher seeking to reach his reader/listener.

Treating Luke as a preacher does not mean that other perspectives will be disregarded. For example, Luke is often examined as a historian, and some very significant studies placing Luke among other ancient historiographers have been produced (see Selected Bibliography). There is no question but that Luke casts a historian's eye on his material, which is evident not only in the broad structures of his narrative about Jesus and the emerging church but also in the many references to the larger context in which the story unfolds. "A decree went out from Caesar Augustus" (2:1); "This was the first enrollment, when Quirinius was governor of Syria" (2:2); "In the fifteenth year of the reign of Tiberius Caesar" (3:1); "Jesus, when he began his ministry, was about thirty years of age" (3:23); "And when he

2

[Pilate] learned that he belonged to Herod's jurisdiction" (23:7); "Judas the Galilean arose in the days of the census and drew away some of the people" (Acts 5:37); "Now Herod was angry with the people of Tyre and Sidon" (Acts 12:20); "But when Gallio was proconsul of Achaia" (Acts 18:12); "Claudius Lysias to his Excellency the governor Felix, greeting" (Acts 23:26): these and numerous other references to time, place, and principal characters are historical in nature and invite the historian's critical evaluation.

However, isolating historical references and pursuing their reliability, or entering into the debate as to the value of Luke-Acts for the reconstruction of early Christian history, is not a primary interest here. Of course, attention will be given to these texts in the course of the commentary but from the perspective of Luke's primary task of proclamation of the gospel. After all, the preacher is, or should be, to some extent a historian, observant of the course of events that has provided the social, economic, and political as well as religious contexts in which and to which the message is presented.

Neither is it the case that the perspective on Luke as preacher precludes consideration of Luke as theologian, a subject of great interest, spawned to a large extent by the publication of Hans Conzelmann's *The Theology of St. Luke* over thirty-five years ago. Of course, Luke is a theologian, as is every preacher; otherwise, what is being said from the pulpit? And as is true of every preacher to whom one is exposed extensively, Luke's proclamation will reveal major themes of his theology: the relation of church to synagogue, of Jesus to the church, and of the church to the larger world; the role of the Holy Spirit in the life of Jesus and of the church; the definition of the gospel; the economic and political implications of the gospel; the authority of Scripture; the identity of Jesus; the meaning of discipleship; and expectations of the end time, to name but a few. However, no effort will be made to distill these themes from the narrative and offer Luke's theology to the reader. Rather, Luke's theology will be treated as Luke offers it, that is, woven into the fabric of his narrative.

What, then, does it mean to explore this Gospel from the perspective of Luke as a preacher? Answers arrive when one reflects on how the work of any preacher becomes a focus for sustained and careful attention. First, it means listening to what is being said, that is, attending to the text of the Gospel as it

3

comes to us. This, of course, is no novel idea, but recall how many studies of Luke, or some other volume, use the text either as a window or as a mirror, to use Murray Krieger's popular phrase (*A Window to Criticism,* pp. 3–4). Using the text as a window means looking through it and behind it, perhaps in search of information, "the facts," about the historical Jesus or the early church. As a mirror, the text functions to effect a better or at least a different understanding of ourselves and our situation before God and in the world. Neither enterprise is unimportant, but they are not the first duty of the reader of Luke.

Second, regarding Luke as a preacher means discerning the form in which the message is cast and reflecting on the significance of that form for understanding what the preacher is doing and saying. Luke's form is a Gospel. "Gospel" can be a word referring to particular content, "the good news," as in Mark's statement, "Jesus came into Galilee, preaching the gospel of God" (Mark 1:14). In fact, some have argued that no writing, whatever the form, qualifies as a Gospel unless it offers a Christ both divine and human. The content of Luke will be unfolded as we move through the Gospel; our present interest is in its form.

Obviously, Luke chose not to present his message in the form of an epistle, as Paul and most other New Testament writers did. An epistle is communication that addresses a person or group directly, often on the pattern of problem/solution. An issue is raised and addressed, in the process of which some reference may be made to a word or an act of Jesus. If certain persons in one of Paul's churches vault themselves into leadership, and impose their authority on the group, Paul speaks directly to that church on that issue. Not so, if one writes in the form of a Gospel. A Gospel is narrative, which means it is indirect communication. In response to the problem just mentioned, a Gospel writer might speak to the church by relating an occasion on which Jesus instructed his disciples about greatness by bringing among them a little child. The listeners to the story make the connection to their own problem. Or is the church resisting open acceptance of persons ethnically different? An epistle writer would move directly to the problem, using logic, tradition, Scripture, and personal appeal. A Gospel writer might recall Jesus' story of the Samaritan who acted as a neighbor. Responding indirectly in this way is usually no less effective than a confrontational style. In fact, the church that lives in and with the Gospels testifies to a sense of being directly addressed by Jesus, so appropriate and forceful are the accounts of what he did and said.

These comments clearly do not engage the ongoing debate as to the literary genre of a Gospel. Is it patterned after ancient biographies of heroic figures? Is it more often the model of historical narrative as one finds in the Old Testament stories of Moses, Samuel, or David? Has the parable, so often on the lips of Jesus, been taken by the Gospel writer as a form for presenting the whole story? Or is it more likely the case that Gospel is a type of literature original with the early church? Was it created because it was congenial to the desire to preserve a number of units of the tradition about Jesus, units that differ from one another as maxims, proverbs, pronouncements, parables, and historical narrations differ from one another but that, taken together, deal "with all that Jesus began to do and teach" (Acts 1:1)? The position one takes in this debate may or may not sharpen the ear to hear more clearly Luke the preacher. What is certain is that the Third Gospel presents to us a writer who has chosen to present his account of Jesus in a form of narrative that we term a Gospel. And we can assume that whatever the nature of Luke's sources, written and oral (1:1–2), the selection, arrangement, and shaping of that material was done so as to satisfy two obligations felt by every preacher: to be true to one's own convictions about an understanding of Jesus, and to be responsive to the needs of the listeners in their circumstances. Throughout the commentary we will be attentive to form; that is, how does Luke communicate?

Consideration of form brings us to a third factor in regarding Luke as a preacher: his craft. Overall, "Form in literature is an arousing and fulfillment of desires. A work has form in so far as one part of it leads a reader to anticipate another part, to be gratified by the sequence" (Kenneth Burke, *Counter-Statement*, p. 124). But how is this achieved by a writer or a speaker? As a whole, the Gospel presents to the reader characters, plot, dramatic action, concrete images, sensory signals, and movement to an ending. But what strategies of communication are built into the parts so as to achieve what is intended? Let us not deceive ourselves here; the material before us is not a Thomas Hardy novel but a Gospel which is not literature in the sense of simply providing an aesthetic experience. Even so, it

5

cannot be denied that Luke or any preacher must gain and hold interest; otherwise, even urgent announcements of matters that have eternal significance will fall unheard to the ground.

That Luke was a literary artist has been recognized since Jerome, who referred to him as the most skilled writer among the Evangelists. To be sure, some New Testament scholars have repeated the general opinion that the early Christians were from the lower classes of society totally innocent of any literary culture. Albert Schweitzer agreed with this opinion but regarded it positively, the writers' lack of skill contributing somehow to the vividness and genuineness of the Gospels. "Jesus stands much more immediately before us, because He was depicted by simple Christians without literary gift" (*The Quest of the Historical Jesus,* p. 6). However, no reader of Luke can miss the artistry of the parable of the father who had two sons (15: 11–32) or of the story of Jesus' appearance to two downcast disciples on the road to Emmaus (24:13–35). And the students of Luke will observe that when Luke and Mark tell the same story, Luke removes redundancies, smoothes awkward lines, broadens the range of verbs to reduce monotony, and rounds off stories that in Mark seem unfinished. We will therefore be giving attention to Luke's communicative strategies throughout the commentary.

Here it might be helpful simply to point to several proven vehicles used by communicators, ancient and modern. We alert the reader in this way so that perhaps some who go to Luke solely for a text to be preached or taught will remain in the Gospel long enough to hear him preach. In both the Gospel and Acts (see below on the relationship between the two), Luke uses several patterns that appear in other literature with such frequency as to indicate their popularity. Among these are travelogues (many chapters of the Gospel are devoted to Jesus' journey to Jerusalem, as is also true of Paul in Acts), trials and courtroom scenes (frequent in Acts), farewell speeches (by Jesus, Stephen, Paul), wonder stories (miracles, appearances by angels, and revelations are common in the ministries both of Jesus and of the early church), and stories within the story (the rich man and Lazarus, the Pharisee and the publican, the persistent widow, the friend at midnight, the dishonest steward, the father with two sons, to name a few found in Luke alone).

In addition to these larger patterns, Luke shows great skill in the use of contrasts, which not only permits him to look at both sides of truth but, as all communicators know, also keeps the audience alert and engaged. Examples are numerous: an old woman and a young girl meet to talk of the destinies of their yet to be born sons (ch. 1), angels and shepherds (ch. 2), blessings and woes (ch. 6), Jesus with the prostitute and Jesus with faithful women (chs. 7; 8), Pharisees reject Jesus and Pharisees befriend Jesus (ch. 13), God hears the prayers of saints and God hears the prayer of a sinner (ch. 18). Luke also knows the power of repetition and the recurring theme. For example, concern for the poor and marginalized extends from Mary's song (ch. 1) through Acts. Repentance and forgiveness of sin is at the center of the sermons of both Jesus and the church. Or again, that unacceptable behavior stems from people "not knowing what they are doing" is expressed by Jesus in his lament over Jerusalem (ch. 19) and from the cross (ch. 23), a theme continued by Peter in Jerusalem (Acts 3) and by Paul among the Gentiles (Acts 17).

Finally, we can expect both to admire and to be captured by Luke's use of restraint so as to create anticipation. Notice, for example, Luke does not jump into the story of Jesus, as Mark does; Jesus is not born until 2:6, not baptized until 3:21, and while the reader is told at 3:23 that Jesus began his ministry at age thirty, the account of that ministry begins at 4:14. At 9:7–9 Herod is perplexed about Jesus and, as Luke says, "he sought to see him." At 13:31 Pharisees warn Jesus to flee, "for Herod wants to kill you," but it is not until 23:8, in Jerusalem at Jesus' trial, that the two meet face-to-face. And no reader of 24:49–53: "But stay in the city, until . . ." expects that to be the end of the story. In Acts 7:58, at the stoning of Stephen "the witnesses laid down their garments at the feet of a young man named Saul." But the reader has to wait to learn who he is and what he is doing. Such restraint is a mark of a masterful storyteller who knows how to capture and hold the participation of the listener. If anyone thinks that such attention to style is inappropriate to the high seriousness of Scripture, it would be well to remember that whoever is concerned only with content dishonors the content.

A fourth and final response to the question, What does it mean to regard Luke as a preacher? is that we will pay attention to how Luke uses Scriptures. Preachers use biblical texts in a variety of ways: to authorize the sermon, to illustrate, to provide precedents, to give continuity, to gain the listener's trust, to prove, and a host of lesser uses. We can expect no less from

Luke. There is no question that for Luke the Scriptures (the Hebrew Scriptures, our Old Testament) are foundational. When the rich man asks father Abraham to send Lazarus to earth to warn his brothers, Abraham says they have the Scriptures and "if they do not hear Moses and the prophets, neither will they be convinced if some one should rise from the dead" (16:31). In other words, the Scriptures are sufficient to generate faith. The law of Moses, the prophets, and the psalms bear witness to Christ to those whose minds have been opened to understand (24:44–45). Both the message and the mission of the church are to be found in these Scriptures (24:46–47). It is not surprising, then, to find the Old Testament in abundance in this Gospel. Most of the songs in chapters 1—2 are composed of biblical lines and phrases; Mary and Joseph see to it that the law of Moses is carefully observed in the rearing of Jesus (ch. 2); Jesus bases his ministry on prophecy (4:16–21); and Elijah and Elisha provided precedents for his behavior (4:25–27).

The fact is that Luke makes more use of the Old Testament than will be observed by a casual reader or by someone not familiar with those texts. The reason is that Luke often uses Scripture in an indirect or allusive way, apparently assuming that the readers will catch the connections. But what is more impressive is that Luke will often tell a story about Jesus or one of the early church leaders after the manner, and sometimes in the very words, of an Old Testament story. For example, Mary's song is Hannah's song (I Sam. 2:1–10); the boy Jesus in the temple is the boy Samuel in the temple at Shiloh (I Sam. 2—3; note especially 2:26); and Jesus raises a widow's son in an account most similar to that of Elijah's raising a widow's son (I Kings 17:17–24). Some will read Luke 9:51–56 and recall II Kings 1:9–16, or Acts 5:1–11 and recall Joshua 7:10–26. The stories are not simply distant cousins; often words and phrases are the same. What an unusual phenomenon! Luke is not trying to prove his point by the Old Testament, nor is he pointing to fulfilled prophecies. If his readers know the Scriptures well enough to read Luke's stories and remember the older ones, what is achieved? If they do not, what is lost? Obviously, trying to discern what Luke is doing and saying in these unusual uses of Scripture will be both a duty and a delight as we move through the Gospel.

8

Perhaps this is the time to say that the reader of this commentary may want to join me as we go along in the reevaluation of an expression popular in the church: "Matthew is the Jewish Gospel, Luke is the Gentile Gospel." If Luke himself is a Gentile, is it not remarkable how knowledgeable he is in the Old Testament and how respectful of its authority? If Luke's audience is Gentile, how remarkable that it is assumed they know the Old Testament so well and respect its authority? If Luke's message is Gentile, is it not remarkable that Luke insists on more continuity between temple and church, between synagogue and church, than any other New Testament writer? To these questions we will be drawn again and again.

Scope: Luke Among the Gospels and Acts

This is a commentary on the Gospel of Luke alone. There will be no attempt to sneak in discussions of the other Gospels at those points where one or more of them tell the same or a similar story. Neither will we be continually rushing ahead to Acts. However, a few comments are in order here.

Because Luke is one of the Synoptic ("viewed together") Gospels, we have long since learned that there is instruction in looking at Matthew and Mark when those Gospels carry parallels. The reasons are two. First, because Luke has a special relationship to both Mark and Matthew (explicated below in the comments at 1:1), noting how Luke concurs or varies from the other Evangelists can help sharpen our insight into what Luke is doing. Second, it is sometimes the case that one remembers an event or a story from one of the Gospels and that memory interferes with one's reading of that event or story in the others. For example, so vivid is the church's memory of Matthew's account of Simon Peter's confession at Caesarea Philippi that one must guard against that account intruding itself into Luke's telling of it, which differs somewhat in content as well as geographic location. Similarly, Matthew's record of Judas' death (he hanged himself) is so vivid in the church's mind that even some teachers and preachers have difficulty reading Luke's report (Acts 1) without importing Matthew into it. Therefore it is sometimes necessary to introduce the other accounts simply in order to say, "However, Luke tells it this way." We do not write one message clearly until the board has been erased of others. Therefore, in discussing a passage in Luke to which there are parallels, the citations of those parallels will be given at the outset. However, commentary on the texts in Matthew and Mark will be offered only if it will help us understand Luke, and

9

then quite briefly. Now and then the Gospel of John will be brought into view when and where affinities are apparent.

As for the relation of the Third Gospel to Acts, that which has been assumed in earlier statements needs here only brief elaboration. That the two volumes are the work of a single writer and addressed to a single audience is now generally accepted by students of the New Testament. The common literary style, the same governing themes, and the overarching theological perspectives, introduced by companion prologues (Luke 1:1-4; Acts 1:1-2) effectively silence speculations to the contrary. Luke-Acts is the largest contribution by a single writer in the New Testament.

However, our present interest is not that of a common authorship or of establishing literary or theological parallels in the two volumes. That parallels are there is quite evident: both Jesus and the church are born of the Holy Spirit; Jerusalem and the temple figure prominently in both; Jesus and Paul journey to Jerusalem in lengthy and dramatic accounts, the destination promising death for each with predictions and forebodings along the way; the accounts of the death of Jesus and of Stephen are companion narratives about martyrs; and the list goes on. But were we faced only with parallels, then Luke and Acts could reasonably be studied separately. The question is, Do Luke and Acts look to each other in sufficiently clear and substantial ways so that in the study of one, references to the other are not only permitted but are most helpful?

The answer is yes. Promise/fulfillment is a pattern characterizing the relation not only between the Old Testament and Luke but also between Luke and Acts. A few examples will suffice here. The reversal of fortunes (mighty–humble, hungry–rich) sung by Mary (1:52-53) not only continued as a social message in the preaching of John the Baptist (3:10-14) and of Jesus (6:20-26) but is a basic agenda for the ministry of the early church (Acts 4:32-37). And in the process, the mighty were pulled down from their thrones (Luke 1:52; Acts 12:1-23). At Luke 9:5 Jesus sends out the apostles with instructions to shake the dust from their feet and leave towns that reject them. At Antioch of Pisidia, Paul and Barnabas "shook off the dust from their feet against them, and went to Iconium" (Acts 13:51). Jesus promised his followers rejection in synagogues, imprisonment, and appearances before governors and kings (Luke 21:12), and the story in Acts fulfills that promise, not in general but

10

specifically, Paul himself suffering expulsion from synagogues, prison, and trials before governors and a king.

The sum of the matter is that the Gospel of Luke anticipates Acts and Acts reflects on the Gospel. Undoubtedly, some of Luke's stories in the Gospel are framed with a story yet to come in Acts clearly in mind. In fact, this has seemed so much the case that a few scholars have conjectured that Luke wrote Acts first, just as preachers often write first the conclusion and then build the way to it. Be that as it may, in the comments on the Gospel, pointing the reader now and then to passages in Acts will be not only justified but often necessary.

Admittedly, this will be a bit awkward, since Luke and Acts are separated by the Gospel of John. The church should not be unduly faulted for the arrangement of the canon. The same leaders who wanted to keep Luke and Acts together also realized that Luke belonged with Matthew and Mark as Synoptics and that Acts could serve as an introduction to Paul's letters. Putting John as the first of the Gospels seemed too high a price to pay for a solution. A loose-leaf New Testament, available in many stores that sell Bibles, could be most facilitating.

Format: Suggestions for the Use of This Book

Let me speak here more directly to preachers and teachers. It is my hope that you will have read the introductory material up to this point. However, I am realistic enough to know that commentaries are often consulted only at the point of the discussion of a particular text for an approaching assignment. I will therefore confine myself to the commentary proper in the following suggestions.

First, have the text of Luke open before you. This commentary was prepared in direct contact with the text and assumes the same of the reader.

Second, read through the entire Gospel of Luke prior to going to work on its parts. For those of you dipping into Luke at a single point for one occasion this may seem a heavy investment for a small return. However, most of you, if not all of you, will at some time teach the Gospel of Luke or preach your way through it. If you follow a lectionary, you will spend one year (Year C) with Luke as the primary Gospel during which at least twenty-three of its twenty-four chapters will receive some attention. Prior to such an extensive use of Luke, it is most important that you read the whole of it, listening, underlining, and experiencing its texture as well as text. Join the early Christians who received this and other New Testament writings first by the ear at public readings in worship: read it aloud to your own ear. Be as open to making discoveries as you can. Do not be embarrassed if you find yourself saying, "I never noticed that before," even in regard to passages that you may have taught or preached more than once. Understanding is a matter not only of intelligence but of character and readiness, and therefore the Scripture releases itself to us over a lifetime, as we are able. Having done this, you will find that the table of contents will be a map, not a maze, and the commentary a colleague.

Third, spend some time with the table of contents; it offers a detailed outline of the Gospel. Let this outline help you to become at home in the text. Notice the movements of the narrative, the critical turns, the transitions. Return often to this outline, for location and arrangement of stories, sayings, and events have a direct bearing on what the writer is doing and saying. The unit on which you are working, however small, is a part of the whole. By the way, those of you who use lectionaries may discover some helpful correspondence at times between the way the text is divided in the outline and the lections for the services of worship. Sometimes, however, this will not be the case. No attempt has been made to negotiate such correspondences; after all, we can here treat all of Luke while the lectionary cannot, the pressure of time necessitating some omissions. Also, factors liturgical and ecclesiastical influence a lectionary in ways they do not a commentary.

Fourth, at the beginning of a major section read the discussions of the whole before proceeding to the parts. Such introductory comments are intended to call attention to clues within that section which will shed light on what the writer is doing in that particular movement of the narrative. Likewise, these discussions of an introductory nature will also appear when a subject or a literary form appears for the first of what will be a number of times. For example, when we first encounter a parable in the text, parables as such will be introduced so that at all subsequent appearances of parables, the commentary can proceed on the basis of some assumed common understandings. I alert you, the reader, to this fact in case your first entry into this commentary happens to be, shall we say, at the point of a later parable and you find that the discussion there assumes what has not at that point been said.

Fifth, do not expect verse-by-verse treatment of the text. Some critical commentaries offer basically word and phrase studies, and Bible dictionaries probe particular names, places, and subjects that appear in texts. While some key verses, as well as some significant terms, will receive considerable attention, my judgment has been guided by keeping the teacher and the preacher before me. Interpretation of the text has been pursued in and for the believing community which lives in both continuity and discontinuity with its tradition and in both tension and harmony with its context in the world. As in every generation, the church interprets the Scriptures by both listening to and seriously interrogating the texts. This commentary seeks to participate in that task.

Finally, regard the references to other secondary literature as invitations for further study at points of interest or need. Within the text of this volume I have occasionally cited a book either as the source of a particular perspective or as an especially helpful treatment of the subject under discussion, offering to anyone who is so inclined the opportunity to do more detailed investigation. The citations are in parentheses and mention only author, title, and page. That is sufficient to lead the reader to the Selected Bibliography at the end of this volume, where the full entries are found. The sources to which I am indebted for my own understanding far exceed the references in the text, and I have tried to make available in these pages the best of that material. In the selections that do appear, I have been guided by two principles. First, it is not helpful to fill the reader's study with strangers, all of them intimidating experts. More learning occurs when one is seated among a few seasoned and clear scholars. Second, references are helpful if they are in the reader's language and accessible in bookstores and libraries. Usually readers with more or different appetites already have the initiative and the means for satisfying them.

LUKE 1:1–4

Luke's preface to his Gospel is unique in the New Testament, having its only similarity at Acts 1:1–2. At 3:1–2 there is another preface or introduction, but it is more in the pattern of opening lines of prophetic books, offering nothing concerning sources, method, purpose, or addressee. The Gospel of John has a prologue, but it is a theological summary, without a word about "how I came to write this book and why." Luke here writes in the style of classical rhetoric, with striking similarities to prefaces found in medical writers and historians of the time. For example, the historian Flavius Josephus begins several of his works in this fashion. "In my history of Antiquities, most excellent Epaphroditus, I have, I think, made sufficiently clear . . . ," he wrote in *Against Apion*. This form is all the more striking here, since Luke shifts at verse 5 to a more Semitic fashion, using not only the vocabulary but also the style of the Septuagint, a Greek translation of the Old Testament, for the entirety of chapters 1—2.

Luke's preface is carefully constructed, consisting of a single sentence in two parts. The first part opens with an introductory clause, "Inasmuch as many" (v. 1), and the second with a concluding clause, "it seemed good to me also" (v. 3). The formality of the writing implies respect for an educated and cultured reader. The recipient is addressed as "most excellent," an expression used again by Luke to refer to the Roman governor of Judea (Acts 23:26). As to the name "Theophilus" (v. 3), scholars are divided in their attempts at identification. The name means "friend of God," and is taken by some as a literary device for addressing Christian readers in general or in a particular community known to Luke. Others regard "most excellent Theophilus" as a Roman official informed about, if not a convert

15

to, the Christian faith. It is unclear whether "you have been informed" (v. 4) means getting information or being instructed as a Christian. In any case, one does not get the impression that either writer or reader fits the popular image of early Christians as being devoid of education and culture. Unlike Mark, who calls his work a Gospel (Mark 1:1), Luke has chosen a term more historical than theological: "an account" (v. 3).

All this having been said, what does the preface tell us? Do we know who the *author* is? No. The writer's self-referencing yields neither a name nor sufficient information to infer a name. However, a general portrait can be sketched. The writer is apparently a member of the Christian community: he writes about what has happened "among *us*," accounts of which have passed on "to *us*." The writer was not an eyewitness but a second- or third-generation recipient of the tradition. He is a student, a researcher ("having followed all things closely for some time past," v. 3), and, judging from the literary style, a person of education and culture. Since the writing style was at home in Greco-Roman culture, the writer may have been a Gentile Christian or a convert from Hellenistic Judaism. The remainder of the Gospel reveals such familiarity with the Greek Old Testament that the latter seems more likely.

But does this sketch identify the author as Luke, a physician and companion of Paul (Col. 4:14; Philemon 24; II Tim. 4:11)? Not really, although it does not eliminate him either. The tradition for Lukan authorship is as early as late second century and widespread: Gaul (Irenaeus), North Africa (Tertullian), Italy (Muratorian Fragment), and Egypt (Clement of Alexandria). But it is not the preface which spawns the tradition, although it is used by some to support it. It was popular in the last century to argue from medical terminology in the Gospel that the writer was a physician, but those arguments have been rather convincingly laid to rest. Equally unclear is the evidence involving the diary-like "we" sections of Acts (Acts 16:10–17; 20:5—21:18; 27:1—28:16). Was the writer revealing himself as a traveling companion of Paul or making use of the records of someone who was? Those who approach Luke theologically find a great deal of distance between him and the Paul revealed in the letters. The end of the matter is that we do not know. However, anonymity is easier to live with now that most of us are persuaded that the question of authorship is not a major

16

factor in understanding the content and accepting the authority of a biblical text.

And what does the preface tell us about *sources* for Luke's Gospel? Quite a bit. The sources were multiple and of two kinds: written (many narratives have been compiled) and oral ("eyewitnesses and ministers of the word," v. 2). As for the oral sources, Luke's "having followed all things closely for some time past" (v. 3) very likely included interviews and other contacts with oral traditions. But oral sources are very difficult to identify. The general tendency has been to attribute to oral sources those portions of Luke for which no other known source exists. This material, unique to Luke (and hence identified in some commentaries as L), accounts for approximately 25 percent of the Gospel and consists primarily of birth and infancy stories, some parables, and resurrection narratives.

As for the written sources, from among the many narratives about Jesus compiled prior to Luke (v. 1), scholars have been rather confident in identifying two, although the relationships among the Synoptic Gospels are so complex as to generate arguments over any single theory that claims to account for their similarities and differences. One is the Gospel of Mark. Mark provides the basic structure for Luke, even though Luke does omit a sizable section of Mark (Mark 6:45—8:26) and insert blocks of non-Markan material (Luke 6:20—8:3; 9:51—18:14). Fully one third of Luke can be found in Mark. The other source is thus far hypothetical and has been called Q from the German *Quelle*, meaning "source." There is a large body of material common to Luke and Matthew but not found in Mark. Two examples are Luke 3:7–9 and Matt. 3:7–10; and Luke 4:3–12 and Matt. 4:3–10. Most of the material designated Q consists of sayings. Did such a source exist? The discovery of the *Gospel of Thomas* in Egypt, a document containing about 114 sayings of Jesus, some of which are not in the canonical Gospels, has encouraged some scholars to think so. More than 25 percent of Luke consists of material in common with Matthew.

To speak of dependence on written sources and the testimony of eyewitnesses is to speak about *date* in the only way the preface permits. When the writer speaks of the things accomplished among us as being "delivered to us" (v. 2) he uses a verb form of the word "tradition." The Gospel is, then, the work of a second-generation, perhaps a third-generation, Christian.

17

And if one of the many narratives about Jesus prior to Luke was
Mark, then that Gospel establishes a "no earlier than" date.
Were we to move beyond the preface to Luke's record of the
fall of Jerusalem (19:41–44; 21:20–24), it could reasonably be
argued that unlike Matthew and Mark, Luke reveals knowledge
of the Roman siege of that city. Therefore 70 C.E. is a "no earlier
than" date. But how much later? The preface reminds us to
keep the date within a generation of eyewitnesses. Therefore,
between 80 and 90 C.E. seems a reasonable conjecture. We do
know that about 140 C.E. Luke was included in the Christian
canon of Marcion, an early Christian leader.

We return once more to the preface to ask about *purpose*.
Since many narratives about Jesus were already in existence,
why did it seem good to Luke to add another? Several possibilities suggest themselves on the basis of what is said in 1:1–4.
Perhaps the answer lies in the address to "most excellent Theophilus." If he is not a symbolic name but a real person, a
Roman official who may someday make decisions affecting
Christians, then a narrative making clear the work of Jesus and
of the church, especially as it made contact with Roman authority, was of prime importance. One would expect that the text
of Luke-Acts would either support or erode such a view. Some
attention will be given to this opinion.

Another answer to the question of purpose may lie in the
expression "orderly account." Luke voices no criticism of the
earlier narratives, but the thoroughness of his research, his re-
cording the events "in order," and his desire to give the reader
certainty in matters about which the reader was already informed combine to argue that Luke found in the prior accounts
something confusing, erroneous, or incomplete.

A third possible purpose may be a literary one, that is, if we
take "you have been informed" (v. 4) in the literal sense of
"being catechized." If the reader's knowledge of Jesus' life and
work came by way of information as offered in a catechism,
then Luke may have regarded that as a form less congenial to
the nature of the event of Jesus and the church than a historical
narrative. Perhaps Luke is putting what Theophilus knew in a
more appropriate literary form. Luke must have known what
all preachers know: some forms of communication can carry a
load of informational freight and still violate the experiences
that the writer or the speaker is seeking to create.

A final theory as to purpose suggested by this preface joined

18

with the preface to Acts has to do with the continuity of history. If the prior narratives were much like Mark in that they began abruptly and ended abruptly, then what really is the relation of Jesus to his own tradition in Judaism, on the one hand, and to the church after him, on the other? Three stories—Judaism, Jesus, and church—need to be related in some way that is both historical and theological. No writer in the New Testament does this except Luke. And perhaps Luke does so, not simply because some person or persons referred to as Theophilus has a need to know. More likely it is because of two realities that impress themselves on Luke. First, the event of Jesus is receding farther and farther into the past. His life and work are matters of history. Second, the church is now a movement, an institution in the world, and Luke assumes that much more time will pass before Christ returns. After all, one does not research and write an orderly account if one is convinced that the day of the Lord is at hand. Enough time has passed and enough time lies before the Christian community to call for a better sense of history. And with that perspective perhaps many questions will be answered, many purposes served. How does Jesus fit in the larger story of God's relation to the world? How did Jesus and how does the church relate to the synagogue and other movements in the name of God? Why was Jesus executed, and why are his missionaries imprisoned and killed? How does it happen that a movement that began among Jews becomes increasingly Gentile? Are there signs that God is bringing in a new age and with it the end of the old? When, where, how will God's purpose for the world be consummated? In the meantime, what sort of persons ought we to be, and what should we be doing?

It is reasonable to approach Luke with the expectation that his thorough research, his obvious literary skills, his love of orderly narration, and his strong desire that the reader know the truth will be joined in such a way as to answer some if not all of these questions.

PART ONE

Infancy and Childhood Narratives

LUKE 1:5—2:52

Before we explore the distinctive and easily identifiable units within chapters 1—2, a sense of the whole will help to facilitate our being ushered into the story of Jesus, perhaps in a way not unlike the experience Luke wanted for his readers. The comments that follow will focus on three subjects: the relation of chapters 1—2 to the remainder of the Gospel, the literary features of this section, and its general structure.

1. The relation of chapters 1—2 to the remainder of the Gospel. Luke 1:5—2:52, referred to as the Prologue by a number of commentators, is not, in the opinion of some scholars, integrally related to the remainder of the Gospel. Some have ventured the theory that it represents a later addition, perhaps inserted to satisfy questions that inevitably arose about Jesus' birth and childhood. The arguments for the separate origin and nature of these two chapters are essentially as follows: These two chapters have their own inner unity, and chapters 3—24 are clear and complete on their own; nothing in chapters 3—24 depends on chapters 1—2 for its meaning; most of the characters in the infancy and childhood stories never reappear elsewhere in Luke or Acts; the virgin birth was not an item in the faith of Jesus' first followers, nor was it preached in the early church, according to Acts; and 3:1 clearly is the beginning of a narrative.

That 3:1 is a beginning, John and Jesus now adults and launching their ministries, is obvious, but was it *the* beginning of Luke's Gospel? It is true that Zechariah, Elizabeth, Simeon, and Anna do not reappear in the subsequent narratives, but the same could be said of most of the apostles, whose names appear but immediately disappear from the story. And the virgin birth of Jesus is absent from all the preaching recorded in Luke-Acts. However, the birth story could have been told for reasons other than satisfying curiosity or other than establishing a ground for presenting Jesus as divine son of God. The birth of Jesus could have been told as a way of distinguishing him from John whose birth was of God, but in a different way. Luke exalts both John and Jesus while making it quite clear who is the lesser and who the greater. Or the birth story could be presented by Luke as a dramatic entry for the reader, generating anticipation: from this one you can expect new and great things. The way the account comes to the reader, as song, story, and liturgy, with Mary pondering it all in her heart, can hardly qualify as an argument or a proof.

But is there any substantive continuity between chapters 1—2 and 3—24? Most definitely. With no attempt to be exhaustive, I offer the following themes and perspectives in evidence: Luke begins the story in the temple (1:8) and concludes it in the temple (24:53); here, as throughout Luke-Acts, Jerusalem is the vital center; the continuity of Jesus with Judaism begins here and continues through the Gospel; in all of Luke, including chapters 1—2, the Greek Old Testament (Septuagint) is used directly and allusively; angels and wondrous revelations are common in all of Luke-Acts; the powerful activity of the Holy Spirit is evident from Jesus' conception through the life of the church in Acts; the theme of universality so commonly associated with Luke begins here; the social messages of both John and Jesus begin in Mary's song (1:46–55); the promise/fulfillment motif which dominates in Luke-Acts is no less evident here; that "today" is the time of God's activity is stated here (2:11) and repeated often (4:21; 5:26; 19:9; 23:43); and these early narratives introduce what becomes the governing affirmation of the whole work: God is the principal character and power in and through all the events of the life of Jesus and of the early church. Luke more than any other New Testament writer reminds us that God is the subject of the entire story, whatever the time, the place, or the cast of characters onstage.

2. The literary features of this section. The style of the infancy and childhood narratives is very much that of the Greek

Old Testament. This is not simply to say that Luke uses count-less citations from the Old Testament but that Luke brings his readers into the world of Judaism's Scripture. Poetry, hymns, prayer, homily, story, and history combine to create that world, and most of it woven from Luke's allusive use of Scripture. The sacred past blends into the sacred present rather than being used as proof of the truth of the sacred present. Continuity prevails; discontinuity must wait for the debates and disagree-ments yet to come in the Gospel. For the present, the reader experiences "the consolation of Israel."

It is evident that Luke wants the reader not to move too swiftly through the narrative. Hence Luke's restraint: eighty verses in chapter 1 and the child is not yet born. First there must be visions and angels visitant; mothers-to-be must wonder and talk and sing; history must roll to a particular moment when Caesar Augustus will put Mary and Joseph in Bethlehem. Hence Luke's poetry, borrowed, some say, from early Christian liturgies. Poetry slows down thought and invites participation in the experience being created. Luke wants the reader to savor new stories that are old stories: an old childless couple are now to have a child; a routine service at the altar becomes a God-filled moment; God turns to the simple and powerless to bring in an era of justice and mercy; God will again put an heir on the throne of David. To say that these new stories are old stories is not simply to say that they are patterned after Old Testament records; rather, it is to say that the writer apparently assumed that the readers would recognize the old in the new. If this is true, then the readers must have had a background in Hellenis-tic Judaism, either as Jews in a Greek culture and using the Greek Old Testament or as Gentiles who were proselytes to Judaism prior to conversion to Christianity; or it might have been that as a general practice instruction in the Old Testament was given to early Christians. In either case, reading chapters 1—2 must have been much like entering a sanctuary and find-ing oneself familiar with the words, the stories, the hymns, even the place.

What could be Luke's reason for creating such an experi-ence at the entrance of his Gospel? Of course, that cannot be known with certainty, but such a beginning does relax the reader even while generating keen anticipation. The reader is made to feel at home, confident of not being ambushed with some new religion that will contradict and violate every convic-

23

tion of the parent faith. The new is at the door, to be sure, as new as the young Mary who visits the old Elizabeth. But for now, it is enough to be assured that the new continues and fulfills the old, with the same God remembering covenants kept and making good on promises made.

3. *The general structure of 1:5—2:52.* This section consists of seven units: annunciation of the birth of John (1:5–25); annunciation of the birth of Jesus (1:26–38); Elizabeth and Mary meet (1:39–56); birth of John (1:57–80); birth of Jesus (2:1–21); Jesus in the temple as an infant (2:22–40); and Jesus in the temple as a boy (2:41–52). There are three noticeable features of this arrangement. First, there are two panels of material: the annunciation of John's birth and the annunciation of Jesus' birth. The two panels are, in a sense, united in the meeting of the mothers-to-be. There follow two other panels: the birth of John and the birth of Jesus. At this point there follow two stories about Jesus in the temple, at six weeks and at twelve years. This parallel arrangement of John and Jesus stories (found similarly at 7:31–35) is the most elaborate handling of the relationship of John and Jesus to be found in the Gospels. All the Evangelists have the double task of honoring John as a man of God and at the same time subordinating him to Jesus. Luke affirms both, making it clear from the outset that, like Esau and Jacob, the older will serve the younger.

The second feature of Luke's arrangement of this section is that the story does begin with John. Not only chronologically but in the plan of God, John was first. Even the Gospel of John, which most vigorously subordinates John, apparently feeling very keenly the "competition" of this powerful and attractive figure who continued to gain disciples as a martyred hero, begins the narrative proper with the testimony of John the Baptist. Mark seems to refer to the ministry of John as "the beginning of the gospel of Jesus Christ" (Mark 1:1).

The third feature of Luke's structure is that by his very arrangement he gradually moves the camera off John and on Jesus alone. By the time the reader has moved through the sadly beautiful story of Jesus' dedication in the temple and has been filled with anticipation by the image of the boy Jesus sitting among the teachers, John has receded into the background. John the preacher of repentance will reappear, to be sure, but Luke has already made the shift: the one who was first is now second; the one who was second is now first.

24

Luke 1:5–56
Annunciations of the Births of John and Jesus

Annunciation of the Birth of John the Baptist (1:5–25)

In a pattern followed throughout the Gospel and Acts, Luke begins by placing the event to be unfolded in the context of contemporary history. As a reward for services to Rome and to Octavius in particular, Herod the Great was elevated to king of Palestine (Luke sometimes refers to the whole land when he says Judea, 4:44) in the year 40 B.C.E. His actual control began in 37 B.C.E. and ended with his death in 4 B.C.E. It is not clear as yet whether Herod is only a date for Luke's story or whether he is mentioned because he and the world he represents will be affected by what follows.

Only Luke tells us the names of John's parents and that he was of the priestly family. Both Zechariah and Elizabeth were of Aaron's line. Aaronic priests had been divided into 24 divisions named for Aaron's 24 sons (I Chron. 24:1–19), and they took turns serving at the altar of the temple in Jerusalem. The couple lived in the hill country (v. 39), but housing in the temple was available for priests on duty. Even though this couple are the picture of Jewish piety, they are childless and now old. Elizabeth, barren in her old age, belongs to a rich tradition: Sarah, Rebekah, Rachel, the unnamed wife of Manoah, and Hannah.

Having introduced the characters, Luke tells the story. It begins in the temple in Jerusalem; Zechariah's division is on duty, and within the division Zechariah is chosen by lot (a method for discerning God's will, Acts 1:26) to burn incense on the altar within the Holy Place. The people attending the hour of prayer wait for the priest's reappearance and his blessing. He is therefore alone in the Holy Place when he is visited by Gabriel, one of the seven archangels of late Judaism and usually given messenger duty. Luke's description fits the pattern of Gabriel's visit to Daniel (Dan. 9:20—10:15): appearance, fear, the message, the recipient stricken speechless. Angels appear as

25

messengers with some frequency in Luke-Acts. Gabriel's message is fourfold: Elizabeth will have a child to be named John (v. 13); the child will give to Zechariah and Elizabeth and to many joy and gladness (v. 14); the child will be reared in the Nazirite tradition (v. 15; Num. 6:3; Judg. 13:2–5); and the child will minister in the spirit of Elijah who was to herald the end time and prepare Israel for it (vv. 16–17; Mal. 4:5). Some scribes taught that Elijah would appear as forerunner of the Messiah (Matt. 17:10). However, unlike Matthew (Matt. 17:10–13), Luke does not specifically identify John as Elijah; after all, Jesus will also be Elijah-like (4:23–26), as will others (Acts 8:26–39) who are moved extraordinarily by the Spirit of God.

Understandably, Zechariah has doubts, and for his unbelief he is stricken speechless (v. 20). The worshipers outside, awaiting the overdue priest, get from him only signs and gestures, but they sense that he has experienced God. His duty ended, Zechariah goes home. Elizabeth conceives, for which she praises God, since barrenness was not only blamed on the woman (not on the man) but was also taken to be a reproach from God. Zechariah is silent, Elizabeth is in hiding, and we are left in a mood of expectation.

Let us reflect for a moment on this story. God is at work here in patterns familiar from the Old Testament: the casting of lots, a vision in the temple, a heavenly messenger, a promise, a sign, and a childless old couple. The "miraculous" portion is experienced by one person alone, but others experience the evidence of God's presence, a perspective that will reappear in Luke-Acts (e.g., Acts 9:3–9). And God is at work from within, not from outside the institutions, rituals, and practices of Judaism. The couple are of Aaron's line, Zechariah is a priest, they are blamelessly pious in all of God's commands and ordinances, and the word of God comes in the temple. For Luke, God works in and through the normal avenues of life in the believing community. Luke will show us later that he knows that those ways can and do become distorted and corrupted, but here he lays out a fundamental conviction: continuity with Israel's institutions, rituals, and faith puts one in position to be used for God's purpose. The old (in this case, an old couple) will usher in the new.

26 **Annunciation of the Birth of Jesus (1:26–38)**

In one sense this story is as different from the preceding story as a young virgin differs from an old couple advanced in years. However, the reader is most aware of how closely parallel the two accounts are. Both are stories of God's initiative of grace and power: of grace in that what is soon to happen will express God's favor toward the world; of power in that God can work through the unable, an old couple and an unmarried girl. Elizabeth and Mary will have sons because God is able; they will have sons for our sake because God is gracious. The word of God's grace and power in both cases comes through the same messenger, Gabriel. The word "angel" is a transliteration of the Greek *aggelos*, "messenger."

Perhaps we should pause to say a word about angels. Rare in early Judaism, they became rather common in the belief system of some areas of later Judaism; for example, Pharisees believed in angels as mediators between God and human beings. They were, however, only one means of communication from God who spoke to our ancestors "in many and various ways" (Heb. 1:1). Matthew, for example, when recalling the birth of Jesus, speaks of dreams as an avenue of revelation (Matt. 1:20; 2:12, 13, 19). Luke has a large place for angels as God's means of announcing, instructing, guiding, and protecting (1:11, 26; 2:8–15; Acts 8:26; 12:7). On the matter of angels, some New Testament writers are silent, while Paul, for instance, speaks of them but not positively at all (Rom. 8:38–39; Gal. 3:19–20; Col. 2:18–19). Apparently angels were widely regarded as free creatures, able to serve or to oppose the work of God.

As in 1:5–25, Luke here introduces the characters, the angel appears, followed by fear, good news, doubt, the sign, response, and the departure of the angel. And as before, Luke dates the event (the sixth month of Elizabeth's pregnancy) and locates it geographically (Nazareth was a small town, of small regard [John 1:46], in south Galilee). However, unlike the earlier story, the announcement of the birth comes not to the man but to the woman. Mary is betrothed but not yet married (v. 34). Betrothals, legal and binding, were usually arranged between families when women were quite young, still only girls. Joseph's importance in the story is that he provides Jesus' legal connection to the throne of David (1:32; 2:4). To the angel's greeting to Mary (v. 28), later scribes added "Blessed are you among women!" (RSV footnote to v. 28), perhaps a borrowing from verse 42.

Throughout chapters 1—2, Mary is portrayed as favored of God (v. 30), thoughtful (v. 29; 2:19, 51), obedient (v. 38), believ-

27

ing (v. 45), worshipful (v. 46), and devoted to Jewish law and piety (2:22–51). Luke names her in the company of believers when the church began (Acts 1:14). To one Lukan scholar, Mary is presented as the ideal Christian and is too much neglected in the Protestant Church (Charles H. Talbert, *Reading Luke*, pp. 22–26). However, we must be careful to notice that none of her qualities is offered as the reason God chose her; that reason lies tucked away in the purposes of God.

Gabriel's message to Mary, as it was to Zechariah, is four-fold: she will have a son to be named Jesus (v. 31); the child will be the Son of God (Ps. 2:7) and will occupy forever the throne of David (vv. 32–33; II Sam. 7:13–16); the birth of the child will be effected by the overshadowing descent of the Holy Spirit (v. 35; Ex. 40:35; I Kings 8:10; Hag. 2:6–9); and as a sign that this will come to pass, Gabriel informs Mary of the pregnancy of her kinswoman Elizabeth (vv. 36–37). As a final word of assurance, the angel recalls the creed behind all creeds, the very words spoken to Abraham and Sarah when they doubted the word that they were to have a child: "For with God nothing will be impossible" (v. 37; Gen. 18:14). Mary bows in humble obedience to the word of God.

Incidentally, churches that follow a traditional lectionary will notice that the Annunciation is on March 25, a date arrived at by moving back nine months from December 25. Interestingly, this tendency in the church to calendarize the salvation story is not unlike Luke's own penchant for times and dates: "in the sixth month"; "about three months"; "at the end of eight days"; "for the space of forty days"; "in the fifteenth year of Tiberius Caesar."

Elizabeth and Mary Meet (1:39–56)

This episode, called in traditional liturgies the Visitation, actually contains very little narrative. It consists almost entirely of inspired speech and song, reminding us of the affective force of literary forms. The visit of Mary to Elizabeth joins the two larger units of the annunciations of the births of John and Jesus and the accounts of their births, thereby accenting the similarities and contrasts between the two sons. In fact, the twin themes of those surrounding narratives are to be found in this beautiful interlude in the hill country of Judah: prenatal and natal signs point to the greatness of both John and Jesus, but the signs are equally clear that Jesus is the greater of the two.

28

The account of the visitation is in four parts. First, there is the brief narrative introduction to the visit itself (vv. 39–41*a*). There is no reason to think Mary's visit was to check out the angel's statement about Elizabeth; Mary had already accepted Gabriel's word as true. The two women, not only kin but drawn by a common experience, meet in an unnamed village in the Judean hills. The one is old and her son will close an age; the other is young and her son will usher in the new. Even the unborn John knows the difference and leaps in the womb when Mary enters. Luke is here offering a historical reminiscence and making a theological point. The historical allusion is to Rebekah in whose womb Esau and Jacob struggled, the message being in both cases, "The elder shall serve the younger" (Gen. 25:21–23). The theological point is that prenatal activity, because it precedes all merit or works, witnesses to the sovereign will of God.

The second unit is the visitation story and consists of the inspired speech of Elizabeth (vv. 41*b*–45). Filled with the Holy Spirit (we will notice throughout the Gospel the variety of activities of the Holy Spirit but will avoid making a list of "things the Holy Spirit does"; after all, it is *God's* Spirit and hardly would submit to such a catalog lest it be taken as an agenda of what the Spirit *will* do), Elizabeth eulogizes both Mary and her child. She blesses Mary on two grounds: she has been chosen to be mother of the Lord, and she has believed the word of God. Elizabeth's humbling herself before Mary is reminiscent of John's humbling himself before Jesus in Matthew's baptismal scene (Matt. 3:13–15).

The third and by far the largest unit of the episode is Mary's song (vv. 46–55), the Magnificat, so termed from the opening word in the Latin translation. In the song, Mary only briefly praises God for the favor bestowed on a handmaiden of low estate (vv. 46–49), and even then, this portion is not solely autobiographical. What God has done for Mary anticipates and models what God will do for the poor, the powerless, and the oppressed of the world, the central theme of the second movement of the song, the triumph of God's purposes for all people everywhere (vv. 50–55). The song draws heavily on and is patterned after the song of Hannah (I Sam. 2:1–10), with other Old Testament phrases and allusions interspersed. Since Hannah was promised and given a child (Samuel) in her old age, some scholars have argued that the song originally belonged to Elizabeth. In fact, some Old Latin manuscripts read "And Elizabeth

29

said" at verse 46, but the earlier Greek texts attribute the song to Mary. Clearly verse 48 refers not to Elizabeth but to Mary.

Two unusual features of the song deserve special attention. First, God is praised in terms of what he has done. To be sure, to speak of what God has done is to announce what God will do; the pattern is a familiar one. However, it is most striking that the lines that clearly refer to God's establishing justice and mercy in the future, in the end time (the eschaton), contain past tense verbs, not future tense verbs. Why? This particular use of the past tense (aorist) of the Greek language here expresses what is timelessly true: past, present, and future without differentiation. But we should also consider the past tense as a way of expressing the confidences and the certainty as though they already were. So sure is the singer that God will do what is promised that it is proclaimed as accomplished fact.

The second unusual feature of the song is found in verses 52–53. Even though the entirety of verses 50–55 is packed with vivid images and has a buildup of momentum through repeated words and phrases, rhythmic lines, and patterned contrasts, the greatest intensity occurs in verses 52–53. In these four lines, Luke expresses in sharpest focus what has been called a classical statement of God's activity: the lowly are raised and the lofty are brought low (John Drury, *Tradition and Design in Luke's Gospel*, p. 50). Mary sings of the God who brings down the mighty and exalts those of low degree, who fills the hungry and sends the rich away empty, and through her Luke introduces a theme prominent in both the Gospel and Acts. More is involved than the social message and ministry of Jesus in behalf of the oppressed and poor. That will follow, to be sure, but here we have a characteristic of the final judgment of God in which there is a complete reversal of fortunes: the powerful and rich will exchange places with the powerless and poor. And this eschatological reversal has already begun; God's choice of Mary is evidence of it. The pattern of reversed fortunes will reappear often in Luke; for example, recall Luke's beatitudes and woes (6:20–26) and his story of the rich man and Lazarus (16:19–31).

The fourth and final unit in the visitation story is a simple narrative in a single sentence: Mary stays with Elizabeth three months and then goes home. We may assume that her three-month stay ended with the birth of John, the record of which will follow immediately. Mary will reappear at the time of her own delivery. Luke is not rushing the story, so we will have to wait, as Mary does.

Luke 1:57—2:21
The Births of John and Jesus

The Birth of John the Baptist (1:57–80)

The reader of Luke may be surprised at the amount of attention given to John; after all, this unit contains 24 verses, while the parallel account of Jesus' birth contains only 21. Why so much free publicity to a man who was later to draw many disciples who apparently chose John over Jesus? Christians have placed John safely in the role of forerunner to the Messiah, and so he is in the early Christian documents, but to the people exposed to the two prophetic figures, John was too strikingly strong and attractive as a man of God to be so easily subordinated. Was Luke, a second- or third-generation Christian of a Gentile or Hellenistic Jewish background, aware of the size and strength of the John the Baptist movement?

Yes, Luke knew; in fact, it is Luke who tells us of the widespread popularity of John. The eloquent Apollos of Alexandria, Egypt, was a disciple of John before becoming a Christian (Acts 18:24–28), and at Ephesus in Asia Minor, Paul found a community of John's followers (Acts 19:1–7). But Luke also was clear in the conviction that Jesus was the Messiah and that John came in the spirit and power of Elijah to prepare the way (v. 76). As to the amount of attention Luke gives to John, four comments are in order. First, Luke is obviously trying to give his reader a more complete and orderly account of the events "which have been accomplished among us" (1:1). Second, Luke has chosen to show the roles of John and Jesus and their relationship not only in their ministries but also in prenatal and natal signs, speeches, and songs. John's parents knew, says Luke; in fact, John knew while still in his mother's womb (v. 41). By thus treating the matter, Luke informs the reader even before John and Jesus appear in the story as adults. Third, Luke makes it quite clear that the views of Elizabeth and Zechariah are not

31

simply their own; they sing and prophesy about their son and Jesus in speech inspired by the Holy Spirit (vv. 41, 67). In other words, Luke is telling us God's definition of the ministries of John and Jesus. And finally, it is only apparently the case that John is receiving a great amount of press in Luke. In the units in which the narrative seems to be about John, actually the songs and prophecies are in the main testimonies to the son of Mary. As we will see, this is abundantly true of Zechariah's prophecy in verses 67–79. The sum of the matter is that Luke is as much aware, if not more aware than most people, of the problem related to but not confined to John and Jesus: that is, persons whose work it is to point others to Jesus can themselves become the objects and centers of the attention, affection, and loyalty of many.

The account in verses 57–80 consists of three parts: the birth, the circumcision, and the naming of John (vv. 57–66); the inspired prophecy of Zechariah (vv. 67–79); and a brief statement about John which serves as both summary and transition to his public life (v. 80). The first unit is a pleasant narrative reflecting the laws and customs of that culture. Relatives and neighbors joined not only in the joy of a birth, and especially if it were of the first male child of older parents, but also in the naming of the child (Ruth 4:17). Apparently in late Judaism the naming was linked to circumcision, the act by which a male child was made a member of the people of God. At least in some quarters, the expectation was that the boy would be named for his father (Tobit 1:9). The releasing of Zechariah's power of speech is to be understood as a miracle, prompting him to praise God and the neighbors to be filled with that fear appropriate to a sense of the presence of God's power. Widespread reports and conversation about these things, joined to quiet ponderings, are Luke's way of creating an atmosphere of anticipation and of the mystery surrounding the ways of God in the world.

Zechariah's inspired prophecy, called the Benedictus after the first word in the Latin translation, falls into two parts: verses 68–75 and 76–79. The first part praises God not for sending John but for raising up "a horn of salvation for us in the house of his servant David" (v. 69), that is, for sending Jesus. Full of Old Testament allusions, those verses are distinctly Jewish, similar to canonical psalms of praise to God as deliverer (Ps. 34; 67; 103; 113) and to the thanksgiving psalms of the Dead Sea Scrolls. Jewish eschatological hopes will be fulfilled, promises will be kept, the covenant with Abraham will be remembered, and all enemies will be overthrown by the "horn of salvation" (power of God, I Sam. 2:10) whom God has raised up. Of course, when read by disciples of Jesus, these verses ring true to the Christian faith.

If, as some scholars have conjectured, the prophecy of Zechariah was originally a hymn circulating among followers of John, then verses 76–79 may be a Christian addition to make it clear that the focus is on Jesus and that John "will go before the Lord to prepare his ways" (v. 76). Whether or not these verses originated outside Christian circles, they are, for Luke and for us, a summary of what John will do and what Jesus will do. This portion of the prophetic song draws heavily on Mal. 3:1–2 and 4:5–6 and on Isa. 9:2 and 42:7. The beautiful line describing the appearance of the Messiah, "when the day shall dawn upon us from on high" (v. 78b), echoes Mal. 4:2 ("The sun of righteousness shall rise, with healing in its wings") but is difficult to translate. The NEB renders it, "The morning sun from heaven will rise upon us," while the TEV says, "He will cause the bright dawn of salvation to rise on us."

The final unit of this section is a brief summary about John's growth, recalling Samson the Nazirite (Judg. 13:24) and the boy Samuel (I Sam. 2:26). That John's life in the desert was within the community at Qumran has never been established. Luke not only rounds off the phase of his account about John but points the reader ahead toward "the day of his manifestation to Israel" (v. 80). When John's story resumes, he will come preaching the approach of God's reign. In the meantime we wait, and we do so with admiration for Luke's communication skills; he knows when and how to break a story so as to hold the reader with a "To be continued."

The Birth of Jesus (2:1–21)

The parallel stories continue. As in the telling of John's birth, Luke again speaks of joy at birth, sings of great expectations, and marks the occasion of circumcision and naming. However, the closing summary statement of the child's growth (1:80) will in the case of Jesus be delayed, one such summary coming after each of two vignettes about Jesus' visits to the temple in Jerusalem (vv. 40, 52). Yet another difference appears. The literary style of 1:5–80 was very much that of the Greek Old Testament. At 2:1, the style is less like the Old

33

Testament and much more like the remainder of the Gospel. Perhaps Luke wanted his writing style to register the shift from the old age, to which John belonged, to the new launched by the appearance of Jesus. This is not to say that Luke ceases to use the Old Testament abundantly. By no means. In fact, Isa. 1:3; Jer. 14:8; and Micah 5:2 nourish the story before us.

The story of Jesus' birth consists of three units: the birth itself (vv. 1–7), the announcement to the shepherds (vv. 8–20), and the circumcision and naming (v. 21). Strikingly simple, brief, and straightforward is the record of Jesus' birth. There is no miracle, no unusual incident. Again, Luke writes as historian, giving the reader date, place, and circumstance. One question is anticipated and answered: How did it happen that Jesus of Nazareth was really Jesus of Bethlehem, David's city? While Matthew (Matt. 2) and Luke agree that Jesus was born in Bethlehem, their accounts of the relation of the holy family to Nazareth and to Bethlehem differ.

To say that Luke writes as a historian here is not to say that extrabiblical sources confirm his account. In fact, Luke's chronology and the census referred to in 2:1–2 do not fit the history to which we have other access. Mary and Joseph were in Bethlehem to be registered for an imperial census and taxation, but historians have been unable to confirm a universal census in the reign of Augustus (Octavius), who ruled from 27 B.C.E. to 14 C.E. There was a census in Palestine when Quirinius was governor of Syria (perhaps the census of Acts 5:37), but that seems to have been later (about 6 C.E.) than the reference in Luke 2:2. However, since Quirinius was a viceroy in that region earlier and since some time elapsed between enrollment and tax assessment, some scholars argue that Luke is generally if not exactly correct in his historical references. Luke's primary aim is to establish Jesus in Bethlehem and in continuity with the royal house of David. Surprisingly, however, he does not quote the messianic prophecy about Bethlehem (Micah 5:2), as does Matthew (Matt. 2:5–6). Beyond any argument as to Luke's historical sources is his basic conviction that emperors, governments, and laws serve the purpose of God, often without knowing it. In this, Luke agrees with Isa. 45:1. Caesar Augustus is more than a date for the story; he is an instrument of God's will. There does not have to be a miracle or an unusual event for God to be at work. God works miracles in Luke, to be sure, but God works without them, too.

During Mary and Joseph's stay in Bethlehem, Jesus is born and, like all newborns, is wrapped with strips of cloth to keep the body straight and to ensure proper growth. The guest room was apparently occupied and hence could offer no privacy, so Mary and Joseph had withdrawn to a stable at the back of or underneath the house, perhaps in a cave. A feeding trough served as a crib. How simple and bare it all seems. At John's birth there was a miracle (speech restored to Zechariah) and an inspired prophetic song. Not so here; Luke has kept the story clean of any decoration that would remove it from the lowly, the poor, and the marginal of the earth. In the history of the church there have been many so poor and abandoned as to be able to identify with this scene. In many quarters, however, the church has not resisted the temptation to run next door to Matthew and borrow his royal visitors with their gold, frankincense, and myrrh (Matt. 2:1–12), place a soft light in the manger straw, and fill the air with angels. Luke has a glow in the story, but it is shining elsewhere, in the shepherds' field.

Verses 8–20 provide the commentary on the significance of Jesus' birth, an angel and the heavenly host being the messengers. It was customary in the Roman Empire for poets and orators to declare peace and prosperity at the birth of one who was to become emperor. In that familiar pattern, but from heaven, comes the good news of joy and peace occasioned by the birth, not of an emperor, but of him called Savior, Christ, and Lord (v. 11). And not in palace halls but in the fields, to the poor and lowly, the news comes first. The prophecy of Isa. 61:1 is fulfilled: the poor have good news preached to them. Two Lukan touches make the story memorable. First, the sign: one would expect that the sign to the frightened shepherds would be some extraordinary proof. For example, as a sign a heavenly host will now appear. Instead, the sign is as common as another baby born to the poor, to be found in a feeding trough. Second, it is from the shepherds that Mary and Joseph hear of the angel and the heavenly host. These two, busy with the chores of childbirth under the most difficult of conditions, do not themselves experience heaven's visit but hear of it from the shepherds. How unusual! But theirs is the baby, and that is enough.

Three matters of theology deserve a word here. First, the angel provides a summary of Luke's Christology: Jesus is of the house of David, he is Savior (neither Matthew nor Mark uses

35

the title), he is Christ (Messiah), and he is Lord. This is the message about Jesus preached by the apostles (Acts 2:14–36). Second, the heavenly host sings of peace, that wholeness of life which God grants to persons and societies through a restoring of balance in all the forces in creation which influence our lives. This eschatological hope (Isa. 9:6; Zech. 9:9–10) will be fulfilled in Jesus. But for whom? Some ancient manuscripts omit "with whom he [God] is pleased" (v. 14), apparently because of objection to what seems to be a restriction, a condition, placed on God's grace. However, the phrase may not be restrictive at all but inclusive of all of humankind. Read the line with a comma (Greek texts had no punctuation marks at all) or a pause after "men" (humankind): "on earth peace among all humankind, with whom God is pleased." This would be consistent with verse 10: "to all the people." All this is not to say that Luke places no conditions on human behavior in his theology. He proclaims God to be "kind to the ungrateful and the selfish" (6:35), and yet more than any other New Testament writer, Luke issues the call to repentance (13:1–5; 15:7, 10; 16:30; 17:3; 24:47; and frequently in Acts). The preacher or the teacher will want to avoid flattening out Luke simplistically, cheapening grace or absolutizing moral and ethical expectations.

The third and final word here on Luke's theology concerns his focus on the shepherds. They belong in the story not only because they serve to tie Jesus to the shepherd king, David (II Sam. 7:8), but also because they belong on Luke's guest list for the kingdom of God: the poor, the maimed, the blind, the lame (14:13, 21). And so the shepherds go to the city of David. The shepherds and the scene are described with some of Luke's favorite words, words he has used before: wondering, pondering in the heart, making known the revelation, praising and glorifying God. The stable is bare, but the glory of God floods the story.

Luke concludes this section (2:1–21) with a simple statement (v. 21) that looks both backward and forward. It looks backward with the reminder that the naming of the child Jesus (Joshua meaning "salvation") fulfills Mary's obedience to the word of the angel prior to her conception (1:31). The story is not disjointed but rolls forward on the pattern of prophecy/fulfillment. Verse 21 looks forward in that the circumcision of the child on the eighth day begins a series of events reflecting the fact that Jesus' parents represent the best of Jewish piety and obedience to the law of Moses. The story beginning to unfold is "according to scripture."

Luke 2:22–52
Two Stories of Jesus in the Temple

With these two stories, the parallel accounts of John and Jesus come to an end, and Jesus alone occupies the writer and the reader. Except for the statements of Jesus' growth (vv. 40, 52) which recall the statement about John (1:80), there are no reminiscences of John. Luke gently subordinates him by silence. We are back again at the temple in Jerusalem, where the action of the Gospel began (1:8). We earlier reflected on the importance for Luke of the continuity between the two Testaments, between Judaism and Christianity, between synagogue and church. All the major writers of the New Testament deal with the issue of continuity and discontinuity. Paul finds continuity in Abraham, discontinuity in the role of the Mosaic law. Matthew finds continuity in the call for a righteousness which exceeds that of the scribes and Pharisees. The epistle to the Hebrews relates the old and the new on the pattern of shadow and substance, finding the perfection of the old in the new. Yet none of them sets Jesus and the church so thoroughly within Judaism, until rejected, as does Luke. It was Jesus' custom to go to the synagogue on the Sabbath; in Acts the missionary Paul customarily went first to the synagogue in every city (although Paul himself never mentions a synagogue). According to Luke in Acts, Paul reported his missionary work to Jerusalem, circumcised Timothy, a half-Jew, observed the days of Unleavened Bread, cut his hair because of a vow, and told the Jewish Sanhedrin in defense of himself, "I am [not "was"] a Pharisee" (Acts 23:6).

Important in the present context is that continuity with Judaism included for Luke the temple, not only the liturgical center but also the center of Israel's hopes and affections. Think for a moment: Luke's Gospel begins and ends in the temple; the church began in the temple area; the apostles observed the

37

hours of the temple prayers; Paul, long after his conversion, prayed in the temple and later was seized while completing rites of purification at the temple. This is, to be sure, Luke's and not Paul's account of events, but that is the point: neither Jesus nor the church rejects the temple, or to say it another way, according to Luke, God has not rejected the temple. Whatever distance is created between Jesus and the temple, whatever discontinuity develops, it will have to be due to the temple's, that is, the priests', rejection of Jesus. Too much Christian preaching turns its back on the temple and its ritual life, and apparently without pain, as though God had experienced a change of mind.

We are now ready to go with Mary, Joseph, and Jesus to the temple.

The Presentation of the Infant Jesus (2:22–40)

On February 2 each year some churches hold a service of the Presentation of the Lord. The Gospel basis for it is the text before us. The story falls into three parts: the framing story (vv. 22–24, 39–40), into which are inserted the response of Simeon (vv. 25–35) and the response of Anna (vv. 36–38). The framing story itself has one governing focus: Jesus grew up in a family that meticulously observed the law of Moses. No fewer than five times in this text Luke tells the reader that they did everything required in the law. Later in life Jesus would be in tension with some interpreters of his tradition, but his position would not be that of an outsider. On the contrary, Jesus' own nurture in his tradition prepared him to oppose flawed and hollow practices in the name of the law of Moses.

Luke here puts together two separate regulations: the purification of the mother after childbirth (forty days after, in the case of a male child, Lev. 12:1–8) and the dedication of the firstborn son to God (Ex. 13:2, 12–16). The purification rite called for the sacrifice of a lamb and a pigeon, except in hardship cases, when two pigeons or doves would suffice. The firstborn son dedicated to God could be redeemed for five shekels (Num. 18:15–16). Nothing is said by Luke about the family redeeming the child from his "belongs to God" status. Jesus is therefore like Samuel, who was dedicated to God and who, after having been weaned, went to live in the temple (I Sam. 1—2). More of Samuel will appear in the next story about Jesus in the temple.

38

Within the story of Jesus' presentation in the temple are two testimonies to who this child really is. The first is offered by Simeon, a devout old man filled with the Holy Spirit and assured by the Holy Spirit that he would not die until he saw God's Christ (vv. 25–26). The Holy Spirit leads him to the temple at the very hour when Jesus is being presented. The scene is a moving one: an old man now ready to die holding a six-week-old baby who is, at long last, "the consolation of Israel" (v. 25). The consolation of Israel refers to the messianic age of which Simeon sings in phrases that draw heavily on Isaiah 40—55. This song, the Nunc Dimittis (so called after the first two words in the Latin translation), is inspired speech, and therefore in it the Holy Spirit is declaring Jesus to be the means of salvation for all people, Jew and Gentile (vv. 30–32). That Gentiles are included is not a new theme: universality was, says Luke, the purpose of God already expressed in Scripture (Isa. 42:6; 49:6). But Simeon's word to Mary (apparently this occurred in the outer court, where women were allowed) is that Israel's consolation and the salvation of Gentiles will not be without great cost. Jesus will bring truth to light and in so doing throw all who come in contact with him into a crisis of decision. In that decision, rising and falling, life and death, result. Jesus precipitates the centrally important movement of one's life, toward or away from God. As much as we may wish to join the name of Jesus only to the positive, satisfying, and blessed in life, the inescapable fact is that anyone who turns on light creates shadows. This is what is meant literally by "making a difference," and it is this reality which causes many to take up the task of preaching with great hesitation; after all, who would casually become an accessory in the radical alteration of the lives of others? And, sad to say, this same deep realization may lie at the root of that preaching which avoids saying anything, lest it "make a difference."

At any rate, Luke as early as 2:34–35 weaves the dark thread into what has been a bright tapestry of hopes, inspired songs, and prophecy. Not surprisingly, Luke introduces the shadow side of Jesus' saving work most beautifully: Simeon has spoken so wonderfully of the child's future that the parents are amazed; Simeon then blesses them (v. 34); and to Mary he speaks poetically of the price both she and her son must pay. In that reversal of nature which carries in it a pain unlike any other, the parent will bury the child. When Jesus returns to

39

Jerusalem as an adult, the journey will be what Luke terms his "exodus" (9:31).

The truth of Simeon's prophetic witness is confirmed by Anna, a devout prophetess of advanced age (v. 37 may mean she is eighty-four or has been a widow eighty-four years). Being a woman with the gift of prophecy who lives in the temple area continually in prayer and fasting, she too comes to the scene precisely where and when Jesus is being presented. She thanks God and witnesses about the child to all who have kept alive hope for "the redemption of Jerusalem" (v. 38). Jerusalem and with it the temple represent the whole of Israel's hope before God. And Jesus will return to Jerusalem because, as these two have testified, God is leading Israel to the Messiah, just as God is giving the Messiah to Israel. But Jesus will weep over the city because it did not recognize the time of the messianic visitation (19:41–44).

These two aged saints are Israel in miniature, and Israel at its best: devout, obedient, constant in prayer, led by the Holy Spirit, at home in the temple, longing and hoping for the fulfillment of God's promises. And they, like Zechariah and Elizabeth, are old, ready to move offstage, to "depart in peace." God is doing something new, but it is not really new, because hope is always joined to memory, and the new is God's keeping an old promise. As the risen Christ was later to say to his disciples, "Everything written about me in the law of Moses and the prophets and the psalms must be fulfilled" (24:44). Anna and Simeon are a portrait of the Israel that accepted Jesus. Those who rejected him misunderstood their own tradition and therefore were not capable of recognizing him as the continuation of their own best memory and hope.

In verses 39–40 Luke returns to his framing story to round it off. The law has been fully kept, Mary and Joseph return with Jesus to their home in Nazareth of Galilee, and the child grows in strength, wisdom, and divine favor (cf. I Sam. 2:26). At this juncture in the parallel story of John (1:80), the reader is told not to expect further word until John's public ministry. Here we are left in anticipation but without a clue as to what comes next. The silence and the parallel lines about John lead us to expect that Luke will now move to the ministry of Jesus. The next story comes, then, as a surprise and as a bonus to those of us hungry for all that can be found about Jesus among records too scarce and too brief for our appetites.

Jesus in the Temple at Age Twelve (2:41-52)

Let us reflect for a few moments on the story as a whole. It could be that we are indebted to Luke for this episode (he alone tells it), because he was a historian trying to be as complete as his sources would allow in writing his "orderly account." More likely, however, Luke's primary interest is to establish that Jesus was a true Israelite, from birth brought up in the moral and ritual life of Judaism. Home, temple, and synagogue formed him, and no subsequent criticisms of his ministry or message could trace charges against him to heretical, unfaithful, or misguided influences on his formation. At every significant period of his life he was in continuity with Judaism. Those periods for a firstborn male child were circumcision at eight days; dedication or presentation to God, in this case at six weeks when his mother was purified; bar mitzvah at age twelve; and public life at age thirty. These are the moments Luke marks in Jesus' life. A final word about this story: anyone familiar with extrabiblical accounts of the child Jesus amazing his friends, helping his parents, and punishing bad neighbors with miraculous feats can appreciate the quiet reserve of Luke's narrative. The event unfolds normally, free of miracles, fulfilled prophecies, and special revelations. There is no indication of any memory of the virgin birth or accompanying miracles, prompting some scholars to suggest that the story came to Luke from a source that did not contain the miraculous birth. But Luke knew and told the birth story and yet sees no need to bring the language of this event ("his parents," "your father and I") into harmony with the virgin birth. The fact is that, for whatever reasons, neither Luke nor Matthew carried the implications of the virgin birth into the remainder of their Gospels, nor did the early church include those stories in the preaching of the gospel.

The law of Moses required pilgrimages for Passover, Pentecost, and Tabernacles (Ex. 23:14), but for people at a distance, only the Passover. Jesus is twelve, and if he has already gone through the ceremony of bar mitzvah ("son of the law"), then he is obeying the command to attend Passover. When the seven-day festival ends, the pilgrims from Galilee return home. In such a caravan it is not surprising that a boy among relatives and friends would not be missed for a day. The reactions of the parents are natural, both in the search and in the reprimand. Jesus assumes they would know he would be in his Father's

41

house and they do not understand; Mary has even more to ponder in her heart.

What is Luke saying about Jesus here? The episode fulfills the earlier act of giving the child to the Lord (vv. 22–23). Jesus now claims for himself that special relation to God which was the real meaning of his dedication as an infant. To this point, all signs of Jesus' special nature or mission have been to or through others: the angel, Mary, Elizabeth, Zechariah, shepherds, Simeon, and Anna, but now he claims it for himself (v. 49). The church has sought to recognize this moment in the lives of young people in the rite of confirmation. Jesus sits in the temple among the teachers as a child of unusual understanding (v. 47), but there is no reason to impute to Jesus full and clear knowledge of his future mission. More clarity on the story comes, not by reading Jesus' future back into this scene, but by reading again Luke's model for this unit, I Samuel 2. The boy Samuel was given to God by his mother Hannah, and in time he was taken to live in the temple (tabernacle). It was in the temple that Samuel came to an awareness of his special mission. And of the boy Samuel it was said that he "continued to grow both in stature and in favor with the LORD and with men" (I Sam. 2:26).

Perhaps this is the time to reflect on this use of the Old Testament by Luke, that is, telling a Gospel story on the pattern of an Old Testament story, sometimes even using exactly the same lines and phrases. We will encounter this style of narration often in Luke. The similarities between the stories old and new are too many and too detailed to be coincidental or to be that unconscious use of a source which one meets in the writing and speaking of every culture. For example, one hears "I saw the handwriting on the wall" or "The team had no chance; it was like a lamb led to the slaughter" or "He washed his hands of the whole business" from persons who do not know they are using Scripture. Luke's use is not that casual, and Luke is certainly not trying to prove his account by citing the Old Testament, as is sometimes the case, especially in Matthew. Nor is Luke following the prophecy/fulfillment motif which is used frequently by him and is structurally important for the whole of Luke-Acts.

What, then, is Luke doing? The answer could be quite simple: Luke knew the stories and found them so congenial to his own literary task that he used them as models. A wealth of Old Testament events and personalities nourish Luke's Gospel:

42

Samuel, Moses, David, Elijah, Jonah, and others, but at no time does the truth or authority of his message depend on the prior stories. In other words, Luke's Gospel stands on its own whether or not the readers know the literary antecedents. The event of the boy Jesus in the temple does not require for its clarity or purpose a knowledge of the boy Samuel; Jesus' raising of the widow's son at Nain (7:11–15) has its own purpose and power independent of its model, Elijah's raising of a widow's son (I Kings 17). Another possibility is that Luke, for whom continuity with Judaism is important, chose to weave together old and new not only historically and theologically but also literarily. A final suggested answer to the question of what Luke is doing has to do with persuasion. Good communicators know the power of recognition. If one is presenting that which is new, framing the material on a familiar pattern so that the message, though new, is recognized by the readers, barriers to acceptance fall easily. Readers almost immediately own what is being said. Luke may here be instructing us in method as well as content.

Returning to the story in 2:41–52, let us at this stage of Jesus' life simply say that there were in him the vague stirrings of his own identity, if not vocation. The circle of his awareness and the sense of a larger duty begin to widen and deepen beyond the home in Nazareth. This growth would, of course, lead to tensions within the family. "Son, why have you treated us so?" (v. 48); "Your father and I have been looking for you anxiously" (v. 48); and "They did not understand the saying which he spoke to them" (v. 50) are statements that reflect this tension. Even so, Jesus returned home with Mary and Joseph and was subject to them (v. 51). As Mark states explicitly (Mark 3:31–35) and as Luke implies in the episode, family love and loyalties have their place and flourish under the higher love and loyalty to God.

PART TWO

Preparation for the Ministry of Jesus
LUKE 3:1—4:13

All who have come under the spell of Mark's Gospel know the impact of a sudden beginning; John preaches, baptizes, is imprisoned, and Jesus is baptized, tempted, and into his ministry within the first 14 verses. But this is not Luke's style. Mark pushes his reader off the high board into the deep end of the pool; Luke leads his reader from the shallow end into the deep. In a way, so does Matthew, but Matthew does it in 48 verses, while Luke takes 134 to prepare us for the ministries of John and Jesus. For Luke, significant events have antecedents, causes, and preparations. The church has learned from Luke in this regard and holds its two central celebrations, Easter and Christmas, only after weeks of preparation. If one does not walk the road, the destination is reduced to half its meaning; withdraw from any occasion the anticipation of it and even an event of great importance is much impoverished.

It was once a familiar claim that Luke too began his Gospel with the ministries of John and Jesus. Some scholars theorized that the original Luke, called Proto-Luke, began at 3:1. There is a new beginning at 3:1, to be sure, but we have already seen that the historical, literary, and theological connections with chapters 1—2 strongly refute the theory. No known manuscript of this Gospel exists without the first two chapters. We will, however, have to pay attention to the form and inquire as to the purpose of a second introduction.

This section consists of four units: the ministry of John the

45

Baptist (3:1–20), the baptism of Jesus (3:21–22), the genealogy of Jesus (3:23–38), and the temptation of Jesus in the desert (4:1–13).

Luke 3:1–20
(Mark 1:1–8)
The Ministry of John the Baptist

As Luke has already made abundantly clear, both the Lord's coming and the preparation for that coming are the initiatives of a gracious God. Traditional lectionaries honor this truth by using Gospel lections about John for the second and third Sundays of Advent.

Luke first identifies John by placing him in historical context. His style for beginning the chronicle of events was not uncommon for the time and, for Luke, was probably patterned after the introductions to Old Testament prophetic books (Jer. 1:1–3; Ezek. 1:1–3; Hos. 1:1; Isa. 1:1). The reader is thereby alerted at the outset to the appearance of a prophet. The historical context consists of time (vv. 1–2a) and place (vv. 2b–3a). The time is the fifteenth year of Tiberius Caesar, that is, 28–29 C.E. Pontius Pilate was procurator (technically not governor) of Judea from 26 to 36 C.E. Luke further dates John's appearance by listing three tetrarchs. A tetrarchy was one fourth of a region, the kingdom of Herod the Great having been divided into four parts following his death. Antipas and Philip were sons of Herod and ruled Galilee, Perea, and the northeast areas of Ituraea and Trachonitis. Still farther to the north of Galilee was Abilene, ruled by a succession of men bearing the name Lysanias. Chief priests were the principal authorities in Israel's religion, their influence centering in the temple in Jerusalem and in the Sanhedrin, the Jewish supreme court. The office of chief priest was for life, but Rome sought to control the authority of the office by appointing and deposing chief priests. Annas served between 6 and 15 C.E.. He was replaced by Caiaphas his son-in-law, who held the office until 36 C.E. but in the minds of the people was the real high priest until he died. According to

46

the Gospel of John, Jesus appeared before each at his trial (John 18:12–28).

Are we to account for this detailed dating by recalling Luke's thorough research and plans for an orderly account (1:1–4)? Only in part. Clearly, Luke is already anticipating Acts and the political and religious arenas in which the gospel will make its way. In its expansion from Jerusalem to Rome, the gospel will encounter not only the poor, lame, halt, and blind but also high priests, synagogue rulers, city officials, leading women, ship captains, imperial guards, governors, and kings, finally appealing to the emperor himself. Luke's universality is not only geographical but also social, political, and economic.

As to the place of John's ministry, Luke is quite brief. John received his prophetic call ("The word of God came" [v. 2] was the traditional introductory expression; cf. Jer. 1:2) in the desert. The desert is not, however, simply a place designation; it recalls Israel's formation as God's covenant people and hence implies a return to God. In all the region about the Jordan, John preached what Luke was soon to designate "the gospel" (v. 18). As we will have repeated occasions to observe, the gospel for Luke is the gift of repentance and forgiveness of sins to Israel and to all nations (24:47). John's baptism was joined to repentance and therefore was not a proselyte baptism which seems to have been practiced by some synagogues when receiving non-Jews. The Qumran sect also practiced baptism, but it was a repeated act of cleansing. John's baptism was within his total ministry of preparing the way of the Lord, making hearts ready for the one soon to come "who is mightier than I" (v. 16).

John's ministry is a continuation of salvation history, the tradition of God's dealing with the covenant people. The prophecy of Isa. 40:3–5 is being fulfilled. In the Hebrew text of Isa. 40:3 the way of the Lord is to be prepared in the wilderness; here, following the Greek text, it is the voice which is in the wilderness (John), but the way of the Lord is not confined to that wilderness (desert). The image of a desert prophet's call to prepare for the salvation of God recalls the exodus and desert journey of Israel. It also recalls the preaching of Elijah. However, unlike Matthew and Mark, Luke does not describe John's appearance as like Elijah (II Kings 1:8), since John is not to be too closely identified with Elijah. After all, Jesus will also be Elijah-like. Luke also omits Mark's awkward insertion of Mal.

47

3:1 into the Isaiah quotation, reserving it until 7:27. Luke also extends beyond Mark the passage from Isaiah. The inclusion of verses 4–5 of Isaiah 40 enables Luke to testify to the universality of the gospel and, as important, to show from the Old Testament that God's embrace of all nations is not a new theme but embedded in the tradition all along.

Luke's statement about John's preaching is much more extensive than that of Mark or Matthew: verses 7–9 contain John's general message of repentance; in verses 10–14 Luke summarizes John's social message; and John's preaching about the Messiah is in verses 15–18. As for John's general call to repentance and reformed life, Luke joins Matthew (Matt. 3:7–10) in content but differs in audience. Not to Pharisees and Sadducees alone but to all the people John pronounces his word of indictment. As snakes scurrying before a spreading fire, John's listeners are portrayed as running to escape "the wrath to come" (Rom. 5:9; I Thess. 1:10). John's message creates a moment of truth: all devices for maintaining an illusion of innocence must be abandoned. "We have Abraham as our father" is neither a valid claim for exemption nor an acceptable excuse for failure. Only life and deeds will enable anyone to escape the fate of fruitless trees. The church has agreed; the Gospel readings about John each year during Advent remind us not only that repentance is an appropriate spirit during that season but also that the way to Christ leads through the desert where John is preaching.

The second unit of teaching (vv. 10–14) is peculiar to Luke. Three groups present themselves for instructions as to what it means to bear good fruit, and John shapes an answer appropriate to the special temptations peculiar to each. John is not simply screaming rebukes, trying to reduce a crowd to a pool of guilt and fear; he has a message of social responsibility. A religious void of ethical and moral earnestness is exactly that, void. "What then shall we do?" the seekers ask. Luke will tell us later that the first preaching of the church prompted many to ask, "What shall we do?" (Acts 2:37). John's answers, which have to do with the injustices and inequities of that society, are continuous with Luke's convictions about the social implications of the gospel, the first glimpse of which we saw in the Magnificat. These social and economic concerns will be built into the agenda of the common life of the early church (Acts 2:43–47; 4:32–35). Food and clothing are to be shared with people who have none; taxes are not to be calculated according

48

to the greed of the people who are in power (take a moment now to read 19:1–10); and the military must stop victimizing the poor people under their occupation by constant threats, intimidation, and blackmail. The peasants of the land do not exist as sources for supplementing soldiers' pay.

The third and last portion of John's message (vv. 15–18) is in response to those who would identify him as the Christ. Both Mark (Mark 1:7–8) and Matthew (Matt. 3:11–12) speak of John's messianic preaching, but only the Fourth Gospel (John 1:19–28) joins Luke in directly dealing with the question in many minds: Is John the Christ? However, all the Evangelists faced the issue directly or indirectly. Luke began to do so, as we have seen, when John leaped in his mother's womb as Mary entered the room (1:41). In the text before us, John distinguishes himself from the Christ in three ways: John is not worthy even to be a slave of the mightier one; the Christ will baptize not with water but with the Holy Spirit and with fire (anticipating Pentecost, Acts 2); and the Christ will bring judgment. Luke here and repeatedly in both the Gospel and Acts will identify the Holy Spirit as the hallmark of Christianity. We will let Luke unfold that theme as we go rather than leaping ahead of ourselves. It does need to be pointed out, however, that the Holy Spirit was a mark of Jesus' work and that of the church (24:49; Acts 1:8; 2:38; 10:47; and others) but not of the community created around John the Baptist (v. 16; Acts 18:24–28; 19:1–7).

In its present context, "Spirit and fire" can also be translated "wind and fire," giving a double meaning to John's words. Wind and fire were symbols for the Holy Spirit, the powerful presence of God (Acts 2:1–4), but also of judgment. Farmers poured wheat from one container to another on a windy day, or tossed the wheat into the air with a fork or shovel so that the chaff would be blown away, leaving the grain clean. The chaff burned with explosive combustion. To this day, farmers know that a fire in a dry wheat field cannot be contained or controlled. The message is clearly one of judgment, just as in the earlier image, "The axe is laid to the root of the trees" (v. 9). The preacher should not, however, use John's message as the permission to launch attacks on listeners, without redemptive content. When repentance and forgiveness are available, judgment is good news (v. 18). The primary aim is to save the wheat, not to burn the chaff.

Luke rounds off the account of John's ministry by brief

49

reference to the response of Herod Antipas who found John's preaching too direct and too indicting (vv. 19–20). Both Matthew (Matt. 14:3–12) and Mark (Mark 6:17–29) offer later and more elaborate records of John's imprisonment and death. The imprisoned John will reappear in Luke (7:18–35) and his greatness extolled by Jesus, but with no account of his martyrdom. Luke will simply quote Herod: "John I beheaded" (9:9). Herod will also reappear several times, a man perplexed, confused, and agitated by both John and Jesus. For the present, however, it is enough to get John offstage in order to make room for the entrance of Jesus. Apparently the directness with which John spoke to the multitudes about repentance and reformation of life he turned on the adulterous tetrarch of Galilee. Rather than responding to the message, Herod tries to silence the messenger.

Luke 3:21–22
(Matthew 3:13–17; Mark 1:9–11)
The Baptism of Jesus

Jesus' baptism is so familiar to the church from the accounts in the other Gospels that the preacher and the teacher will have to call deliberate attention to Luke's text in order for him to be heard. Luke does not mention the place of the baptism (although the Jordan was named at v. 3) or the one who baptized Jesus. Luke already has John in prison (v. 20). This way of telling the story, which seems to subordinate history to theology, is certainly not to create doubt about who baptized Jesus but rather to move the camera off John and on Jesus alone. Also, Luke is clearly not interested primarily in the baptism itself. He mentions the baptism in a dependent clause in which Jesus is part of a crowd who have been baptized. In fact, Luke does not focus on the scene until Jesus has already been baptized (v. 21). Why? This minimal attention to Jesus' baptism may be due in part to some early Christian difficulty with, if not embarrassment over, the fact that Jesus was baptized. Matthew 3:13–15 deals with the problem, and later Christian writings dismissed any problem with Jesus being baptized by converting the baptismal scene into a grand miracle with bright lights, fire on the surface of the water, and a voice proclaiming Christ's divinity. However, it is more likely that Luke's slight attention to the baptism itself is due to his desire to highlight the postbaptismal revelatory character of Jesus' experience. The first main clause of the text is "The heavens were opened"; here Luke's principal affirmation begins. It is for this reason that the church has long understood the Gospel accounts of Jesus' baptism as Epiphany texts, that is, as proclamations of God's Christ to the world.

The revelatory drama of Jesus' postbaptismal experience is in three parts. First, "the heavens were opened." The expression recalls Isaiah's prayer for heaven to open and for God to come again as in the exodus (Isa. 64:1–4). A new exodus would be the beginning of a new age. Second, the Holy Spirit comes upon Jesus, and thereafter marks his ministry (4:1, 14, 18, and many others) and will be his gift to the church to enable its ministry of witness and service (24:49; Acts 1:1–4). It is difficult to know from what background, if any, the Holy Spirit was associated with a dove. It may have been a connection made by early Christians but not from Judaism. If Luke's readers were familiar with Hellenistic literature, then they may have recalled stories of birds as harbingers of divine choice or destiny (Talbert, *Reading Luke*, p. 40). The phrase "in bodily form," unique to Luke, is especially difficult, since in bodily form is the only way a dove can descend. Perhaps it is Luke's way of asserting the certainty of the experience, not to be confused with thought or feeling alone. One recalls Luke's risen Christ eating fish (24:42–43); perhaps this is similar. Since Luke's account of the experience is not so much a public event as in Matt. 3:13–17, "in bodily form" is probably not to be taken as a proof to others who might have been present.

The third part of the revelatory drama is the voice from heaven, "Thou art my beloved Son; with thee I am well pleased" (v. 22). This heavenly attestation combines Ps. 2:7, used at the coronation of Israel's king as son of God, and Isa. 42:1, a description of the servant of God. The two texts join sovereignty and service. There is no justification, however, for pouring into this moment all the implications of Isa. 42:1, that Jesus here becomes aware that he is to be a suffering servant Messiah. A few manuscripts add to verse 22 the remainder of Ps. 2:7: "Today I have begotten thee." This slim testimony was taken by some early Christians to support the adoptionist view

51

that Jesus became Son of God at his baptism. In agreement with Mark, the voice is addressed to Jesus and not to others as a public announcement, as in Matthew. The voice from heaven affirming Jesus' relation to God is important in the overall structure of Luke's Gospel. Here at 3:21–22 that voice precedes the beginning of Jesus' public ministry; at 9:35 on the Mount of Transfiguration, the voice will confirm Jesus as Son of God preceding the journey to Jerusalem and to death.

The coming of the Holy Spirit does not make Jesus the Son of God; Luke has told us who Jesus is from the time of the annunciation. The Holy Spirit comes to empower Jesus for his ministry. He will soon be led by the Spirit into the desert (4:1), and then he will return "in the power of the Spirit into Galilee" (4:14).

A final word about this text: notice the reference to Jesus praying (v. 21). The prayer life of Jesus is very important to Luke and, through Luke, for his readers. Jesus will be presented often in prayer, and especially at critical moments, such as when choosing the Twelve, when asking his disciples to say who he is, or on the Mount of Transfiguration (3:21; 6:12; 9:18–22; 9:28–29; 11:1; 22:32, 41; 23:34, 46). But it is not the prayer life of Jesus alone which concerns Luke as though it were a matter of historical interest. Just as Jesus was praying when the Holy Spirit came upon him, so the church was in prayer awaiting the promised coming of the Holy Spirit (Acts 1:8, 14), and, after the manner of Jesus, they continued in prayer (Acts 2:42; 3:1; 4:31; 6:4; 12:12; 13:3). There is no reason the church should think that the Holy Spirit and prayer are data of history and not available for life and ministry until the close of the age. Luke's history is more than history; it is witness.

Luke 3:23–38
(Matthew 1:1–16)
The Genealogy of Jesus

52   While it is evident that Luke is now following the outlines of Mark, he does insert a genealogy between the baptism and the temptation of Jesus. Luke's intention in giving the geneal-

ogy is not clear, nor is his reason for placing it here. Some scholars have theorized that Luke's pattern was suggested by the fact that Moses' call and ministry are separated by a genealogy in Ex. 6:14–25. Matthew, whose genealogy is different and differently structured, opens his Gospel with a list of the generations of Jesus, beginning with Abraham. Luke's placing of the genealogy does not seem to be a purposive separation of the baptism and the temptation but rather a closing of the accounts in chapters 1—3. Viewed in this way, what of value to Luke's reader is offered in verses 23–38? First, we are told Jesus was approximately thirty when he began his ministry. This is one of only two Gospel references to Jesus' age as an adult (John 8:57). Up to this point, Luke has marked the significant periods in Jesus' life as an Israelite: eight days, six weeks, twelve years. Is thirty years of age an important milestone? Perhaps Luke is recalling David's age when he began to reign (II Sam. 5:4) or perhaps the age when a priest could begin to serve God (Num. 4:3).

Second, the genealogy links Jesus to God through Adam. Luke is not developing a Christology of Jesus as the Second Adam, as Paul did (Rom. 5:12–21); rather, he is again expressing the universal reach of God's purpose. In other words, Jesus is related to creation and Adam (humankind) as a reaffirmation not simply of the extent of the ministries of Jesus and the church but of God's original and never abandoned purpose. This theology will reappear in Acts, especially in Paul's preaching in Athens (Acts 17:22–31).

Finally, the genealogy dramatizes a point repeatedly made by Luke: Jesus is in continuity with his heritage, a true child of Israel. The family line is traced through Joseph, the legal but not the biological ("as was supposed," v. 23) father of Jesus. The differences between the names here and those in Matthew should not distress the reader. Genealogies were framed for particular reasons and tended to become stylized and even symbolic. For example, Luke has eleven series of seven names each, a total of seventy-seven. One immediately suspects that symbolism has seasoned history. Anyone wishing to pursue further the nature and functions of genealogies could profitably read Joseph A. Fitzmyer, *The Gospel According to Luke,* 1:488–498. It is enough for our present purpose to say that the genealogy, given its location, gives us a literary release to follow the now adult, now anointed with the Holy Spirit, Jesus of Nazareth

53

in the direction in which he will be led by the Spirit. One would expect that the genealogy would be used by Luke to separate preparation from ministry, but the preparation has not yet ended. The Spirit is leading Jesus, but not yet to Galilee; the devil will not let him move that easily into the service of God. It probably was no surprise to Jesus, nor should it be to us: good news always has its enemies. Love generously and hatred will pull on boots and helmet; speak truthfully and falsehood begins to charm its auditors; live simply and extravagance sets up a carnival across the street; serve faithfully and self-interest renews its seduction of human pride.

Luke 4:1–13
(Matthew 4:1–11; Mark 1:12–13)
The Temptations of Jesus

That Jesus was tempted has strong attestation in Scripture, being recorded in all three Synoptics and in Hebrews 4:15. The writer of Hebrews recalls Jesus' temptation to underscore his total identification with all of us. Here, however, the story has a different function. But first, to be true to Luke's style, we need to locate Jesus' temptation in relation to its antecedents in Judaism: Moses' forty days on the mountain without food (Ex. 34:28; Deut. 9:9); Elijah's forty days in flight to the mountain of God (I Kings 19:4–8); and, of course, Israel's forty years of struggle in the wilderness (Deut. 8:2–6). In fact, the wilderness trials of Israel, especially as recited in Deuteronomy 8, are clearly the immediate background to Luke 4:1–13, and in that passage Deuteronomy is quoted by Jesus three times (Deut. 8:3; 6:13; 6:16). Of course, the general background is the Garden of Eden (Gen. 3:1–7). There will be more on that later. The New Testament brings the wilderness trials of Israel forward not only into the life of Jesus but also into the life of the church (I Cor. 10:1–10). Subsequently, the church has reflected on temptation as the common human lot during the forty days of Lent, the Gospel reading for the first Sunday always being one of the accounts of Jesus in the wilderness.

54

Since all three Synoptics tell this story, the preacher would do well to separate Luke's record and focus on its particular accents. Even though Luke has much in common with Matthew, noticeable differences appear. In Luke, Jesus' not eating "in those days" (v. 2) is not formalized into a forty-day fast, as in Matthew 4:2. Luke says the devil's showing Jesus the kingdom of the world is a temporal experience ("in a moment of time," v. 5), whereas it is spatial in Matthew ("to a very high mountain," Matt. 4:8). Luke seems to have reserved mountains for experiences of prayer and revelation. Also in Luke's order of the temptations, Jerusalem and the temple are the site of the final struggle. This is an appropriate climax, since Jerusalem and the temple are so central to Luke-Acts, being the destination of Jesus' journey and the scene of both triumphs and trials for Jesus and the church. Finally, it is noticeable that Luke, for all his comfort with angels, has none here, as do Mark and Matthew. Luke concludes the temptations not with relief but with foreboding: the devil "departed from him until an opportune time" (v. 13). This expression anticipates the passion, for the tempter will reenter the narrative through Judas (22:3).

The experience of temptation is between one who is full of the Holy Spirit and is led by the Holy Spirit, on the one hand, and the devil ("the slanderer"; Mark has Satan, "the adversary"), on the other. The Scriptures variously characterize the power of evil in the world: tendencies within ourselves; a personal being outside ourselves, apparently a powerful angel gone astray; a cosmic power; and organized forces arrayed against the will of God for the world. In whatever images or concepts, Scripture agrees with experience that there is in us and among us strong opposition to love, health, wholeness, and peace. Being committed to the way of God in the world does not exempt one from the struggle. In fact, it is those who are most engaged in the way of God who seem to experience most intensely the opposition of evil. If Jesus struggled, who is exempt? Nor did the presence of the Holy Spirit mean the absence of temptation; rather, the Spirit was the available power of God in the contest.

Give the tempter his due: the timing is perfect. Jesus has not preached a sermon, cast out a demon, or healed a sick person. He is alone and hungry in the desert, poised at the edge of his ministry. What will be its nature and shape? Scripture

55

does not give psychological profiles of its characters but permits the reader to see them through action and conversation. Here the temptation is presented as a conversation, as in Genesis 3. We may surmise that Jesus is struggling with what it really means to be about God's business. This first temptation is not only personal but social: Will Jesus' ministry be one of turning stones to bread? The second is political: Will Jesus submit to the ruler of this world in order to achieve good for the people of this world? The third is religious: Will Jesus win Jerusalem by coercing faith, avoiding death by the display of supernatural power? It is important to keep in mind that a real temptation beckons us to do that about which much good can be said. Stones to bread—the hungry hope so; take political control—the oppressed hope so; leap from the temple—those longing for proof of God's power among us hope so. All this is to say that a real temptation is an offer not to fall but to rise. The tempter in Eden did not ask, "Do you wish to be as the devil?" but, "Do you wish to be as God?" There is nothing here of debauchery; no self-respecting devil would approach a person with offers of personal, domestic, or social ruin. That is in the small print at the bottom of the temptation.

If anyone is having trouble believing that Jesus was *really* tempted, then he or she needs to keep in mind that temptation is an indication of strength, not of weakness. We are not tempted to do what we cannot do but what is within our power. The greater the strength, the greater the temptation. How fierce must have been Jesus' battle! And very real; this is no cartoon with pitchforks, red suits, and horns. Temptation is so deceptively attractive. It was not to a malicious opponent but to a very close friend that Jesus said, "Get behind me, Satan!"

But Jesus, full of the Holy Spirit, is armed with Scripture. In Luke's theology, Scripture is adequate to generate and to sustain faith. If Scripture is set aside, not even miracles will help (16:27–31). Three times Jesus counters the tempter with Scripture. To be sure, the devil also quotes Scripture to support a temptation (Ps. 91:11–12), an indirect testimony to the central importance of Scripture in Jesus' life. But Jesus discerns the difference between appropriate and inappropriate uses of Scripture; as Shakespeare has put it, "There is no error so gross but that some sober brow will bless it with a proper text."

The struggle ends. Jesus has rejected the way of flaunting miracles and he will not take up the political sword. The way of God's response to human need is otherwise. Jesus leaves for Galilee, but the trials are not left forever in the desert; the tempter will watch and wait for the "opportune time."

PART THREE

The Ministry of Jesus in Galilee

LUKE 4:14—9:50

This section is one of the two major movements of Luke's narrative about Jesus' ministry prior to his entry into Jerusalem, the other being the extensive account of the journey to the Holy City (9:51—19:28). In this section we can anticipate basically two types of material: that which gives the reader stories of typical activities of Jesus as he moved freely about Galilee: teaching, preaching, healing, exorcism, and controversy; and that which gives the reader some sense of movement and development in Jesus' ministry: beginning alone, growing in popularity, choosing helpers, preparing them, and facing growing anxiety among his followers and opposition from established leaders.

Luke prepares the reader and creates anticipation by providing a kind of summary at the outset (4:14–15). Luke is very fond of summaries, for they function to round off one section, provide transition to another, and prepare the reader to make a new beginning. There are many summaries both in the Gospel (4:14–15; 8:1–3; 11:53–54; 19:47–48; 21:37–38) and in Acts (2:43–47; 4:32–35; 5:7; 9:31; 12:24). In fact, there are in the Gospel and in Acts brief summaries of Jesus' ministry that apparently were a part of the church's preaching, especially in its encounters with followers of John the Baptist and with the synagogue:

> Go and tell John what you have seen and heard: the blind receive their sight, the lame walk, lepers are cleansed, and the deaf hear, the dead are raised up, the poor have good news preached to them.
>
> Luke 7:22

59

> Men of Israel, hear these words: Jesus of Nazareth, a man attested to you by God with mighty works and wonders and signs which God did through him in your midst, as you yourselves know.
>
> Acts 2:22

> The word which was proclaimed throughout all Judea, beginning from Galilee after the baptism which John preached: how God anointed Jesus of Nazareth with the Holy Spirit and with power; how he went about doing good and healing all that were oppressed by the devil, for God was with him.
>
> Acts 10:37–38

With this characteristic of Luke in mind, we are prepared to look at the summary with which the Galilean ministry is introduced.

Luke 4:14–15
(Matthew 4:12–17; Mark 1:14–15)
Opening Summary

This brief unit functions in three ways. First, it provides a transition in terms both of location and of activity from Jesus' temptations in the desert to the launching of the Galilean ministry; second, it continues to hold the attention on the power of the Spirit in Jesus' ministry in Galilean synagogues; and finally, it sets the general context of Jesus' ministry in synagogues. It is important for understanding the rejection of Jesus in Nazareth and the attempt on his life (vv. 28–29) to see the Nazareth episode against the backdrop of a broad reputation (v. 14) and a favorable reception (v. 15).

Unlike Matthew and Mark, Luke does not relate Jesus' Galilean ministry to the imprisonment of John. Neither does Luke report Jesus preaching an eschatological message of the approaching reign of God. Instead, he offers the most concise sketch: Jesus teaches in the synagogues of Galilee, the report of him spreads, and he is everywhere praised. Clearly, Luke wants nothing of major substance to be reported prior to the visit to Nazareth.

As we move farther into 4:16—9:50, two structural matters will become apparent. First, Luke will be following in general

60

the outline of Mark 1:14—9:39, although some events will be rearranged. We will note these shifts and explore possible reasons as we go. Second, Jesus' ministry according to Luke will be confined to Galilee. Therefore Mark's stories of trips to peripheral regions and north to Tyre and Sidon are omitted.

Luke 4:16–30
(Matthew 13:54–58; Mark 6:1–6)
Jesus in the Synagogue at Nazareth

So different is Luke's account from those of Matthew and Mark that many commentators have reasonably supposed that Luke used a different source. Whether or not that is the case, Luke certainly has a different purpose for the story. This is evident in its location within the Gospel. Rather than placing it late in Jesus' Galilean ministry as do Matthew and Mark, Luke puts it at the beginning. True, in verses 14–15 he has already spoken generally of the Galilean ministry, but this is the first specific event related. It is also true that this story assumes that Jesus has already had a ministry in Capernaum (v. 23), the account of which is yet to be told (vv. 31–37). Luke is not confused; he is sacrificing chronology for another purpose. Just as he told of John's imprisonment before he told of Jesus' baptism (3:19–22), thus leaving the reader with a historical question, so here Luke places the Nazareth visit first because it is first, not chronologically but programmatically. That is to say that this event announces who Jesus is, of what his ministry consists, what his church will be and do, and what will be the response to both Jesus and the church.

It is important first of all to allow the passage to remind us of that which Luke never tires of telling: all that Jesus says and does is within the bosom of Judaism. By his faithfulness, Jesus affirms the Sabbath, the Scriptures, and the synagogue. Jesus not only attends synagogue services regularly but he participates, as all male adults were permitted to do, by reading Scripture and commenting on it. The synagogue services were rather informal, consisting primarily of prayers, reading of Scripture, comments, and alms for the poor. This institution of

61

Judaism apparently arose during the exile as a temple surrogate, but of course without altar or priest. Led by laity, the Pharisees being the most prominent among them, the synagogue became the institutional center of a religion of the Book, not of the altar, and in time became and remains today the dominant form of Judaism. While there was only one temple, synagogues arose everywhere, wherever ten adult males wished so to constitute themselves. The synagogue was not only an assembly for worship but also a school, a community center, and a place for administering justice. Among relatives and friends, in the synagogue Jesus is at home.

By reading Isa. 61:1-2, Jesus not only announces fulfillment of prophecy (v. 21) but defines what his messianic role is. Isaiah 61 is a servant song, and "anointed me" means "made me the Christ or Messiah." When understood literally, the passage says the Christ is God's servant who will bring to reality the longing and the hope of the poor, the oppressed, and the imprisoned. The Christ will also usher in the amnesty, the liberation, and the restoration associated with the proclamation of the year of jubilee (v. 19; Lev. 25:8-12). At the close of the reading, Jesus said, "Today this scripture has been fulfilled in your hearing" (v. 21). It is interesting that in Luke's Gospel, the first public word of Jesus as an adult, apart from reading Scripture, is "today." The age of God's reign is here; the eschatological time when God's promises are fulfilled and God's purpose comes to fruition has arrived; there will be changes in the conditions of those who have waited and hoped. Those changes for the poor and the wronged and the oppressed will occur today. This is the beginning of jubilee. The time of God is today, and the ministries of Jesus and of the church according to Luke-Acts demonstrate that "today" continued. Throughout these two volumes, "today" never is allowed to become "yesterday" or to slip again into a vague "someday." The history of the church does not, however, bear unbroken testimony to Jesus' announcement, "Today this scripture has been fulfilled."

The response to Jesus is mixed: admiration, wondering, doubt. At verse 23, the narrative takes such a negative turn that some scholars have wondered whether Luke has joined two visits of Jesus to Nazareth, one in which he was favorably received and one in which he was rejected, this second perhaps being the one reported in Mark 6:1-6. In the text as we have it, whatever resistance was latently present is evoked by Jesus' quotation of two proverbs: "Physician, heal yourself" and "No prophet is acceptable in his own country." The proverbs indicate that Jesus understood the people to be expecting a demonstration of his extraordinary work reported from Capernaum, but the people's proximity and familiarity tended to be privileges that blinded them. Luke reports as much on other occasions: the people of Nineveh and the queen of the South will judge this generation which did not listen to one greater than either Jonah or Solomon (11:29–32); and those who seek entrance to the kingdom on the grounds that Jesus once taught in their streets or ate in their homes will be turned away (13:26–27).

The problem, however, lies far deeper than blind familiarity. If the people of Nazareth assumed privileges for themselves, that error is joined to a more serious one: resentment that Jesus has taken God's favor to others beyond Nazareth, especially Capernaum, said to have had a heavy non-Jewish population. Jesus defends his ministry to outsiders by offering two Old Testament stories. Both Elijah (I Kings 17:8–14) and Elisha (II Kings 5:1–17), prophets in Israel, took God's favor to non-Jews. That these two stories were in their own Scriptures and quite familiar perhaps accounts in part for the intensity of their hostility. Anger and violence are the last defense of those who are made to face the truth of their own tradition which they have long defended and embraced. Learning what we already know is often painfully difficult. All of us know what it is to be at war with ourselves, sometimes making casualties of those who are guilty of nothing but speaking the truth in love. For Luke, the tension that erupts here and will erupt again and again elsewhere is not between Jesus and Judaism or between synagogue and church; it is between Judaism and its own Scriptures. Luke's point throughout Luke-Acts is that Israel should have understood and embraced Jesus' message. Israel knew of God's grace toward all peoples as early as the covenant with Abraham (Gen. 22:18; Acts 3:25). And Jonah stands forever as the dramatic embodiment of that capacity in all of us, Jew and Christian alike, to be offended by God's grace to all those of whom we do not approve. The reason I did not want to preach to Ninevites, said Jonah to God, was "I knew that thou art a gracious God and merciful, slow to anger, and abounding in steadfast love" (Jonah 4:2).

The synagogue, now a mob, attempts to stone Jesus. Hurl-

63

ing a person against stones was as acceptable a form of stoning as was hurling the stones against the person. Yet this is far from official procedure; it is angry mob reaction. Even so, it foreshadows not only the trial and death of Jesus but also the fate of many of his followers. If it foreshadows Israel's rejection of Jesus and the taking of the message to Gentiles, then it is important to notice that Jesus does not go elsewhere because he is rejected; he is rejected because he goes elsewhere. Jesus' escape, stated without detail (v. 30), is reminiscent of the elusive Elijah who is mysteriously caught away by the Spirit of God (I Kings 18:7–12), and it anticipates the escapes of Peter (Acts 12:6–11) and Paul (Acts 16:25–28).

Luke 4:31—5:16
A Ministry of Growing Popularity in Galilee

All the Synoptics agree that Jesus was favorably received in Galilee (Nazareth excepted), drawing huge crowds with a reputation that extended beyond his itinerary. In the last century when it was popular to write novels about Jesus, this period of his life was called "The Galilean Spring" in contrast to the later period which was entitled "The Jerusalem Winter." The division is, of course, too neat, but even so, the Gospel records witness strongly to an early popularity in Galilee. Even the Fourth Gospel, quite different in perspective and selection of materials, agrees that Galilee was for Jesus welcome relief from the unbelief in Judea (John 4:43–45).

In this section Luke offers six vignettes from Jesus' ministry, not only indicating the range of his activity—teaching, preaching, healing, exorcising demons, and calling disciples—but also providing reasons for his immense favor among the people. In these six stories Luke follows Mark (Mark 1:16–45) except for the relocation of the call of the first disciples to a later time (Mark 1:16–20; Luke 5:1–11). Following Mark, the first four stories could almost be entitled "A Day in the Life of Jesus," beginning with a synagogue service, moving from there to a home, the coming of the sick at sunset, and departure the next morning. However, given the variety of reasons an Evangelist had for a particular selection and arrangement of events, not too much should be made of chronological markers in the Gospels.

An Exorcism in a Capernaum Synagogue (4:31–37) (Mark 1:21–28)

While Mark is followed rather closely here, the reader, by making a comparison, will see how Luke puts his own mark on a story. For example, given Luke's emphasis on Jesus' continuity with Judaism, the contrast between the teaching of Jesus and that of the scribes (Mark 1:22) is omitted. This event occurs in Capernaum, a town on the north shore of the sea of Galilee and the center of much of Jesus' activity. The foundation of an ancient synagogue has been excavated there, perhaps on the site of the one visited by Jesus. The account of what occurred is in three parts: Jesus teaches with authority in the synagogue (vv. 31–32), the exorcism (vv. 33–35), and the response of the crowd to Jesus' authoritative word and the spread of Jesus' fame (vv. 36–37). That the episode opens and closes with statements about the authority and power in the word of Jesus is very important and will be given attention shortly. First, however, a word about demons and exorcism.

The entertainment industry has made so much in recent years of demons, exorcisms, witches, vampires, black cats, and Friday the thirteenth that it would be helpful for the teacher and the preacher to take time to read the articles on demons and on exorcism in a good Bible dictionary (I recommend *Harper's Bible Dictionary*). A major part of learning is unlearning. Luke joins Matthew and Mark (no exorcisms occur in the Fourth Gospel) in reflecting the widespread belief in demons (evil spirits) and the power of Jesus over them. Belief in demons was not native to Judaism and therefore entered through contact with other cultures. Demons were said to inhabit deserts, large bodies of water, the air, and the subterranean regions. When they entered a person they were considered to be the cause of blindness, muteness, and all kinds of physical problems as well as mental disorders. Matthew distinguished between demoniacs and epileptics (Matt. 4:24), "epileptic" being a translation of the word meaning literally "moonstruck" ("lunatic"). That the moon and the stars adversely affected human conditions was also a popular belief. We should not generalize too

65

broadly, thinking that all people in Jesus' time believed in demons or that all physical and mental maladies were due to demons. People in that time and place were not unlike those of other times and places in experiencing a great deal of hostility in the universe and in having to deal with forces hidden in mystery, lying outside the usual avenues of cause and effect. What is important to keep in mind is that in the Gospels the influence of demons is physical or mental, not moral. This distinction is important. For example, we will meet Mary Magdalene in 8:2, of whom it is said that Jesus exorcised seven demons from her. It is erroneous to assume that because of the seven demons she was an immoral woman, as she is so often portrayed. Luke will tell us in 8:26–33 of a man whose demons were legion, they were so many, but their influence was not in the realm of morals; he lived among the tombs, without clothing, often frightening local citizens by his bizarre behavior.

Since demons were from the supernatural world, it is not surprising that they recognized Jesus as a person of God and therefore an opponent of all forces that hurt, cripple, oppress, or alienate human life. In his inaugural message in Nazareth, Jesus announced clearly his intention to relieve, release, heal, and restore life. All persons or powers to the contrary must view him as an enemy. But Jesus was not alone as an exorcist; among the Jews there were exorcists (11:19), some even using the name of Jesus in their ritual of exorcism (9:49; Acts 19:13–17). Jesus also gave the power to cast out demons to the apostles (9:1), and, according to Luke, this was also a dimension of Paul's ministry (Acts 19:12). The act of exorcism involved the confrontation, the calling of the name, since speaking someone's name was an exercise of power over that person or power; sometimes a shouting match between the opponents; calling out the demon by a stronger power; and the recovery, sometimes gradual, of the one now set free. Physical contact between the demoniac and the exorcist may or may not be a part of the process. All this may seem very primitive to an enlightened modern, but we have not, by the announcement that we do not believe in demons, reduced one whit the amount of personal and corporate evil in the world. The names of the enemies have been changed, but the battles still rage.

66   Apparently it was Jesus' authoritative teaching that stirred the demon in a man who was present in the synagogue. The unclean spirit in the man recognized that the word of God

could destroy not only him but "us" (v. 34), that is, the whole realm of demons. The demon sought to gain power over Jesus or at least to neutralize Jesus' power by calling Jesus' name. But the powerful word of Jesus prevailed in the command to be silent and to depart. The man convulses and is thrown to the floor, but once set free, he bears no permanent damage.

The exorcism itself is framed on either side by statements about the authority and power of Jesus' word. Primary attention is not on the exorcism; no rituals or incantations are described. Luke is saying that Jesus is a teacher of the word of God and that word has power. It is that which the world of demons must now face; it is that which amazes the crowd; it is that which the church after him proclaims. This episode is the first vivid demonstration of what Luke meant when he said Jesus came into Galilee "in the power of the Spirit" (v. 14) and the first implementation of the Nazareth sermon (vv. 16–30).

Healing Simon's Mother-in-Law (4:38–39)
(Matthew 8:14–15; Mark 1:29–31)

Luke tells this story in such a way as to give the impression that he assumed the reader had heard it or read it in Mark. For example, he assumes we know who Simon is, but it is Mark (Mark 1:16–20), not Luke, who has introduced Simon. And Luke assumes we know who "they" are who intercede in the mother-in-law's behalf (v. 38), but it is Mark (Mark 1:29), not Luke, who names four people in the room. However, Luke makes his own contribution to the event by describing it not as a healing by touch (Mark 1:31) but as an exorcism. Jesus "rebukes" the fever, the same word used earlier in his word to the demon (v. 35). Luke is following the exorcism in the synagogue with another account of the power of Jesus' word.

Healing the Sick at Evening (4:40–41)
(Matthew 8:16–17; Mark 1:32–34)

We are to assume that this episode occurred in the same city and on the same day as the two immediately preceding. With the sunset the Sabbath is ended and people are free to carry a burden, in this case a sick relative or friend. The sick are healed by the laying on of hands, and demons are exorcised by being "rebuked" (v. 41). Earlier a demon had recognized Jesus as "the Holy One of God" (v. 34); here, as Son of God and Christ (v. 41). Jesus silences the demons, perhaps because the use of

67

such titles could predispose the crowds to a wrong understanding of his mission. After all, they had, as we do, their own definitions of what a Son of God or a Christ was to be and do, and those definitions, like ours, may not have coincided with Jesus' own understanding of his mission. Or it could be that Jesus did not permit the demons to speak, because he would not tolerate confessions from evil spirits. That Luke saw good confessions from questionable sources as a problem is evident in subsequent stories. Paul and his companions were trailed in Philippi by a slave girl with a spirit of divination by which she made money for her owners. For several days she followed them, announcing, "These men are servants of the Most High God, who proclaim to you the way of salvation." Paul exorcised the spirit, not because the slave girl's words were wrong, but because the messenger did not fit the message (Acts 16:16–18). Luke later tells of unbelieving exorcists who try, with disastrous results, to imitate Paul's success by using the name of Jesus (Acts 19:13–17).

Jesus Leaves Capernaum (4:42–44)
(Mark 1:35–39)

The next morning after the events described above, Jesus leaves the town and goes to a lonely place. While the image of "a lonely place" may conjure up the vision of a pensive Jesus in meditation and prayer, the fact is that Luke, who most often speaks of the prayer life of Jesus, does not do so here. It is Mark who says Jesus was praying (Mark 1:35), but even that does not clearly illumine the scene. The key may be the expression "a lonely place," which is, literally, "a desert place." The expression may be more theological than geographical. Jesus was in a desert earlier, in temptation, struggling with the nature of the ministry before him. Now that ministry has begun, he has become famous, the crowds are swelling, and now the people search for him, find him, and do not want him to leave. He is ministering to their needs, to be sure, but is there something in their praise and pleading for him to stay that sounds familiar from the earlier desert experience? It is not an easy call for him or for anyone to make. However, one thing is clear: just as Nazareth had no claim on Jesus to the exclusion of others, neither does Capernaum. The good news of the reign of God—that is, of the time and place of God's favor as shown in Jesus' ministry—is to be shared widely (Luke uses "kingdom of God" here for the first time). That the widespread dissemination of the gospel of God is the very purpose of Jesus' life is clear to him. Yet even so, large crowds of needy people pleading for his service is an experience that has its "desert" side.

The summary statement to the effect that Jesus was preaching in the synagogues of Judea does not necessarily mean that he went to the region to the south of Galilee and of Samaria. Some manuscripts, however, felt the awkwardness of the statement and substituted "Galilee." We know from elsewhere in Luke that Judea was sometimes used as a synonym for Palestine as a whole. For example, in 1:5 Luke calls Herod king of Judea when, in fact, he was king over the entire country, including Galilee and Perea. This seems also to be the use of the word in Acts 10:37. Luke apparently is giving a general statement of the broad range of Jesus' ministry, but he is also saying where Jesus did not go, that is, outside the country, as Mark indicates (Mark 7:24–30). Luke's Gospel is for the world, but first the synagogues must hear it.

The Call of the First Disciples (5:1–11)
(Matthew 4:18–22; Mark 1:16–20)

Both Matthew and Mark place quite early the call of the first disciples, making it all the more remarkable since the backdrop for their call to leave everything to follow Jesus consists only of a brief general statement about Jesus preaching in Galilee. In Luke, the call comes after such wide fame and growing popularity that one can understand the fishermen following such a commanding figure. Also, as our text will unfold, these disciples are responding to a Christ who, in their presence, demonstrates a power to which they are witnesses. They follow a transcendent, compelling Christ in Luke, not a new preacher of an approaching kingdom, as in Mark and Matthew. That the church has traditionally regarded Luke 5:1–11 as an Epiphany text along with Isaiah's vision of God (Isa. 6:1–8) and Paul's vision of Christ (I Cor. 15:1–11) is not surprising. Here Simon Peter gets a glimpse of the power and knowledge of Christ and falls before him in the profound grip of his own sinfulness.

In fact, the miraculous catch of fish, which precedes the actual call, seems very close to the account in John 21:1–23

69

which is a resurrection appearance narrative. In both there is not only a large catch of fish at Jesus' instruction but also a focus on Simon Peter. Simon was mentioned earlier (4:38–39), but here he appears for the first time on full camera. The story so thoroughly centers on Simon that his partners are unnamed until the end, and then Andrew, Peter's brother, if present, is not mentioned. The remarkable catch of fish recalls stories of miraculous provisions in the Elijah-Elisha stories (I Kings 17; II Kings 4), the prophets who have already appeared as a favorite resource for Luke. Luke's comfort with miracles is well known. However, even he is aware of the ambiguous role of miracles in the generation of faith, since non-Christians can also work wonders (11:19; Acts 8:9–11).

A few details need to be noted. While the four preceding episodes in this section seem chronologically joined (a Sabbath, sunset, the next morning), there is no reason to assume any such connection here. It is, however, set in this period of Jesus' great popularity. In fact, he uses the boat of Simon to give himself room, since the crowd is pressing him to the edge of the sea (Gennesaret is Luke's name for the Sea of Galilee). The centrality and efficacy of Jesus' word is again much in evidence: the people come to hear the word of God (v. 1), and Simon responds to Jesus, "At your word I will let down the nets" (v. 5). The call to follow, "Henceforth you will be catching men" (v. 10), is addressed to Simon, but his partners hear the word as also to them, for "they left everything and followed him" (v. 11). Fishing, along with shepherding, became lasting images of ministry in the church. Notice also that Simon's response to the power and knowledge of Jesus is not a fisherman's response; that is, he did not say, Why did I not know where the fish were? Rather, his response is that of a human being in the presence of one he now calls Lord. Simon's skill is not the issue; the issue is his life. Yet in Jesus' eyes his sin does not disqualify him; the same power that prompted Simon to fall at Jesus' knees now lifts him into God's service.

Luke's location of this story of the call of the first disciples implies that Jesus' popularity and the size of the crowds made it necessary to have helpers. This becomes more evident later in the sending out of the Seventy (10:1–2). The work of Jesus is thus prophetic of the church's successful spread of the gospel, a condition that also required the enlisting of more workers (Acts 11:19–26).

Healing a Leper (5:12–16)
(Matthew 8:1–4; Mark 1:40–45)

Luke's introduction to this healing story, "While he was in one of the cities," is quite general, which is a way of saying, "Also typical of Jesus' ministry is the following." We have been shown Jesus in contact with the sick and the demon-possessed; now we see Jesus ministering to a person with a social disease. Leprosy was a name given to a range of maladies from mildew in houses and on clothes to skin diseases in humans (Lev. 13; read the article on leprosy in *Harper's Bible Dictionary*). Much more and much less was classified as leprosy than what we know today as Hansen's disease. But into every culture sooner or later come diseases so mysterious and so threatening that they are met primarily with fear and ignorance. Having no explanation or treatment, religious, social, and political forces join in the demand that the diseased persons be removed from sight, isolated from all domestic, religious, and commercial contact. And so the law said,

> The leper who has the disease shall wear torn clothes and let the hair of his head hang loose, and he shall cover his upper lip and cry, "Unclean, unclean." He shall remain unclean as long as he has the disease; he is unclean; he shall dwell alone in a habitation outside the camp.
>
> Leviticus 13:45–46

Obviously this man violated the law of isolation by approaching Jesus, evidence not only of his desperation but of his belief in what he must have heard, that Jesus could help him.

That Jesus *could* help him seems not to be a question in the leper's mind; the question is, *will* he? After all, his problem is not only one that evokes compassion, such as blindness or a withered limb; his disease is social, evoking repulsion. Yet the leper soon learns that joined to Jesus' power is his selfless caring, for by touching the man, Jesus entered into the man's isolation and shame. No long-distance relief here; Jesus gives himself to those to whom he ministers. Just as one cannot forgive without appearing to condone the very sin forgiven, neither can one help a leper without entering the colony. This realization prompted one New Testament writer to say of Jesus, "For we have not a high priest who is unable to sympathize with our weaknesses" (Heb. 4:15).

71

To the leper now healed, Jesus gave two instructions. First, he was to tell no one. Several possible reasons come to mind. Jesus is already swarmed by crowds, finding little place for privacy, and so he needs no more attention. Jesus does not want any single dimension of his ministry to become so well known that he is defined by it: a healer, an exorcist, a preacher. He is not one of these, nor all of these. To be misperceived is to be robbed of effectiveness in the totality of his work, as outlined in Isa. 61:1–2. Or it could be in this case that Jesus does not want the man to broadcast his healing and thereby be delayed or distracted from his immediate obligation. And that obligation is Jesus' second instruction: go to the priest and go through the ritual required by the law (Lev. 14). Jesus supports the law and will not be accessory to its violation.

But the report of this and other acts of compassion bring to Jesus even greater acclaim and popularity. The people are not to be faulted; they want to hear and to be healed (v. 15). But Jesus will not permit himself to be defined by the people or be so occupied as to be cut off from the source of his power. He is in the desert again, praying and perhaps, as in the desert before, struggling. It was no simple or easy matter to turn away, even for prayer, so long as even one diseased or possessed person asked for help. Some of us regard turning from evil to good a victory; only persons of extraordinary spiritual discernment can at times turn from good to the power necessary to resource the good. In verse 16, Luke says literally, "But he was withdrawing in desert places [plural] and praying." This is not a reference to a single instance but to a pattern of repeated behavior. This is as customary for Jesus as going to the synagogue on the Sabbath.

Luke 5:17—6:11
Early Controversies with Religious Leaders

Some New Testament scholars have gone to the field of folklore to learn how a community preserves and orally passes on stories that are important to the identity and life of that community. This approach quite reasonably assumes that prior to being written in the Gospels, stories of Jesus circulated in Christian communities, became fixed in form with little variation, and were preserved because they were useful for the church's self-understanding and its mission. For example, some stories were used in worship, some in evangelism, some in teaching new converts, and so on. Those who study the Gospels in this way have identified one type of material as having been preserved for use by the church in defending its beliefs and practices before critics. Materials cast in this form are called controversy stories, and that is what occupies us in this section.

Again, Luke follows Mark (Mark 2:1—3:6), but with modifications appropriate to Luke's theology and purposes. Against the backdrop of great popularity, Jesus here is responding to critics. Just as there were six vignettes portraying the types of ministry in which Jesus was engaged, so here there are six stories of controversy. However, since the six units actually involve only four issues, we will treat them as four controversies. The issues are forgiving sin, socializing with publicans and sinners, fasting, and Sabbath observance. Apparently these were very live issues in the early church, and the remembrances from the ministry of Jesus gave the church a response to critics and opponents and a defense of its practices.

First a word to those who may think of the Gospels as biographies of Jesus. The location of these stories within the Gospel of Luke is not to be taken chronologically, that is, as though they occurred early in Jesus' ministry and in this order. Luke wants us to understand them as typical controversies that Jesus faced throughout his ministry. Notice the way the events are introduced: "On one of those days"; "After this"; "On a sabbath"; "On another sabbath." Luke is saying, "I have related to you some of Jesus' activities that generated great popularity; now here is the other side of what was going on." Not only honesty in reporting dictated this procedure but also the need to allow readers to come to informed decisions about Jesus and their relation to him. A yes to Jesus is hardly valid unless one is given the opportunity to join those who say no. This is not to say Luke is doing purely objective reporting; he is an advocate, he is proclaiming the gospel. Yet any preacher who is not afraid, insecure, or silly knows that to Jesus, to the gospel, and to the church many say no. After all, something about Jesus' person and work got him killed, and for twenty centuries many of his followers have paid the same price. Old Simeon said it when Jesus was still a baby: "This child is set for the fall and rising of many in Israel" (2:34).

73

INTERPRETATION

There seems to be no particular order to these stories, not chronological and not in an order of increasingly important issues or of growing intensity of opposition. In fact, the first controversy involves the issues of greatest weight and consequence. We will therefore discuss them as matters distinct and separate from one another.

One final introductory word. In these stories we will meet Pharisees and with them a gathering of scribes, teachers of the law, and disciples. Because Pharisees figure so prominently in Jesus' ministry and because in Luke they relate to Jesus sometimes favorably, sometimes unfavorably, it would be time well spent to go to a Bible dictionary (I have recommended *Harper's*) and read the article on Pharisees. Many of us need to do so much unlearning about them. Widespread in the church is the notion that Pharisee is a synonym for "hypocrite." No doubt many Pharisees were; not only Jesus so accused them but in rabbinic writings some were so charged by other Pharisees. Those whose lives did not correspond to their teachings were called "sore spots." Yet to generalize from that fact to hold all of them guilty is no more fair than to condemn all clergy because of the scandals associated with a few. Pharisees were not priests, as were Sadducees; their center of activity was the synagogue, and the center of their religion was the law, both written and oral. Much of their time was spent spelling out in detail what the law meant in particular situations. For example, the law said, "Remember the sabbath day to keep it holy," but what did that mean if this or that situation arose? They determined meanings for particular cases, and thus attached to a given law might be scores of case-by-case regulations. And why? Because of their basic conviction that the will of God was to be done in every situation twenty-four hours a day. Thus they tried to keep the faith, preserve the community, and protect it from compromise and foreign influence. One does not have to strain to find much in common between Jesus and Pharisees.

The Healing of a Paralytic (5:17–26)
(Matthew 9:1–8; Mark 2:1–12)

It is not surprising that the ministry of Jesus has attracted not only the sick and the demon-possessed but also Pharisees and teachers of the law from all parts of the country. No motive for their presence is stated, but as religious leaders they certainly would want to check for themselves the truth of the

74

stories circulating about this teacher, preacher, healer, and exorcist. They are present on an occasion Luke introduces only in a general way: one day while he was teaching and healing. What happens is very dramatic and most unusual. A group of men trying to bring a paralytic to lay before Jesus are frustrated in their effort and so they lower him through the roof (Luke says "tiles," v. 19, reflecting his own Greco-Roman background rather than Palestinian architecture). In Jesus' ministry to the paralytic (seeing "their" faith, v. 20) he is both healed and forgiven. It is this double blessing which makes the account complex and generates speculation about the meaning of the event.

Some interpreters have concluded that since the first word of Jesus to the paralytic was, "Man, your sins are forgiven you" (v. 20), the clear implication is that his illness is related to his spiritual condition. That some biblical writers make a direct correlation between one's spiritual state and one's physical, or even financial, condition is beyond question. Psalm 1 is a good example: serve God and you prosper; choose the way of wickedness and you fail. In John 5, after healing the paralytic, Jesus said to him, "Sin no more, that nothing worse befall you" (John 5:14). Later, in Acts, Luke will speak of the punishments that come on the sinful: Judas, Ananias and Sapphira, Herod Agrippa. On the other hand, Luke will record Jesus' blessing on the poor and hungry and woe on the rich (6:20–26), the very opposite of the observation of Psalm 1. Luke will also say that Jesus flatly denied any correlation between the tragedies that people experience and their spiritual condition (13:1–5). Of course, the crucifixion of the one without sin is the final argument against the notion that bad things always happen to bad people, or as one noted American clergyman once put it, "Show me a poor man and I will show you a sinner." Clearly the Bible argues with itself on this matter, but in the case before us it is clear that the forgiveness of the man's sin did not cure his paralysis. Whatever one's view of the relation of sin and sickness, this story has a complexity about it not clarified by modern views of psychosomatic diseases.

The complexity of the passage is both literary and logical. From a literary perspective, Luke is obviously using Mark's story (Mark 2:1–12), which many students of the passage regard as a conflation of two stories. According to this view, the account of Jesus forgiving sin is inserted within a healing story. The healing is reported in verses 17–20*a* and resumed at verse 24*b*.

This account, when read without the intervening verses 20*b*–24*a*, is complete, smooth, and clear. Stories within stories are not uncommon in the Gospels (Luke 8:40–56, e.g.). Logically, the complexity lies in verses 23–24. How can one say whether healing or forgiveness is easier, and how can healing prove the authority to forgive? The difficulty of tracing this interweaving of healing and forgiveness forces us to back away and recognize that both have their source in a God who both heals and forgives, and this text announces that God is present in the ministry of Jesus.

In fact, three statements can be made about what Luke is saying here. First, the church is claiming that Jesus had the power of God both to heal and to forgive sin. Second, Jesus commissions his followers to a ministry of healing (9:1–2; Acts 3:1–16) and offering in Christ's name the forgiveness of sins (24:47; Acts 2:38). And finally, Luke understood that there was a relationship between healing and forgiveness. This is evident not only in the story before us but elsewhere as well. For example, Luke uses the same verb in Jesus' statement to a forgiven woman ("Your faith has *saved* you," 7:50) and to a healed woman ("Your faith has *made you well*, 8:48). In the Acts account of the cripple at the temple, the man is described with the same word as both healed and saved (Acts 4:9, 12). Perhaps the tendency to think of persons as composed of body, mind, feelings, and soul hinders our understanding of Jesus' ministry to the whole person.

Eating with Tax Collectors and Sinners (5:27–32)
(Matthew 9:9–13; Mark 2:13–17)

This unit opens with the call to discipleship of the man in whose home Jesus will sit at table with persons regarded as social and religious outcasts. The man is Levi, called Matthew in the First Gospel (Matt. 9:9). Whether Levi had previously known Jesus and has now come to full-time discipleship is not known. What Luke presents is a radical call and a radical response, no less so than the earlier call of disciples. The power of Jesus' word, noted previously on occasions of exorcism and teaching, is again demonstrated here. There is no need to imagine unrecorded gradualism in Levi's decision, nor is there justification for projecting on to the brief account a psychological profile of Levi: a wealthy man still empty, guilt-ridden and sleepless in his silken ease, haunted by the hollow eyes of the poor, searching for the market where real life can be bought, spiritually bankrupt and alone. Why not let the text say what it says: a wealthy man ("Levi made . . . a great feast," v. 29) with a host of friends ("a large company," v. 29) meets the word of Jesus calling him to a life entirely different in which God's care for the oppressed, the imprisoned, the blind, and the poor heads the agenda. Unlike many preachers who wait for the rich and powerful to experience a reversal of fortune before speaking to them of God's reign, Jesus' word to the rich and powerful *creates* the reversal of their lives: "He left everything, and rose and followed him" (v. 28).

The banquet that follows Levi's call to discipleship is not one to which Jesus has also been invited; "Levi made *him* a great feast" (literally, "for him"; that is, Jesus). Jesus is being honored, and at table with a large gathering of Levi's old associates, tax collectors, and "others." These "others" will be identified by critics among the Pharisees and scribes as "sinners" (v. 30). This and other such associations earned for Jesus frequent criticism as "a friend of tax collectors [publicans] and sinners" (7:34). In our society in which a tax collector is on salary and is but one person in a network of financial checks and balances, the teacher and the preacher will have to define the tax collector of the Gospels. In the Roman Empire, local residents, unless enjoying some rare exemption, were subjected to many taxes. There were on occasion poll taxes, road and bridge tolls, taxes on merchandise, and what we would call property taxes. The task of collecting taxes was usually given to a wealthy and powerful figure in a geographical area, most often someone who was not a native of that area. He in turn divided the area into tax districts with chief collectors who in turn used locals for the actual collections. The system allowed for extra tax to be collected above the amount to be sent to the government. The doors to corruption stood wide open. In the literature of the period, including the New Testament, publicans were despised. Add to the financial oppression the ceremonial impurity of such contact with Gentiles and the element of treason for working for foreigners against one's own people and the outcast status is understandable. As for "sinners," this was not simply a personal opinion about someone's life-style; it was a term for those whose breach of the Mosaic law was known in the community, their violations having been formally or informally noted, and who were therefore excluded from the synagogue. Given the

77

central place of the synagogue in the community, to be a sinner was to be an outcast.

The story before us, then, is one that tells of Jesus including the excluded. Jesus' inclusiveness is religious, economic, and political. It is an error to use the Gospel of Luke, with its strong and repeated accent on Jesus' embrace of the poor and oppressed, as permission to be *against* any person or group. One does not have to hate some in order to prove love for others. As Luke will tell us later in a parable of Jesus, a certain man had two sons, and he loved both, and he went out to welcome both (15:11–32).

Jesus' acceptance of publicans and sinners is total, as evidenced by his eating with them. In the cultures and subcultures of that time and place, table customs were identifying marks of a group, whether philosophical, literary, or religious. As expressed in a Near Eastern proverb, "I saw them eating and I knew who they were." Luke will soon tell us that the basis for the rejection of both John and Jesus by many of their contemporaries was the eating habits of these two prophets: John ate with no one and Jesus ate with everyone (7:31–35). Inviting others to one's table could be a sign of affluence or status, but it could also be an act of service. In the early church, common meals were a way of meeting physical needs but in such a manner as to embarrass no one. Those who had and those who did not have sat at table together without distinction (Acts 2:43–47). It was for a violation of this principle, creating an economic division of the table, that Paul sternly rebuked the church at Corinth (I Cor. 11:17–22). After all, table fellowship meant full acceptance of one another. Even today in a pluralistic culture with a range of table customs, eating together has important social meanings, both expressing and creating a community.

Notice that the criticism of Jesus is directed toward Jesus' disciples (v. 30). This does not indicate fear of Jesus but rather reflects the use of this and similar occasions of attack in the life of the early church. That is, the church (Jesus' disciples) was criticized for its inclusive table fellowship which seemed to condone the behavior of publicans and sinners. The answer to the charge is given not by the disciples but by Jesus (vv. 31–32). The church found its defense for its behavior in the example of Jesus' table fellowship and in his words. Jesus responds to the attack with a proverb (v. 31) and a declaration of his vocational purpose (v. 32). The manner of Jesus' words is not only striking in clarity but inescapable in its demand. No one is directly addressed or indicted; rather, Jesus speaks of two categories of persons in two sets of metaphors: the well and the sick, the saint and the sinner. Jesus is clear as to whom his ministry is extended, but his listeners have to decide whether they are well or sick, saint or sinner. Indictments are self-inflicted. And the reader is also caught and can no longer be a spectator at the banquet: Am I at table with Jesus, tax collectors, and sinners, or am I among the critics?

Unlike Mark 2:17 and Matt. 9:13, Luke adds to his version of the story the word "repentance." No other writer in the New Testament approaches Luke's frequency of reference to repentance. One should not be lulled by Jesus' acceptance of all persons, including social and religious outcasts, into thinking that life in God's reign is without any ethical expectations. Repentance is both a gift and a demand of the age ushered in by the presence and the preaching of Jesus.

Debate About Fasting (5:33–39)
(Matthew 9:14–17; Mark 2:18–22)

Unlike Mark, who separates the question of fasting from Levi's house and has unidentified people raise it, and unlike Matthew, who also separates this debate from the preceding one and has John's disciples raise the issue, Luke implies at least that "they" who question Jesus are persons present at Levi's banquet. Here the issue is addressed to Jesus, but it is about his followers (the church), whereas earlier the disciples were asked about their behavior and Jesus answered. In both cases, the matters involve the church. The question is not whether fasting is right or wrong, or whether Jesus' followers are to fast. Fasting, along with prayer and alms, was one of the three good works of Judaism, and the church should not be so adolescent as to reject an act simply because it was practiced in the synagogue. Matthew not only described Jesus' fasting (Matt. 4:2) but assumed it to be an act of Christian piety: "When you fast" (Matt. 6:16–18). Luke speaks of fasting in the early church (Acts 13:2–3; 14:23). In fact, in the Lukan text before us, Jesus says, "The days will come, when the bridegroom is taken away from them, and then they will fast in those days" (v. 35). At issue seems to be the matter of appropriateness. Announced public fasts (II Chron. 20:3; Ezra 8:21–23; Lev. 16:31–34) and routine fasting on Mondays and Thursdays ("I fast twice a week," 18:

79

12), which Pharisees observed, could very easily be separated from a sense of God's grace and generosity toward the world. Living in God's realm involves not only mourning and sorrow for sin but also joy and thanksgiving. Weddings and banquets are also proper analogues for the kingdom of God. However, as verse 35 makes clear, the death of Jesus did later prompt fasting among his followers, and the church will continue until the end of the age remembering his cross as well as his resurrection. The question of appropriateness, of what is fitting on a given occasion, is not answered by Jesus. Were he to say exactly when to fast and when to celebrate, some followers might be relieved at being told exactly what to do and when, but the matter of fittingness would have been denied. The church must wrestle with its proper responses to life and to gospel, just as the loving father struggled with his older son over the question, Is it appropriate to make merry when a lost son and brother returns home (15:25–32)?

Jesus elaborates with a parable. The word "parable" is used to refer to simple figures of speech, to analogies, and to metaphors extended into narratives. It seems best to wait until we meet parables in their fuller and more complex forms to discuss what parables are and what they do. In this case, the parable is a rather straightforward analogy. Jesus tells his critics that his disciples can no more join to old rituals their new sense of life in the age now begun than one can successfully tear up a new garment to patch an old one or put new wine in old skins. New cloth and new skins are alive, changing, not fixed in form or size, and therefore are not to be treated as though they were dead and unchanging. Christian rituals of worship and forms of activity must always be appropriate to the liveliness of the new age. The followers of Jesus have not, however, been able to hear this word as an ever-present word. Rigidity sets in, often for the worthy motives of maintaining identity and defending the faith. Then when this text is rediscovered, its implementation meets with great resistance and division occurs. Under such circumstances the matter of appropriateness is often lost, while "old" and "new" are trumpeted as values in themselves.

Luke's verse 39 is unique and unusual. Is it humor or irony? The statement is certainly discontinuous with the preceding verses, having in common with the prior discussion only the words "wine," "old," and "new." It may be a recognition that many who heard Jesus found it very difficult to abandon the old

ways of Judaism—respected, traditional, confirmed with Scripture—and to take up the new, which was still finding its way,
its voice, its shape, its own identity. Luke may be looking ahead
to Acts, in which he records this very struggle in the church.
Many sincere believers in Jesus insisted on keeping in place the
practices of the law but with Jesus added on as the Messiah. The
issue will not go away: Seventh-Day Adventists remind us that
not all are yet of the same mind. Luke himself is not exempt,
for old and new, continuity and discontinuity, are for him two
values, and he will not relinquish one as the necessary price for
holding the other.

Debates Concerning the Sabbath (6:1–11)
(Matthew 12:1–14; Mark 2:23—3:6)

That Luke locates these stories quite generally—"on a sabbath" (v. 1) and "on another sabbath" (v. 6)—is not only to say
that these are just two examples of conflicts over Sabbath observance but also to underscore that what is important is not
where or when these events occurred but the kind of events
they are: they are Sabbath stories. This is to say that these
incidents from the life of Jesus present him in conflict with
Jewish leadership over practices that were central to piety and
to identity as God's people. So very much of what it meant to
be the faithful community was tied to the table customs and
Sabbath observance. In this section of controversy stories, two
have dealt with Jesus' eating habits (he ate with sinners; he ate
when others fasted). Now we have two that deal with Sab-
baths—that is, the seventh day of each week and certain other
designated holy days. Support for Sabbath observance was both
theological ("God rested on the seventh day," Gen. 2:1–3; Ex.
20:11) and practical (workers and animals need rest, Ex. 23:12;
Deut. 5:14–15). Naturally, questions would arise in the community: "But what if this or that happens on a Sabbath?" The law
gave specific instruction to cover many contingencies, but as
others arose, tradition provided precedent and interpretation.
The Pharisees and the scribes were knowledgeable and skilled
in such details.

Luke follows Mark in relating two Sabbath conflicts back to
back, perhaps representing two different kinds of answers the
early church used in responding to criticism from the synagogue or from some of its own members who continued to be
faithful to the law of Moses. In the first, Jesus defends the actions

of his disciples (vv. 1–5); in the second, his own, which, we may assume, was, for the early Christians, an argument for its own behavior from the precedent of Jesus (vv. 6–11). In the first, the disciples are not accused of stealing; one was allowed to eat from a field while traveling (Deut. 23:25). The charge is apparently harvesting (plucking grains) and threshing (rubbing the grains in the hands to remove the chaff). Jesus' defense is by a precedent from the life of David who, in a crisis, acted contrary to the law (I Sam. 21:1–6). Extreme human need, hunger, made a claim prior to that of sacred ritual. Luke does not, however, follow Mark (Mark 2:27) in an expansion on that incident into a broad principle: "The sabbath was made for man, not man for the sabbath." Perhaps such a principle was regarded by Luke as opening the door to and blessing many easy violations of the Sabbath in favor of Christian preferences. We have already observed that Jesus was too interior to Judaism to suggest any permission to disregard its laws and customs. Rather, Luke concludes the episode with a pronouncement: "The Son of man is lord of the sabbath" (v. 5). This strong christological statement asserts that Jesus is superior to Sabbath laws and can determine where, when, and how they apply. For the church, this means that Jesus Christ, his words, and his actions determine the church's understanding of the Sabbath. This is understandable, given Luke's position that the Old Testament bears witness to Christ (24:27, 44). The church is not, then, bound by the Sabbath, but it is not free to treat it cavalierly; rather, it is bound to Christ who interprets the Sabbath for the church.

In the second Sabbath conflict, Jesus' behavior provides for the church another interpretation of the use of the law for good. Jesus is teaching in the synagogue on the Sabbath; that is, he is faithfully observing the law and ministering within Judaism. The crisis arises when he is confronted by a case of human need. Will he teach now and heal later, or will he join teaching and healing now? Must he delay meeting a need because it is the Sabbath? Mark says Jesus was angry (Mark 3:5); Luke says the Pharisees and the scribes were (v. 11). Jesus poses the issue so as to make inactivity before human need no real option at all. One will be *doing* something: to act is to do good (save life); to refuse to act is to do evil (destroy life). The choice is not whether to do or whether not to do but *what* will I do? Jesus answers his question by his act of doing good: he heals the man. The message is clear: it is never the wrong day to help another, to minister to human need.

82

This incident equipped the church with its second way of responding to criticism, within or without, over its interpretation of Sabbath observance. Luke will later provide two additional cases of Jesus healing on the Sabbath but with slightly different supporting arguments. At 13:1–17, following the healing of a woman with a severely curved spine, Jesus will argue that if it was permitted on the Sabbath to loose a tethered animal in order to take it to water, why not allow the loosing of this woman so long tethered by infirmity? At 14:1–6, Jesus will support a Sabbath healing by an appeal to the recognized allowance for emergency action on the Sabbath: If it is permitted to rescue from a well a son or an ox, then is not this case covered by that same exception? One can hear in these critical incidents echoes of the early church's struggle not only with the synagogue but with itself over this ancient and sacred tradition.

Both Matthew and Mark conclude this section of controversies with the opposition taking counsel against Jesus, how to destroy him. Luke draws this material to a close with an anticipation of the cross but not yet indicating a definite death plot. The critics are angry and discuss "what they might do to Jesus" (v. 11). These opponents are Pharisees and scribes; no high priests from Jerusalem are yet in the picture, and so the pot has not yet come to a boil.

Luke 6:12–16
(Matthew 10:1–4; Mark 3:13–19)
Choosing Twelve Apostles

With the expression "In these days" (v. 12), Luke pulls the reader back into the longer narrative of the Galilean ministry. After several units that relate intense conflicts with Pharisees and mounting opposition to Jesus, the reader may feel distant from the accounts of great popularity into which Luke had set the controversies. Perhaps a return to 5:16 will restore the larger picture: overwhelming public approval, with Jesus withdrawing for times of prayer in the desert. But the opposition is not to be forgotten. Popularity and conflict form the twin backgrounds for calling the Twelve: the apostles can help with an ever-increasing ministry and they can assure continuity when

83

opposition becomes hostility and Jesus' life is taken. In fact, these twin backgrounds also provide the apostles with a sense of the kind of contexts in which they will be working.

Luke again reminds the readers that the ministry of Jesus moves along on a life of prayer. None of the other Evangelists is so attentive to this pervading factor in Jesus' ministry. At his baptism Jesus was in prayer (3:21); at the peak of his popularity he withdrew for prayer (5:16); the choice of the Twelve came after an entire night of prayer (6:12); and we will be reminded of Jesus' practice of praying when he asks his disciples to say who he is (9:18), when he goes up on the mountain and is transfigured (9:28), as well as on other occasions (11:1; 22:41–46). There is no way the reader of Luke can think of the choice of the Twelve as an act to expedite matters when the job is too big for one person. The might of prayer elevates the act into the larger purpose of God. Luke will say this again when he sets the commissioning of Barnabas and Saul in a context of worship, fasting, and prayer (Acts 13:1–3). In fact, says Luke, the choice of Barnabas and Saul was the work of the Holy Spirit. This certainly was no less the case with the Twelve.

Unlike Matthew and Mark, for whom the selection of the Twelve is a commissioning for work which is described, Luke here describes nothing but the choice of twelve from among the disciples, twelve whom Jesus names "apostles." Mark uses the verb "sent out" (Mark 3:14) from which the word "apostle" is derived. The other Gospels use this name only once, but with Luke it is a title for the Twelve and he uses it frequently (6:13; 9:10; 17:5; 22:14; 24:10). Luke is certainly looking ahead at this point to his second volume, in which the apostles are principal figures. Not only is the name "apostle" important for Luke but so also is the number twelve, symbolic for the twelve tribes of Israel. When Judas Iscariot fell away, Luke says a divine election was held to replace him, bringing the number again to twelve (Acts 1:15–26).

As for the names of the Twelve (cf. also Matt. 10:1–4; Mark 3:13–19; Acts 1:13), Luke has a second Judas, a son of James, but no Thaddaeus, and he uses no nicknames, such as "sons of thunder" (Mark 3:17) or "the Twin" (John 11:16). While all the Evangelists identify Judas Iscariot as the one who betrayed Jesus, Luke alone labels him with the rare noun "traitor" (v. 16). Although the New Testament provides four lists of these twelve, Luke himself the source for two of them, little or nothing is known about several of these men. We have learned already that several were fishermen and that Matthew (Levi) was a tax collector. There are two Simons, one called Peter (Luke makes nothing special of that) and the other called the Zealot. The term in its religious sense referred to one zealous for the law of God (Num. 25:13; II Kings 10:16), as was Paul (Acts 22:3). Or the word could be used here in a political sense, one who vigorously opposed the Roman occupation of Palestine, one who was a strong nationalist. Later legends filled in the lack of information about the unknown ones among the Twelve, and Christian scribes standardized the four lists, as later manuscripts indicate.

Luke 6:17—9:6
Ministry Between the Choosing and the Sending of the Twelve

Jesus has been making disciples for some time now, and some of them have "left everything and followed him" (5:11, 28). Being with Jesus has been, among other things, a time of preparation for them. From among these disciples, after a night of prayer, Jesus chooses twelve to be apostles, that is, those to be sent out as his representatives. One might suppose that these twelve were the ones from the larger body of followers who were qualified and now ready to go out and minister in Jesus' name and power. But not yet. In fact, Luke has not yet indicated why the Twelve were chosen or what they were to do. Because Luke places a number of teachings and events between their being chosen and being sent out, we may safely assume that the period is one of preparation for them. This is certainly not to say that what Jesus now says and does is to be construed simply as pedagogy for the Twelve. So to interpret this section would be reductionistic and would empty words and acts of much of their meaning. Jesus' ministry continues as it was, fully with and for those who seek his word and his healing. Never is there the slightest hint that Jesus said or did anything as an exhibition of what or how, as though to say, "Now watch and listen, you twelve; this is how it is done." It is not the

85

person trying to be an example who is a good example; rather, it is the person who gives full attention to others and to the opportunity to serve. The good example is the person surprised to discover later that he or she has been viewed as an example. The Twelve are with Jesus; that is opportunity enough to learn what to be and to do, whether or not any intentional pedagogy is taking place.

The Sermon on the Level Place (6:17–49)

So much more familiar to the church is Matthew's Sermon on the Mount that we might be aided in listening to Luke if we take time to set these teachings in his context. First, Luke has reversed Mark's order (Mark 3:7–19) by placing the call of the Twelve (6:12–16) prior to the healing of the crowds (6:17–19) and has moved the scene from the sea (Mark 3:7) to a level place (6:17). Luke has placed the sermon later in his Gospel than Matthew does in his, but even so, the contexts are similar. Matthew's version comes after the call of four disciples and a general statement about Jesus' ministry (Matt. 4:18–25), while Luke's follows the call of the Twelve and a general statement about Jesus' ministry (6:12–19). Luke's sermon is but one-fourth the length of Matthew's, and there are noticeable differences in the common subject matter, but it is evident that the two Evangelists had a common source (Q; see Introduction). Matthew's sermon contains much material found elsewhere in the Gospels and offers such interpretations within the sermon that many students have concluded that Luke follows more closely their common source.

Luke's sermon is given on a level place (6:17), not on a mountain (Matt. 5:1). Both Matthew and Luke seem to be making a theological use of geography. For Luke, the mountain is a place of prayer, and there he chooses the Twelve. Now he moves to the plain below to be with the people, with whom Jesus identifies, as at his baptism (3:21). The crowd on the level place is made up of three groups: the apostles, the disciples, and the people (v. 17). By saying that the people came from as far as Jerusalem and Judea to the south and Tyre and Sidon to the north, Luke may be saying that Jesus' ministry and message are for all. In fact, the mention of Tyre and Sidon may imply a Gentile as well as a Jewish audience. Certainly the audience includes the sick and the distressed, persons of special concern to Luke's Jesus. Within the large audience, the sermon itself

86

seems addressed in particular to the disciples ("And he lifted up his eyes on his disciples, and said," v. 20). However, at the close of the sermon, Luke says, "After he had ended all his sayings in the hearing of the people" (7:1). How shall we understand the indication of two audiences? Perhaps Luke means that these teachings are for Jesus' followers (the disciples) and for all who would be disciples (the people). Certainly nothing here is exclusive or secretive; the entire ministry of Jesus contradicts that.

The sermon (that is our word, not Luke's; verses 20–49 are a collection of teachings of Jesus on a wide range of subjects) consists of five parts: (1) blessings and woes (vv. 20–26); (2) on love of enemies (vv. 27–36); (3) on judging (vv. 37–42); (4) on integrity (vv. 43–45); and (5) on hearing and doing (vv. 46–49).

1. Blessings and woes (vv. 20–26). Unlike Matthew's nine blessings and no woes (Matt. 5:3–12), Luke has four of each, set in parallels: poor–rich, hungry–full, weeping–laughing, rejected–accepted. Even in English translation one can see how carefully symmetrical is the construction. Notice the use of "now" in the second and third blessing and woe, and the same clause that closes the blessings (v. 23) and the woes (v. 26). The reader is reminded of the blessings and the woes set before Israel (Deut. 11:26–28), but there is a major difference: In Deuteronomy the blessing or the curse was contingent on behavior, while here there is no contingency, no urging, no exhortation to act so as to receive a blessing or to avoid a woe. In our text, Jesus is pronouncing that condition which is in fact the case. Although blessings and woes are in form akin to the wisdom tradition of proverbs, they are not proverbs in the sense of being observations on the way life is. As pronouncements on the lips of Jesus, these statements are performative; that is to say, the words have power and perform or make true the kinds of life presented in the statements. Jesus is making the official proclamation of the way life is inside and outside the reign of God. These are not suggestions about how to be happy or warnings lest one become miserable; blessings and woes as words of Jesus are to be heard with the assurance that they are God's word to us and that God's word is not empty.

The reader of Luke is not surprised to hear God's word of favor on the poor, the hungry, those who weep, and those who are despised, nor is it surprising that woes are pronounced on their opposites. Luke stated as early as the Magnificat (1:46–55) that the arrival of God's reign will be marked by a complete

87

reversal of fortunes for the rich and the poor, the powerful and the powerless, the full and the empty. But these terms and these reversals are drawn from an eschatological frame of reference. Does this mean that this entire passage is descriptive of a condition still in God's future? Luke's answer is yes and no. Both the blessings and the woes are anchored in the present. Notice: "Blessed are you poor, for yours *is* the kingdom of God" (v. 20) and "But woe to you that are rich, for you *have received* your consolation" (v. 24). Both of these conditions are realized, not promises for the future. However, in blessings and woes two and three, "now" is contrasted with "you shall," clearly indicating future fulfillment. This joining of present and future reminds us that the eschatological reality is already beginning with the advent of Jesus. Jesus has already announced as much: "Today this scripture has been fulfilled" (4:21). The "today" that Jesus declared in the synagogue in Nazareth still prevails; the Messiah who will come has come, and the prophecy of Isaiah (Isa. 61:1–2) concerning the poor, the imprisoned, the diseased, and the oppressed is no longer a hope but is an agenda for the followers of Jesus. The church in Luke's second volume so understood it, as Acts amply testifies (Acts 2:44–46; 4:32–37; 6:1–2; 11:29–30).

In collections of sayings such as we have in Luke's Sermon on the Plain it is extremely difficult, if not impossible, to identify original audiences. However, the use of "you" (plural) throughout the blessings and woes seems to imply the presence of both rich and poor in the group addressed. That is no clear certainty, and scholars continue to debate the matter (Eduard Schweizer, *The Good News According to Luke,* p. 120). Matthew does not use the "you" of direct address in the blessings until the ninth and last one. The difference between "blessed are those who" and "blessed are you" is striking, but we could be dealing with different literary forms with no real clues about audiences. The fact is that to say "Woe to you that are rich" does not necessarily mean the rich were present. By means of a literary vehicle called an apostrophe, a speaker or a writer may address persons who are absent. To say "Woe to you that are rich" to an audience of the poor was a rather popular way to encourage the poor. Very likely James 5:1 provides an example of such an apostrophe: "Come now, you rich, weep and howl for the miseries that are coming upon you." Fortunately for us, while a reconstruction of the original audience for Luke 6:20–26 would

88

be satisfying historically and sociologically, the truth and the force of Jesus' words do not depend upon such a reconstruction.

Let us make one final observation. Luke is clearly addressing the poor and the despised of the earth in the literal sense of those words, not the "poor in spirit" or "those who hunger and thirst for righteousness," as in Matthew (Matt. 5:3, 6). It is true that "poor" in some quarters had clear spiritual overtones, becoming a synonym for "saint." In Hellenistic religious circles "rich" described life with God in eternity and "poor" stood for one's miserable existence on earth. Paul so used the terms to speak of Christ: "Though he was rich, yet for your sake he became poor, so that by his poverty you might become rich" (II Cor. 8:9). However, in treating Luke's text, the preacher and the teacher would be advised not to sail above economic realities into such spiritual realms. Luke does join material and spiritual conditions ("Blessed are you poor, for yours is the kingdom of God"), but he does not allow in the process the evaporation of "poor" into some condition other than being without food, without shelter, without hope of anything better tomorrow. Luke will later etch in our minds what it is to be poor and to be rich in his story of the rich man and Lazarus (16:19–31). There the reversal of fortunes will be inescapably clear.

2. *On love of enemies (vv. 27–36).* Love of enemies is but one theme among many in this unit, but it is the dominant one: "Love your enemies" opens the series of instructions (v. 27), and the phrase is repeated at the close (v. 35). In between is a compilation and not a single sermon. This judgment is supported by the shifts in the Greek text from plural "you" (vv. 27–28), to singular (vv. 29–30), and back to plural (vv. 31–36), coupled with the fact that some of these sayings are found elsewhere in the Gospels, and where paralleled in Matthew, they are in a different order (Matt. 5:39–42, 44–48; 7:12).

This unit contains two parts. The first, verses 27–31, lays down the general principle that Jesus' followers do not reciprocate, do not retaliate, and do not draw their behavior patterns from those who would victimize them. Following the statement of principle are numerous examples of forms of mistreatment: hating, cursing, abusing, striking, stealing, begging (pressuring one's sense of compassion). Two observations are in order. First, the teachings assume that the listeners are victims, not victimizers. Jesus offered no instruction on what to do after striking, stealing, hating, cursing, and abusing others. Such behavior, it

89

is assumed, is foreign to those who live under the reign of God. Second, followers of Jesus may be victims, but they are not to regard themselves as such, being shaped and determined by the hostilities and abuse unleashed on them. Rather, they are to take the initiative, but not by responding in kind, or by playing dead, or whining. They are not to react but to act according to the kingdom principles of love, forgiveness, and generosity. Such behavior is not a covert strategy for a soft kill ("Whip them with kindness") but is a pursuit of that life one learns from God who does not reciprocate but who is kind even to the ungrateful and the selfish (v. 35). This part of the unit concludes with Luke's version of the Golden Rule (v. 31), found not only here and in Matthew (Matt. 7:12) but also in Homer, Seneca, Tobit, II Enoch, Philo, and elsewhere. If anyone is disturbed that the saying is not unique to Jesus, remember that the universal embrace of a principle does not make it any less true, any less valid, or any less binding.

The second part of this unit (vv. 32–36) repeats from a different perspective the principle of the first part; that is, one is not to reciprocate in one's response the behavior of the other. However, here the principle is applied to our relationships with those who love us and do good for us. In other words, just as one's life-style is not determined by the enemy, neither is it determined by the friend. Rather than a person hating in response to hatred and loving in response to love, Christian behavior and relationships are prompted by the God we worship who does not react but acts in love and grace toward all. This is what it means to be children of God (v. 35). Luke's "For he [God] is kind to the ungrateful and the selfish" (v. 35) expresses Matthew's "He [God] makes his sun rise on the evil and on the good, and sends rain on the just and on the unjust" (5:45). Both affirm the radical grace of God which finds its reason in God and not in the merits of its recipients. Both Evangelists are also sensitive to the offense felt by those who regard God's impartiality as unjust. Matthew expresses this offense in the parable of the vineyard workers (Matt. 20:1–16), focusing the issue with the question, "Do you begrudge my generosity?" Luke dramatizes the offense of grace in the older brother's reaction to his father's party for the returned younger brother, an offense met by the father's simple justification, "It was fitting to make merry and be glad, for this your brother was dead, and is alive; he was lost, and is found" (15:11–32). The difficulty many of us have

90

with God's kindness is therefore twofold. First, God behaves with favor toward persons whose life-style does not merit such favor; and second, we are to relate to others with this same graciousness. God's people do not so often quarrel with God about how they themselves are treated as they do about how God is too generous toward others. Remember Jonah's complaint about God's grace toward the people of Nineveh. It is not an overstatement to say that Luke 6:35 expresses the essence of the whole gospel.

3. On judging (vv. 37–42). That this subunit consists of teachings held rather loosely together is evident not only internally but in the fact that Matthew has scattered these sayings in several contexts (Matt. 7:1–5; 15:14; 10:24–25). The preacher and the teacher will help the listeners by pointing out that such constellations of sayings are found in all the Gospels, and the recognition of that fact is the first step in treating individual units and subunits without giving the impression of tearing texts from contexts. Those especially who use lectionaries, which often suggest lengthy readings, will need to distinguish between lengthy readings that are single narratives and those which consist of collected teachings. The key is to be sensitive to the integrity of a text—that is, its inner unity, whether it is one verse or fifty. In the verses before us, two images serve as magnets for gathering the sayings: the controlling image in verses 37–38 is the measure, a container of known capacity; for verses 39–42 the image is the human eye.

From what has been said in verses 27–36, it follows naturally that Jesus' followers are not to judge or condemn. Luke says literally, "Stop judging" and "Stop condemning" (v. 37), indicating that in the audience were those who handled life's inequities and injustices by judging and condemning those whom God seems to be letting off the hook. Apparently God's gracious and forgiving treatment of others leaves the work of judging unattended and so we must take care of it. Or so it seems to many who are not comfortable in a kingdom where parties are given for prodigals and where tax collectors and sinners are welcome at table. After all, many argue, does not forgiveness abrogate justice? Mercy and justice are, and always have been, in tension. And justice is an appropriate topic among Jesus' followers; verses 37–38 make that clear. Without justice and fairness, grace degenerates into permissiveness, just as justice without grace hardens into cruelty. After teaching about

91

kindness and mercy in verses 27–36, Jesus now talks of fairness, of measure for measure, of reward and punishment. But even here, the balanced fairness of "The measure you give will be the measure you get back" (v. 38) is broken by the image of abundant generosity poured into the lap of those who give. The phrase "into your lap" (v. 38) refers to the large pocket created by the belt and the fold in a robe just above the belt. But even this huge pocket will not be an adequate container for the pressed down, shaken together, running over blessings that come to the generous.

Verses 39–42 have their center in the image of the eye, verses 39–40 speaking of blindness and verses 41–42 speaking of impediments in the eye which hinder seeing. The first part is called a parable, but again, as at 5:36, parable here means a simple analogy or figure of speech, and we will wait until we arrive at a more extended comparison, such as the parable of the sower, to discuss this literary genre. If verses 39–40 are taken together (it could be that these two sayings once existed separately and in other contexts had other meanings), the message is a warning about that leadership which presumes to guide others in matters that the leader has not personally understood, believed, or appropriated. Disciples who follow such blind and hypocritical leaders can expect to be no different. In our culture it is argued that a leader's personal life be kept separate from his or her professional life, but in Luke's culture, modeling behavior, especially by a teacher, was a primary responsibility. Example was a major factor in pedagogy, and imitation of one's teacher was the basic mode of learning. Many New Testament texts support this understanding of the teacher-disciple relationship (Acts 20:17–35; I Cor. 4:15–17; 11:1; Phil. 3:17; Titus 2:7). And it is fair to say that most congregations do not separate behavior in a leader from skills for leadership. Luke is not saying that imperfections disqualify a leader. On the contrary, Luke's point is that the disqualifying factor is not flaws but blindness to one's flaws, an unwillingness to be self-critical and honest with oneself.

This is the point of the tragicomical image of a person with a log in the eye trying to improve the condition of another with a speck in the eye (vv. 41–42). The issue is moral superiority, a quality found in persons without the faculty of self-criticism. The problem often resides in persons sincere and without faulty motives. Helpers of all kinds can easily be deceived by the altruism of their efforts ("Brother, let me help you by removing the speck in your eye"), unaware that looking always to others can be a socially and religiously approved way of never looking at oneself.

4. On integrity (vv. 43–45). In the preceding verse Luke has used the word "hypocrite," that is, one who pretends, acts, wears a mask. It is a word from the theater. Luke now strikes it down as totally inappropriate as a description of Jesus' followers. What one is, what one does, and what one says are an inseparable union, as are a tree and its fruit. More specifically, the accent in this teaching is on one's speech: what one says reveals what one is as surely as the appearance of fruit announces the nature of the tree. "For out of the abundance of the heart his mouth speaks" (v. 45). Luke is not alone in this attention to the importance of one's word (Matt. 12:33–35; James 3:11–12). In fact, the entire New Testament objects to the popular expression, "It's not what you say but what you do that counts." Throughout Luke-Acts, from the inspired songs before Jesus' birth to the sermons of Christian missionaries, the most common evidence of the presence of the Holy Spirit is in the speaking of persons filled with the Spirit. Our speech reveals who we are and whether the Holy Spirit is present.

5. On hearing and doing (vv. 46–49). A pattern we have met and will meet again in Luke is the bold statement of a quality to be found in disciples of Jesus and then immediately a modifier of that statement. God's people are to be gracious, but grace does not void the need for justice in our dealings; helping others is applauded, but altruism does not replace the need for critical attention to oneself; and now, having said that deeds and words are inseparable in human character, Luke reminds us that Jesus himself realized that some of his followers would speak but not do. The confession of Jesus as Lord was, of course, appropriate, being one of the earliest forms of the Christian creed (Rom. 10:9; Phil. 2:9–11). However, this confession no matter how exuberant, when unaccompanied by obedience will not hold one's life when the storms hit. It is in the storms, and the faithful seem to face more of them than anyone else, that the difference between interested listeners and obedient disciples will be evident. Luke's image of the storm is the swelling of a stream, not quite the same as Matthew's wind, rain, and flood (Matt. 7:24–27). Perhaps the differences reflect the climate and weather in the locales of the two writers. But to

93

anyone who has returned, once the water has receded, to a house still standing or to a house now fallen in the mud, differing descriptions of the storm will not be of primary interest.

Healing the Centurion's Slave (7:1–10)
(Matthew 8:5–13; John 4:46–53)

This story opens a section in Luke (7:1—8:3) sometimes called "the little insertion" because it consists of material (six units) inserted at this point into the framework of Mark. Some of the content is found also in Matthew but not in Mark. Luke will at 8:4 return to the Markan structure which in general provided the frame for Luke's Gospel.

Luke begins this section with a literary transition (the Sermon on the Plain is ended) and a geographical move (Jesus goes to Capernaum). Matthew and John agree on the location for this healing. In fact, Matthew and Luke tell the story with more than sixty identical words, but all three contour the episode according to their own theologies and purposes. We attend here only to Luke.

The centurion is a Gentile, perhaps in service to Herod Antipas, tetrarch of Galilee, or to Pontius Pilate, procurator of Judea, headquartered at Caesarea. He represents the believing Gentile living within Jewish territory. Luke's practice of relating parallel events from the life of Jesus and the life of the church is evident here. Remarkably similar to 7:1–10 is Acts 10. The Acts account begins, "At Caesarea there was a man named Cornelius, a centurion of what was known as the Italian Cohort, a devout man who feared God with all his household, gave alms liberally to the people, and prayed constantly to God" (Acts 10:1–2). What is important about these parallels is that 7:1–10 both foreshadows the mission to the Gentiles which is unfolded in Acts and provides an authoritative precedent for that mission in the ministry of Jesus himself.

The centurion is a man of admirable qualities. That his slave is gravely ill is a concern to him and that Jesus can heal him is held in firm faith (vv. 3, 7, 10). According to leaders of the Jewish community, the centurion is worthy, he loves the Jewish people, and he built a synagogue for them (vv. 3–5). According to friends, presumably Gentile, the centurion feels himself unworthy of Jesus' presence in his home (vv. 6–7a). In addition, he believed there was power in Jesus' word. After all, as a military officer, he knew the power of a command given and received

94

(vv. 7*b*–8). Jesus praises the man's faith as unmatched in Israel, and the slave is healed.

The centurion himself never came in contact with Jesus; that fact is important to the story in at least two ways. First, the centurion anticipates all those believers yet to come who have not seen Jesus but who have believed his word as having the power of his presence (v. 7; John 20:29). Such faith is not disadvantaged as though it were secondhand or belief at a distance, a consideration of major importance to those of us who believe in Jesus Christ but who are of another time and another place. The word of Christ, effective and present to faith in all times and places, creates and sustains the church. The church could not otherwise survive, having a past but no present, finding small comfort in a Book of fond memories of what Jesus once said and what he once did.

Second, and more immediate to Luke's purpose, is the fact that the centurion had his contact with Jesus through two sets of intermediaries, some Jewish, some Gentile. The officer himself is probably a proselyte-at-the-gate, a person who accepted Judaism's faith but who had not submitted to the rites whereby a Gentile became a Jew. The two sets of delegates dramatize his situation as a bridge between two worlds, Jew and Gentile, believing in the God who is the God of both and trusting that the word of Jesus had the power to move past any barriers between the two. The time would come when missionaries would take that word into the Gentile world (Acts 1:8); Simon Peter himself would, reluctantly and with the prodding of the Spirit, enter into a centurion's house, preach, baptize, and break bread with Gentiles (Acts 10). But that story is yet to unfold; Luke is moving the reader in that direction. The healing of the centurion's slave not only anticipates that story but begins it; in fact, it authorizes it by the healing word of Christ.

Raising the Widow's Son at Nain (7:11–17)

Without parallel in the other Gospels, this story has its connections in the cycles of Elijah (I Kings 17:17–24) and Elisha (II Kings 4:32–37), early established as two of Luke's favorite prophets (4:25–27). In form, Luke 7:11–17 is very similar to miracle stories told in Hellenistic culture, but it is Luke's story here and we will explore it for Lukan accents, literary and theological. Details of the account correspond to what we know of burial practices in Palestine at the time: the use of a stretcher

95

(Luke says "bier" from his Greek culture), the procession of bearers and mourners, and the burial outside the city wall. This particular city, Nain, may have been the ancient name of a town southeast of Nazareth, but that remains a question. We will give attention to four elements in the story: Luke's use of the Elijah antecedent; the act of Jesus; the response of the crowd; and the location of this story in the Gospel.

Both Elijah and Elisha restored life to young men. In the case of Elijah, the parallels to Luke are remarkable: the mother was a widow, the prophet met her at a city gate, and after life is restored, "he gave him to his mother," an exact quotation by Luke (v. 15) from the Greek text (Septuagint) of I Kings 17:23. We have previously and will again observe what could be called Luke's *literary* use of the Old Testament, that is, a use of the Old Testament not to offer proof of an argument, not to establish the prophecy/fulfillment pattern, but so as to allow the Old Testament narrative to provide the way of telling. Luke does not bring I Kings 17 to the reader's attention; it remains beneath the surface, and if the reader does not know the Old Testament, the Elijah story will not come to mind at all. What, then, is Luke doing? It could be simply a case of imitation, a guiding principle of literary art in that culture, widely practiced and widely respected. Our modern sensitivities about plagiarism, developed in support of laws of copyright which assume that an individual and not a society owns words, do not pertain here. As the English Bible has been a conscious or unconscious tutor of poets and novelists, perhaps the Greek Bible was a literary influence on Luke. But if Luke's readers did know the Greek Old Testament, passages such as 7:11–17 could give a sense of continuity, of being at home, of knowing a truth at the powerful level of recognition. All good teachers and preachers know not only the pedagogical value of repetition but also the effectiveness of recognition in the communicative transaction.

Second, this episode offers a dramatic example of Jesus' ministry of compassion. The object of his compassion is the mother. His total attention is on this woman who is a widow and whose only son, her sole means of support as well as being her whole family, is dead. There is sadness enough when children bury parents, but it does not compare to the grief attending nature's reversal, when parents bury children. Jesus' whole attention is on the woman; the storyteller seems unaware of the disciples, the crowd, the bearers, the mourners. Jesus acts without drama, ritual, or even prayer. The same word of Jesus that from a distance healed a centurion's slave (v. 7) here has the power to raise the dead.

Third, when the crowd enters the story (v. 16), it is almost as a chorus, registering and expressing the fear and praise of God appropriate to such an event. However, their principal role is to give voice to the faith generated by Jesus raising the dead. Their faith expressions are two: "A great prophet has arisen among us!" and "God has visited his people!" (v. 16). It would be a mistake to speak pejoratively of the crowd's estimation of Jesus as a prophet as though that were somehow reductionistic. Regrettably some Christian traditions, zealous to label Judaism's view of Jesus as "only a prophet" and to debate certain liberal Protestants as holding Jesus to be "only a prophet," have thereby miniaturized the image of prophet. Luke embraced the term as descriptive of Jesus whose ministry was reminiscent of that of the prophets, especially Elijah and Elisha (4:24; 7:39; 13:33; 24:19). The early church, says Luke, preached Jesus as the prophet like Moses (Acts 3:22–23; 7:35–37). To say Jesus "was a prophet mighty in deed and word before God and all the people" (24:19) is not, to be sure, to say all that Luke or we believe about Jesus of Nazareth. Sometimes, however, the rush to insist on how much more than a prophet he was leaves neglected the rich meaning of the role of the prophet in the tradition of Israel. The prophet spoke for God and brought by speech and act the word of God to bear on the life of the people. If some of Jesus' contemporaries taught that the age of prophecy had closed, then the crowds around Jesus announce that God has reopened it. The phrase "has arisen among us" may possibly be a faint allusion to Jesus' resurrection, but more likely it is drawn from Deut. 18:18: "I will raise up for them a prophet like you [Moses] from among their brethren."

The second expression, "God has visited his people," is also a favorite of Luke (1:68; 19:44; Acts 15:14). God's visitation may be in wrath (Ex. 20:5) or in mercy (Ps. 106:4), but for Luke it is always an act of grace. In 19:41–44 Jesus will predict the destruction of Jerusalem but not as a divine visitation. On the contrary, the destruction comes because the city "did not know the time of your visitation."

Finally, let us give attention to the literary location of 7:11–17. In addition to having its own message, this unit anticipates the next story about Jesus' message to John the Baptist. It does so in two ways. First, the raising of the son of the widow of Nain provides concrete support for Jesus' word to John, "The dead are raised up" (v. 22). When Matthew (Matt. 11:2–6) records Jesus' message to John, he has already told of Jesus raising the daughter of a ruler (Matt. 9:18–26). Luke has not; that story will be told later (8:40–56), so the raising of the dead at Nain serves Luke as preparation for the summary statement of Jesus' activity sent to John, a statement that includes raising the dead. Second, this unit anticipates the following story about John by referring to Judea in verse 17: "And this report concerning him spread through the whole of Judea." Rather than the expected "Galilee," the reference to Judea permits the report of Jesus' ministry to reach John whose ministry was in Judea.

We have thought about anticipation of an upcoming event as a literary function of location and arrangement of materials. Preachers and teachers can learn from Luke the preacher in this matter. Yet having said that, it should further be said that all Christians reading Luke 7:11–17 have their minds run ahead to the climax of the Gospel: God raises Jesus from the dead. Luke must have had similar thoughts; after all, the whole story of Jesus is being narrated from the perspective of one who is looking back through an empty tomb. But Luke would correct us by saying that while the resurrection of Jesus was the climax, it too was anticipatory in the sense that the Spirit which empowered Jesus was now to be given to the church for its life and mission. It is understandable that a major story of Luke describes the ministry of Jesus as being the middle and not the end of the story (Conzelmann, *The Theology of St. Luke*).

John and Jesus Again (7:18–35)
(Matthew 11:2–19)

Because the lives of John and Jesus have been intertwined since birth, and even before birth, an approach to this unit could well involve a review of what Luke has said thus far about the two and their relationship. Chapters 1—2 contain parallel stories about them which prophesy of their adult lives. And just as important, one has to be aware of what Luke has *not* said. For example, John has preached that a stronger one was coming (3:16–17), but Luke has given no clue that John identified that stronger one as Jesus. Matthew indicates that at Jesus' baptism, John recognized Jesus to be greater and that their roles should be reversed, Jesus baptizing John (Matt. 3:13–15), but Luke tells of John's imprisonment before his brief account of Jesus' baptism (3:19–22). The fact is that only in the Fourth Gospel does John have the revelation that the Messiah to come is Jesus (John 1:24–34). These observations are important for interpreting the text before us. For example, it is not uncommon to hear sermons on Luke 7:18–23 in which John is pictured as depressed, despondent, having second thoughts and growing doubts about Jesus. "Are you he who is to come, or shall we look for another?" thus becomes the question of a man who once preached Jesus as the Messiah but who now, because Jesus has made no messianic power moves and because John himself is suffering the loneliness, the abuse, the neglect of a prison cell, grows pessimistic about Jesus and his own grand announcements of the approaching reign of God. That jails, reversed fortunes, and disappointed hopes can erode faith is a fact well supported by experience, but this text does not support such an interpretation. In Luke, this is John's first contact with Jesus, and the reports about Jesus' ministry embolden him to ask, "Are you the one I have been talking about? My disciples bring me reports that point to that conclusion."

The unit before us (vv. 18–35) consists of two parts: the interchange between John's disciples and Jesus (vv. 18–23), and Jesus' words concerning John (vv. 24–35). In the first part, we assume John is in prison. Unlike Matthew who says John sent a message to Jesus from prison (Matt. 11:2), Luke offers no such word; we have to recall 3:19–20 and assume John is still there. Both Matthew and Mark say John remained in prison until his execution, which both relate at length (Matt. 14:1–12; Mark 6:14–29); Luke will say only briefly that Herod beheaded John (9:7–9). We know that Luke knows the fuller account in Mark, and therefore we can only guess that he either regarded it as unimportant to his point or chose to praise John for his ministry rather than for his martyr hero's death. We do not know from the New Testament where John was imprisoned. Since he was arrested by Herod Antipas, it must have been in Galilee or in the area identified in Matthew, Mark, and John as Perea, a corridor lying along the eastern side of the Jordan. The Jewish historian Josephus says that in southern Perea, in a mountain fortress called Machaerus, high above the Dead Sea, John was imprisoned and there he was killed.

99

Why John's question, "Are you he who is to come, or shall we look for another?" One interpretation has been eliminated.

It has been suggested that John may be attempting to prod Jesus into a public declaration of who he is. Perhaps. In forming a judgment, we must not overlook two elements in the account. One factor is the tenacity of John's faith. He is not asking, Are you the Messiah or shall we give up? Rather, he is saying, God has promised one to come whose ministry will be marked by Holy Spirit and fire. We have confidence in that promise, and if you are not the one, we will keep looking. The second factor lies in what prompted the question. It was not his imprisonment that gave rise to his inquiry; Luke does not even mention prison. Rather, the question is in response to what Jesus is doing. Two of John's disciples come and remain long enough to observe. They report to John what they have seen and heard: the blind see, the lame walk, lepers are cleansed, the deaf hear, the dead are raised, and the poor hear the good news (v. 22). In other words, Jesus is carrying out what he announced as his program in the synagogue at Nazareth, the fulfillment of Isa. 61:1–2. Such a ministry is evidence enough to evoke the question, Is Jesus the Messiah? However, such a ministry is not evidence enough to settle the question: Jesus is the Messiah. The issue is not whether or not one believes that Jesus really is doing these things; the issue is, Are these the things a Messiah does? It is not one's view of Jesus that may need adjustment but rather one's view of a Messiah. "When the Messiah comes" is the introduction to all kinds of wishes, dreams, and hopes, but what will God's Messiah do? How will he relate to the leaders and the institutions dedicated to the preservation of faith in God? Will he be politically active? And now most pointedly the question arises, Can someone who gives time and attention to the dead, the very poor, the outcast, the acknowledged violator of the law, and the diseased be God's Messiah? John has to decide in the same way all of us decide, on the basis of witnesses reporting what they have seen and heard. If faith hesitates, it is not because it waits on one more witness bringing further proof. That route is a detour, in pursuit of another question about whether Jesus could or could not perform miracles. Many gallons of afternoon tea have been poured over that one, and the results are disappointing when those who say yes and those who say no discover that their answers have no bearing on their lives or the lives of others. But if one says that Jesus is the Messiah, then one is saying that in the ministry of Jesus we are seeing what God is doing in the world, what the reign of God

100

really is. And that, of course, is to say what we are to be doing in the world if we confess that Jesus is God's Messiah. This is the crucial question raised by John, and Jesus cannot answer it for him. Jesus can only say, "Blessed is he who takes no offense at me" (v. 23).

The second part of this unit of verses 18–35 consists of Jesus' words about John and the people's response to him (vv. 24–35). Jesus' audience had been in the audience of John ("What did you go out into the wilderness to behold?") and therefore were able to compare and contrast the two prophets, and John was, says Jesus, a prophet of God. As a prophet, John was neither a voice echoing public opinion nor the spokesman for the wealthy and powerful. In fact, John was not only a prophet, he was the prophet of Mal. 3:1: "Behold, I send my messenger before thy face, who shall prepare thy way before thee." In other words, John is the prophet preceding the Messiah. Malachi identified this one who was to prepare the way for the coming of the Lord as Elijah (Mal. 4:5), and Matthew takes that as justification to call John Elijah (Matt. 11:14). Luke does not make that identification, because, as we have seen, both John and Jesus were Elijah-like. Yet for all of John's greatness, this child of old parents belongs to the old age, even though he announces the advent of the new. His greatness lies in this unique mission, to point to and prepare for the reign of God. But it is Jesus, the child of the young virgin, whose ministry makes present the kingdom toward which John pointed. Jesus' statement that the one "who is least in the kingdom of God is greater than he" (v. 28) does not rob the earlier praise of its meaning or importance. These words simply echo what John himself recognized as the immense difference between his own work, and by implication that of his followers, and that of Jesus and his disciples: "I baptize you with water; but he who is mightier than I . . . will baptize you with the Holy Spirit and with fire" (3:16).

In a parenthetical statement (vv. 29–30) Luke says the audience was divided. The RSV puts verses 29–30 in parentheses to indicate a narrator's comment inserted into the comments of Jesus. Jesus' voice breaks at verse 28 and resumes at verse 31. Matthew has the content of verses 29–30 as a statement of Jesus, and in a much clearer form (Matt. 21:32). In Luke's statement, the audience is divided between "all the people and the tax collectors" (an awkward expression; Matthew has "tax collectors and harlots") and "the Pharisees and the lawyers," and the ground of the difference is not that some followed John and some followed Jesus but whether or not they accepted John's baptism. Accepting or rejecting John's baptism was, says Luke, accepting or rejecting the purpose of God. Those who received John's baptism "justified" God; that is, they confirmed by their acceptance the active presence of God's purpose for them. Regardless of the confusion and the competition that developed in some quarters between disciples of these two prophets, all the Evangelists agree that John was a prophet of God and his baptism was "from heaven."

Jesus' words about John conclude with verses 31–35 which really offer commentary on the way the people "of this generation [age]" responded to John and to Jesus. The negative tone of the passage is apparently prompted by the preceding verse which comments on the rejection of John by Pharisees and lawyers. Those of "this age" are obviously those not of the eschatological age, the age of God's reign. These verses, then, are not addressed to the crowds (v. 24), who were generally favorable both to John and to Jesus. The observations of Jesus in this passage are framed on two proverbs, both relating to children (vv. 32, 35). Those in the audience who rejected John and Jesus are compared to children who refuse to be satisfied: they will not play wedding, they will not play funeral; they will not dance, they will not mourn. All parents know what Jesus is saying. Even children normally happy have days when no game is fun, no food is good, no trip is interesting, no book contains good stories. But Jesus is talking to adults, not to children, and these adults find John too austere and Jesus too sociable. These unhappy people stand at sufficient distance from both ministries to criticize and to justify their refusal to participate by attacking the life-styles of the two prophets.

The focus of criticism of both John and Jesus is their eating habits. We cannot stress too strongly the central importance of table fellowship in that culture, in the ministry of Jesus, in the life of the early church, and among New Testament writers, Luke most especially. We considered this fact earlier in commenting on 5:27–32, but here it is even more sharply the issue because two prophets are summarily dismissed with strong attacks at a point that seems to many moderns as of no consequence. About no candidate for political office, for a teaching position, or for a pulpit would we ask, But what about his or her

102

table customs? What we have to keep in mind is that table fellowship and Sabbath observance were identification marks for a community struggling to maintain identity among many foreign and some hostile influences. What was eaten and with whom one ate it were critical questions. Luke will tell us later that after Simon Peter went to the house of a Gentile Cornelius at Caesarea, he was called on the carpet by certain persons in the Jerusalem church. Their concern was not that Simon had preached to Gentiles, or that he had baptized Gentiles, but, "Why did you go to uncircumcised men and *eat with them?*" (Acts 11:3). The act of Simon had violated their opinion of who is and who is not in the Christian fellowship. Simon had, by eating with Gentiles, radically redefined the identity of the church. When, therefore, critics of John say that he eats with no one they are saying that he has removed himself from the covenant fellowship of God's people. When the critics say of Jesus that he eats with anyone they are saying that he violates the sacred distinctions as to who is and who is not within the covenant fellowship. To what shall we compare table customs in the community of faith today? Do we have any distinctive identifying mark, or are we rather casual about all such things lest we seem exclusive? Would embrace of a creed be a reasonable comparison? Or Baptism? Perhaps Holy Communion? This text which seemed at first so distant and unusual has turned on us and made us uneasy.

The concluding proverb (v. 35), "Yet wisdom is justified by all her children," recalls passages such as Prov. 8:32 and Ecclus. 4:11. Wisdom (Sophia) was the eternal principle or truth by which God created and sustains the world, and all who follow her or take her into their lives become like her and are called her children. Just as Luke said earlier that God was justified by those who accepted God's purpose as expressed in John's baptism (vv. 29–30), so here wisdom is justified by those who accept John and Jesus. Wisdom or truth cannot be confirmed at a distance except by those who embrace wisdom. There is a kind of knowing which does not precede a decision or an act but which comes in the deciding, in the acting. The truth of the principle expressed in Luke 7:35 is stated in the Fourth Gospel in this way: *"If anyone wills to do God's will, that person will know* the teaching, whether it is from God or I am speaking on my own" (John 7:17; trans. mine). 103

In Jesus' words about John (vv. 24–35), the principal characters have been Jesus, Pharisees, and sinners, and one of the principal subjects has been table fellowship. Now Luke joins Jesus, a Pharisee, and a sinner in a story that takes place at the table. Luke is an excellent communicator: he moves from a discussion of an issue to a story that dramatizes the issue, as though Luke were saying, "For instance."

Jesus Anointed by a Sinful Woman (7:36–50)

Perhaps the first act in interpreting this passage is to separate it from the anointing stories of Matthew 26:6–13, Mark 14:3–9, and John 12:1–8; otherwise those accounts may bleed through into Luke and hinder a proper listening to this text. Clearly Luke's is not a parallel story, but hints and similarities are enough to tease the mind. For example, Matthew and Mark agree with Luke that the name of the host was Simon, but they identify him as a leper. John agrees with Luke that the woman anointed Jesus' feet, not his head; but John also agrees with the others that the anointing was in Bethany, while Luke's story is apparently set in Galilee. Matthew and Mark agree with Luke that the woman is unnamed; John says she was Mary sister of Lazarus in whose home the incident occurred. The three others place the event late in Jesus' ministry and relate it to his death; Luke's story is one of love and forgiveness. What can we say about all of this? It may be that the Gospels reflect sources oral or written that spoke of one, two, or even three anointings, but as we receive the traditions, Luke must be understood as sufficiently distant from the others in location, time, and purpose to be considered entirely on its own.

That a Pharisee asked Jesus to dinner should be met with neither suspicion nor surprise: not suspicion, because there is no evidence a trap was being set; nor surprise, because Jesus had much in common with these lovers of the law of Moses and leaders of the synagogue. This is not a solitary instance of Jesus dining in the home of a Pharisee (11:37; 14:1). And besides, no general image of Pharisees matched any one of them in particular. Furthermore, for Jesus to eat with tax collectors and sinners and refuse table fellowship with Pharisees would have made him as guilty of reverse prejudice as some of us who discover in our zeal to right wrongs we develop prejudices against the prejudiced, a condition that places us in the camp of those we charge with standing in the way of God's reign on earth. We learn from the story that the Pharisee's name is Simon (v. 40);

104

there is no reason to identify the woman as Mary Magdalene (8:2). Houses in that culture were so constructed that the woman's entrance required no break-in, and since dining occurred in a reclining position, anointing Jesus' feet should not conjure up the image of a woman crawling around under a table.

Let us think of the account as a small drama. The setting is a Pharisee's home where the host Simon, Jesus, and others (v. 49) are dining. The context, especially verses 29–30, 34, creates in us an anticipation of tension, but there is none at the outset. We do not learn until later that for some reason Simon had not extended to Jesus the customary courtesies of hospitality: foot washing, anointing, and a kiss (vv. 44–46). The crisis in the drama is created by the entrance of "a woman of the city." That Jesus does not expel her is proof to Simon that Jesus is no prophet; if he were, he would know that the woman is a sinner. Simon thinks this but does not say it. However, Jesus knows Simon's thoughts, proof by Simon's own criterion that Jesus is a prophet.

The solution of the crisis (vv. 40–47) is a bit surprising. The reader is inclined to see in the story one sharp contrast, that which is so evident between Simon and Jesus. Here are two religious leaders suddenly in the presence of a sinful woman. One has an understanding of righteousness which causes him to distance himself from her; the other understands righteousness to mean moving toward her with forgiveness and a blessing of peace. However, the context should have alerted us that the contrast Luke has in mind (vv. 29–30) is between Simon and the woman in their response to Jesus. They make specific the earlier statement to the effect that sinners receive and Pharisees reject the purpose of God offered by John and Jesus. The irony here is that even though Jesus is a guest in Simon's home, it is a sinner who extends hospitality. Even though some commentators speak of the erotic implications of this woman's behavior toward Jesus (letting her tears fall on his feet, wiping his feet with her hair, kissing his feet, anointing them with ointment), it is clear in Luke's telling that she is extending the hospitality Simon had withheld. This is Jesus' interpretation of her actions: water for the feet (tears), the kiss of welcome, and the anointing for one coming in from a journey exposed to the heat of the day. The brief parable of the two debtors ensnares Simon in a recognition of the difference between his behavior toward Jesus and

105

that of the woman. Her behavior is that of a person who has been forgiven. Verse 47 is awkward, seeming to say that her love earned her forgiveness. The contrary is more likely: because she was forgiven much, she loved much. The NEB translates it: "And so, I tell you, her great love proves that her many sins have been forgiven."

The drama concludes in a christological dispute (vv. 48–50), bringing into sharp focus questions of Jesus' identity and authority to forgive sins. The murmuring among the other guests recalls the controversy reported at 5:17–26. The final word to the woman, "Your faith has saved you; go in peace," seems a bit out of place and may have once existed as the conclusion to another episode. The use of floating sayings to round off stories is not infrequent in the Gospels (cf., e.g., Matt. 19:30 and 20:16), and this may be one of them. After all, the commendable quality in the woman in this story is not her faith but her love. Setting the question of proper context aside, the word of Jesus "Go in peace" adds considerable pathos to the event. Where does one go when told by Christ "Go in peace"? The price of the woman's way of life in the city has been removal from the very institutions that carried the resources to restore her. The one place where she is welcome is the street, among people like herself. What she needs is a community of forgiven and forgiving sinners. The story screams the need for a church, not just any church but one that says, "You are welcome here."

Women Share in Jesus' Ministry (8:1–3)

With this note about Jesus' Galilean ministry Luke concludes the insertion into the Markan framework which began at 7:1. At 8:4 Luke returns to the structure that Mark's Gospel provides. This small unit is in Luke alone and may, in addition to any other purposes, serve as a contrast to the preceding story about the sinful woman. The women here are disciples and participants in Jesus' mission. Luke seems to be fond of arranging materials so as to create sharp contrasts. For example, after a parable about God vindicating the elect (18:1–8) he has one in which God hears the prayer of a tax collector (18:9–14), and he places back to back Jesus blessing a blind beggar and the rich Zacchaeus (18:35—19:10). This seems to be more than literary preference; Luke could also be impressing on us that God is not "either/or" but "both/and."

106

The most striking feature of this summary of a mission tour

through Galilee is the presence of women who participate in Jesus' ministry along with the Twelve. Joanna is mentioned here and at 24:10; Susanna, nowhere else. Mary of Magdala, prominent in the resurrection narrative, has been relieved of seven demons. Only popular legend has made her a prostitute. According to Gospel records, demon possession caused various maladies of body and mind but not moral or ethical depravity. These women are said to have been healed, to have been with Jesus and the Twelve, and to have provided financial assistance. Joanna was the wife of a domestic administrator in Herod's government, and we may assume the others were also women of means. Given the seductions and traps of money and power, it is not only commendable but remarkable that they found ways to put both money and power in submission to the gospel. No doubt there were social and political costs in their commitment. Even more remarkable is the fact that the risks associated with discipleship are compounded for them as women. Yet they are not out of sight sending money from a distance; they are with Jesus and the Twelve. Luke's favorable reports about women began with Elizabeth and Mary and will continue through Acts, where Luke will comment on the presence of "not a few of the leading women" in the church at Thessalonica (Acts 17:4); and at Berea, "not a few Greek women of high standing as well as men" (Acts 17:12).

The Parable of the Sower (8:4–18)
(Matthew 13:1–23; Mark 4:1–25)

Even though Luke twice earlier used the term "parable" (5:36; 6:39) and once earlier told a brief parable without designating it as such (7:41–42), it is here in the parable of the sower that this literary form comes center stage for the first time. In fact, in this unit we are given the parable (vv. 4–8), the reason Jesus spoke in parables (vv. 9–10), the interpretation of the parable (vv. 11–15), and a general statement on the purpose of parables (vv. 16–18). This is the teaching form most commonly associated with Jesus. In fact, Mark says that Jesus did not speak to the crowds without a parable (Mark 4:34), and Matthew, who agrees with Mark (Matt. 13:34), says that this pedagogical method of Jesus was to fulfill the prophecy: "I will open my mouth in parables, I will utter what has been hidden since the foundation of the world" (Matt. 13:35; Ps. 78:2). We have therefore reached the point where we can no longer delay discussing

107

the nature and function of the parable. We will do so prior to considering the parable of the sower, because what is said here will pertain not only to this parable but to the many others we will meet in Luke. To avoid unnecessary repetition, the reader will be referred back to this discussion when subsequent parables are being explored.

The word "parable," from the Greek word *parabolē*, means, literally, "that which is tossed alongside," implying a comparison, an analogy, an elaboration, or an illustration. Perhaps the best-known and most helpful definition of a parable has been provided by C. H. Dodd: "At its simplest, the parable is a metaphor or simile drawn from nature or common life, arresting the hearer by its vividness or strangeness, and leaving the mind in sufficient doubt about its precise application to tease it into active thought" (*The Parables of the Kingdom*, p. 16 of 1961 rev. ed.). This definition is most appropriate for the more extended or narrative parables (the sower, the widow and the judge, the Pharisee and the publican, etc.) rather than for the single sentence or single phrase comparisons which are also called parables (5:36; 6:39; Mark 7:17). In fact, in the Scriptures the word "parable" has a wide range of uses, referring to proverbs, bywords, allegories, riddles, figurative speech, and stories. However, since Luke contains so many narrative parables, Dodd's definition may prove illuminating. It reminds us that the sources for these stories are both nature (the mustard seed) and common experience (the prodigal son) and that their function may be as a simile (he is like a bulldog) or as a stronger, implied comparison called metaphor (he is a bulldog). Dodd also points to the attention-getting quality of the parable, joined to its refusal to make its meaning easily accessible to the hearer. In other words, parables are not simple little stories Jesus told so that everyone, even the children, could understand everything he said. On one level, of course, these stories are intellectually within the reach of all. As we will observe shortly, the parable of the sower is so vividly the way life was known and observed that it would seem to carry in its bosom no mystery at all. Yet, if it is that obvious, why did Jesus tell it?

The parable puts a burden on the listener that is not intellectual; rather, it teases the mind into active thought. The hearer has a feeling of strangeness in a very familiar narrative, and some interpretation is not only invited but urged. The hearer thus becomes an active participant in the communication and begins to offer interpretations. Because the parable generates meanings for which the listener takes responsibility, it seems a particularly appropriate literary form for communicating the gospel, since each hearer must take responsibility for his or her own faith. It is easy to understand, therefore, why parables are not used by speakers who wish to control listeners by telling them exactly what to think and to do and why parables are not well received by persons who wish to be told directly what to think, to believe, and to do. Control is lost, participation is gained in the use of parables, because parables must be interpreted. They are interesting, and, as is true of most stories, they disarm and engage, but still they must be interpreted. In this sense they are like poetry, lying between the opaque and the obvious, evoking meanings and feelings. However, a parable may also at times function as a proverb, impressing the hearer with some neglected conventional wisdom. Yet further, nothing can exceed the parable in prophetic force; recall Nathan's parable which convicted King David of his sin (II Sam. 12:1–10). In other words, parables are somewhat elusive, revealing and yet concealing, having no single form or function, always drawing something from the listener, asking for an interpretation.

The church has always had some difficulty with the parables of Jesus in the Gospels (there are none in the Fourth Gospel; John prefers to speak of Jesus using "figurative speech," John 10:6; 16:25, 29). Interpretations began early; some of the parables have interpretations within the biblical text itself. For centuries the most popular method of interpreting parables was by allegorizing, this being the way some of Jesus' parables are explained within the Gospels themselves. In an allegory, each significant item in a story is assigned a meaning. For example, in the parable of the prodigal son allegorically interpreted, the father represents this, the older son that, the younger son this, the inheritance that, the far country this, the swine that, the party this, the fatted calf that, and on and on. Some allegorizing was restrained; some was uncontrolled and exaggerated, biblical texts being used to authorize all manner of doctrines and demands on the hearers. Late in the last century the German scholar Adolph Jülicher radically changed the way parables were interpreted. Breaking with allegorization, Jülicher insisted that a parable has not many but one single point. Interpreters after him disagreed with Jülicher and with one another as to what the single point of a parable was, but they agreed with the principle: a parable has but one meaning.

Jülicher's interpretive principle prevailed among scholars until fairly recent times. Amos Wilder, professor of New Testament at Harvard Divinity School, in a very influential book, *The Language of the Gospel: Early Christian Rhetoric,* examined the forms and function of the parable and called for the preservation of the form of a parable as essential to what it does as well as says. It is not enough to distill a parable into a theme sentence, just as it is not enough to reduce a poem into a prose statement of its meaning. A parable *does* as well as says, and therefore adequate interpretation will attend to what parables do in the minds and hearts of listeners. After all, if a single sentence will state the meaning, why the parable? Most American interpreters of parables have been strongly influenced by Wilder. However, viewing parables as literary art has meant that what a parable says and does is to a very large degree determined by the listener, just as a work of art means different things to different viewers. The result is that the old question from allegorizing days has returned: Are there any boundaries, any limits on what a parable may mean, or are its meanings as multiple as its readers or hearers? After a period of celebrating the autonomy of a parable and its freedom to convey limitless messages, scholars are now speaking of guidelines of meaning. Among the restraints on parable interpretation, the most persuasive are the character of Jesus' life and mission, the context of the parable within a Gospel, the community of faith to which the listener belongs, and the sobering recognition that the interpreter must accept responsibility for what is heard in the parable. These guidelines still permit a great deal of freedom in hearing a parable, more freedom, in fact, than many want to accept. These persons join the disciples who frequently asked Jesus in private following his use of a parable, What did you mean?

Anyone who wishes to read further about parables will find helpful the article "parables" in *Harper's Bible Dictionary;* John D. Crossan, *In Parables;* Pheme Perkins, *Hearing the Parables of Jesus;* Robert H. Stein, *An Introduction to the Parables of Jesus;* and John R. Donahue, *The Gospel in Parable.*

110   We return now to the parable of the sower. Or perhaps we should say the parable of the seed or even of the soil; titles can predispose the reader to a particular interpretation and thus

violate the openness of a parable. Only Matthew calls it the parable of the sower (Matt. 13:18). Of the three Evangelists who relate this parable, Luke tells it most briefly and sets it in the most general context. The audience is a great crowd and the story itself is clear enough in its own terms; it is a scene that all of them have observed year after year. It may help the modern reader to know that sowing preceded plowing, and therefore seed did fall on paths and among weeds. But when the story ends, what has been said? It invites some interpretation; the question, So what? arises. For Jesus to say "Let the one having ears to hear hear" implies there is more to his words than their apparent and obvious meaning. In fact, who Jesus is, what he has been doing and saying, the very reasons the crowds have gathered, argue that he is saying something very important which lies buried in an event as commonplace as sowing seed, in a story that every child in the crowd thinks it understands.

While the crowd wonder why Jesus has told them what they already know, or why they may not really know what they think they know, or what might be the key to deeper insight—the sower? the seed? the soil? the harvest?—the disciples among them raise their hands. Teacher, what does this parable (in Matthew and Mark they ask about parables in general) mean (v. 9)? The fact that they asked is very important. Real understanding—significant learning and communication in matters of value and relationship—is antiphonal; it does not occur without response. The parable is a form of communication which permits: it permits the listener to bear some responsibility for what is heard and it permits others to be spectators, not curious enough to push forward, to raise the hand, and to say, "It is important for me to understand what you are saying." Some truths are not available to the casual passer-by. After all, the word of God is located not simply at the mouth of the speaker but at the ear of the listener. In giving Jesus' response to the disciples (v. 10), Luke noticeably softens Mark (Mark 4:10–12). Luke has in mind two general groups, "disciples" and "others." The disciples ask and to them the secrets of the kingdom are given. They will receive some clarification. As for the others, Luke omits Mark's "Lest they should turn again, and be forgiven" (Mark 4:12) based on Isa. 6:9–10 which Matthew quotes (Matt. 13:14–15). Matthew and Mark seem willing to dip into the ancient writer's view that the reason some hear and some do not lies hidden in the purposes of God. The same word that

111

softens some hardens others. When a stepping-stone for one became a stumbling block for another, some thinkers among the Hebrews were content to say God causes some to step across and some to stumble. In other words, the *result* of an action was stated as having been the *purpose* of the action. This perspective could speak of the *result* of Jesus' teaching (others did not understand) as a purpose of his teaching (so that they not understand).

To repeat, Luke has softened Mark here, but still verse 10 shows that Luke is struggling with a matter every teacher and preacher has faced: Why is it that in the same audience some hear and some do not? Is it intelligence? Sin? Predestination? God's grace? Whatever the conclusion reached, whatever the theological underpinnings of that conclusion, one thing is clear in the text: in a crowd of auditors, some disciples ask for help in understanding. They have a great deal invested in Jesus and his ministry and Jesus will not let them walk away empty and confused.

In the interpretation (vv. 11–15) the parable is made into an allegory, that is, a story in which each item in the narration is said to represent something else. Most scholars take this interpretation to represent the situation of the early church in its missionary preaching to a variety of conditions. As an explanation of the parable, however, the interpretation is less than clear. For example, the seed is identified as the word of God, and one would expect that the different kinds of soil would be identified as different kinds of hearers. But that is not the case. The interpretation speaks of the ones sown on the path and the devil takes away the word; the ones sown on the rocks are those without roots; the ones sown among thorns have the word choked out; and those sown in good soil receive the word and bear fruit. It is inexplicable that the word of God is sown and the different kinds of listeners are also sown. Most interpreters of the parable choose to ignore this awkward and confusing quality of the interpretation provided and speak of the listeners not as seed but as soil. One could almost wish the parable alone was given, without an explanation! Even so, one can easily understand how the parable could speak effectively to the followers of Jesus. The parable says not all teaching and preaching will be fruitful. The parable encourages those who have experienced failures in their ministries, reminding them that some seed will yield abundantly. The parable says to everyone that

112

it is in the honest, good, and patient heart that the word of God comes to full fruition.

The unit concludes with three separate sayings (vv. 16–18), sometimes called "floating sayings" because they are found elsewhere separate from one another and in different contexts (Matt. 5:15; 10:26; 25:29; Luke 11:33; 12:2; 19:26). Placed together here, all three are appropriate to parabolic communication. The first saying, in this context, reminds the reader that even though parables require some initiative and responsibility from the listener, Jesus' purpose was not to conceal but to reveal. The second likewise underscores the conviction that Jesus came not to keep secrets but to bring to light what had previously been unknown: the reign of God and the nature of life within that reign. The third saying reminds the reader, however, that Jesus' parables do not bless all alike, without distinction. Those who lean forward to hear, who invest trust and commitment, who come to the altar of the word seeking, asking, and hungering—these are the ones to whom "more will be given." Those who think they already know, who acknowledge no blindness, who listen with ears that register only likes and dislikes, who fold the arms across the chest waiting to be convinced or entertained, who want information without obligation—these are the ones who discover painfully that even what they thought they had has been taken away.

The Real Family of Jesus (8:19–21)
(Matthew 12:46–50; Mark 3:31–35)

This episode provides for us an excellent opportunity to observe the influence of context on the meaning of a passage. Mark tells this story in a setting of intense controversy in which the tension between Jesus and his critics extends to Jesus and his family. Mark also locates it prior to the parable of the sower. In Luke's location immediately after the parable of the sower, the episode illustrates the truth of the parable: hearing and doing the word of God is the way into the fellowship created by Jesus. And by removing the event from an atmosphere of controversy, and reducing it, Luke has the coming of Jesus' mother and brothers become the occasion for Jesus to teach that the family of God includes all who hear and do God's will. Unless one is remembering Mark while reading Luke, there is no reason to take Jesus' comment as a distancing from his mother and brothers or as reflecting tension between them. Luke has made

113

it clear from the beginning that Jesus' mother heard and obeyed God's word (1:38, 45) and that the family were models of faithfulness (2:21–51). Luke says, therefore, that the family of God is created by hearing and doing the word; this included Jesus' Nazareth family. It will be quite clear in subsequent passages in Luke that this criterion for membership in God's family will create severe tensions in some biological families.

Jesus Calms a Storm (8:22–25)
(Matthew 8:23–27; Mark 4:35–41)

This story is the first in a series of four episodes in which Jesus performs wonders: stilling a storm, healing a demoniac, healing a sick woman, and raising a dead girl. The order is Mark's, but there seems to be little if any connection with what precedes. Luke simply says "One day" (literally, "on one of the days"). Since these episodes will be followed immediately with the commissioning of the Twelve, it may be appropriate to view these four selections as examples of Jesus' ministry during the period of their preparation. The four events are related to one another in a broad geographical sense: in the boat crossing the Sea of Galilee (Luke says "lake"; for a non-Palestinian, "sea" meant the Mediterranean), an exorcism on the eastern side of the sea, and the return to the western side, where the healing and raising of the dead occur.

Of the four miracle stories before us, the calming of the storm is in a class by itself. This is not a reference to this being the first demonstration of Jesus' power over nature. It is no more an exercise of power over "nature" than were the healings or the raising of the son of the widow at Nain. The concept of "nature" belongs to a scientific age which speaks of laws of nature and is comfortable saying "It rained" or "It was very windy," not "God sent a rain" or "God stirred the wind in the trees." The calming of the storm is, like the story that immediately follows, an exorcism. Notice the customary language of an exorcism: "He rebuked the wind and the raging waves" (v. 24; recall 4:35, 39, 41). From ancient times and in many cultures large bodies of water were believed to be the abode of evil spirits which sometimes stirred up storms against sailors. The belief was as old as Near Eastern flood stories in which the water tried to take over and destroy the land. The book of Revelation echoes that belief in its description of the final triumph of God: "And the sea was no more" (21:1).

114

To say this episode is in a class by itself is to say that Jesus is with his disciples alone, away from the crowds or the critics, and Jesus ministers to them. It is rare in the Gospels for the disciples to be beneficiaries of Jesus' power; usually they are present as he ministers to others or they join him in that ministry. The usual posture of the church is serving others in the name of Jesus, but the church also is the recipient of Christ's ministering presence. Otherwise it could not sustain itself in the long haul. Without some belief in and experience of the presence of Christ, or of the Holy Spirit, the church collapses under the weight of its institutionalism or goes astray with self-promoting programs.

Two other striking features of this story are the two questions with which it concludes. Jesus asks his disciples, "Where is your faith?" (v. 25). What is he asking them? He certainly is not saying that if they had had faith, there would not have been a storm; after all, Jesus was in the boat too. And most likely he is not saying that, with faith, they could have stilled the storm themselves. They have not yet been given power and authority to exorcise and to heal (9:1–2). Jesus seems by his question to be addressing their fear during the storm—fear, not doubt, being the opposite of faith. They had been with Jesus long enough to have adequate ground for trust in God and in Jesus' access to God's power. Notice that with Jesus' calming of the storm they are said to be afraid, perhaps even more so. They have just witnessed a power greater than the storm; why would they not be afraid? It is sheer sentimentalism that supposes that being in the presence of Jesus is total comfort. The question, "Where is your faith?" has the additional force of signaling a new level of expectation from Jesus. They have not been asked anything like that previously, but they are soon to be sent out to preach, to heal, to overpower demons. And it will not be too long before they are asked a variation on this same question: *What* is your faith? Who do you say that I am? (9:18–22).

This leads us to the second question, the one the disciples asked one another: "Who then is this?" (v. 25). Surely that question has been forming itself in their minds during their time with him, but now the question is clear, and it is out in the open: Who is Jesus? Of course, Luke has the reader in mind as well, not only in the asking but in the anticipation of an answer. It will have to be asked, but who will ask and who will answer? Will they ask Jesus, Who are you? or will Jesus ask them, Who

115

do you say that I am? If they ask him, as John did from prison, we can imagine his answer would be much the same (7:22). But if Jesus asks them, what will they say?

Healing the Gerasene Demoniac (8:26–39)
(Matthew 8:28–34; Mark 5:1–20)

The RSV of 8:26 says this exorcism occurred in the country of the Gerasenes; the NEB and TEV say "Gergesenes." Matthew, in all three translations, has "Gadarenes." These translations are registering differences in the Greek manuscripts, and more is involved than spelling. If this event occurred in the country of Gerasenes, then Jesus was in or near Gerasa, thirty-three miles southeast of the Sea of Galilee, in the mountains of Gilead. It was a large grand Roman city, founded by Alexander the Great. Even today one can see remains of the city gate, the triumphal arch, the forum, the hippodrome, theaters, and pagan temples. If Matthew is correct, then Jesus was in or near Gadara, located about six miles southeast of the Sea of Galilee, a city given to Herod by Caesar Augustus. It was basically Gentile in population, with some Jewish inhabitants. Gadara seems more likely. Even so, this is Luke's only record of Jesus ministering in a place primarily Gentile.

The account itself is of an exorcism, and though the demon possession is extreme, the usual pattern for an exorcism is followed (4:31–37). The abyss was the netherworld, the abode of spirit powers (Phil. 2:9–11), the dead (Rom. 10:7), imprisoned spirits (I Peter 3:19), and the place of Satan's prison (Rev. 20:3). The demons did not want to be sent back to the abyss, either because it was for them a prison or because they knew that the abyss was not beyond the power of Christ (Phil. 2:9–11; Rom. 8:38–39; I Peter 3:18–22). If they thought going into unclean animals and causing them to go into the sea was an escape from Jesus' power, they were mistaken. The episode immediately preceding this has shown Jesus' power at sea. This story prefigures the Gentile mission much more forcefully than the healing of the centurion's slave (7:1–10), because the centurion was within Jewish territory, was a God-fearer, and had built a synagogue. Now Jesus has moved out among Gentiles, among swine keepers (recall the swine in the far country in the story of the prodigal, 15:11–32). His power is no less effective even in an area where demons were most numerous and most destructive. Luke wants us to remember this when the Christian mission-

116

aries go into Gentile country and confront the power of evil spirits (Acts 16:16–34; 19:11–20). The demons are not able to withstand those who preach, teach, and heal in the name of Jesus who sent them out with power and authority (9:1).

However, the story is not without its negative fallout. Upon hearing what happened to the demoniac and to the herd of swine, the people of that area asked Jesus to leave (vv. 34–37). In Luke's characteristic way of telling things twice, Acts 16: 16–39 records Paul's experience in Philippi: he casts out a spirit from a slave girl, and the conclusion of the matter is that Paul is asked to leave the city. In both cases the reasons for the negative responses are two: fear and economic loss. The fear is evoked by the recognition of a power present which was greater than the power of evil spirits. If it is surprising that there was not unanimous joy at the arrival of a power greater than evil, a moment's reflection will cause the surprise to subside. In the case of the Gadarene demoniac, the people knew the locus of the evil, knew where the man lived, and devoted considerable time and expense trying to guard and to control him (v. 29). A community thus learns to live with demonic forces, isolating and partially controlling them. If it is not "spiritualizing" the story too much to say so, this partially successful balance of tolerance and management of the demonic among them also allowed the people to keep attention off their own lives. But now the power of God for good comes to their community and it disturbs a way of life they had come to accept. Even when it is for good, power that can neither be calculated nor managed is frightening. What will God do next in our community? People who understand this fear are best prepared to understand the running fear created by Easter.

Of course there was also the factor of economic loss. It remains the case to this day that a community becomes very much involved when the impact of Jesus Christ affects the economy. And the gospel does stir the economy, because healings, conversions, and the embrace of Christian ethics radically influence getting and spending. The Gerasene people are not praising God that a man is healed; they are counting the cost and find it too much. Likewise, Paul felt not only in Philippi but in Ephesus as well (Acts 19:18–34) the powerful economic forces that array themselves against the good news. It continues to be a painful part of the education of young ministers to discover that the reign of God has its enemies, that those ene-

117

mies reside not only over against us but also within and among us, and that no one is untouched by the conflicts that follow. Being asked to leave by those you seek to help is a pain unlike any other.

Naturally, "the man from whom the demons had gone, sitting at the feet of Jesus, clothed and in his right mind" (v. 35), wanted to continue to be with Jesus. However, his brief but dramatic experience with Jesus was sufficient to be the content of a witness, and the behavior of the people of his area certainly reveals their need for such a witness. Jesus tells him to perform the one ministry for which he is qualified: "Return to your home, and declare how much God has done for you" (v. 39). The man did so, except he talked of what *Jesus* had done for him (v. 39). His experience had been with Jesus; he apparently was unable to think beyond Jesus to the power of God which was in Jesus. However, the reader of Luke's story should note that Jesus was, here and elsewhere, pointing his listeners to God, not to himself. God is the subject of the entire story, from Adam to the eschaton, the story within which Luke places both his Gospel and Acts.

Raising Jairus' Daughter
and Healing a Woman with a Hemorrhage (8:40–56)
(Matthew 9:18–26; Mark 5:21–43)

Geographically, these two events are located on the western side of the Sea of Galilee, Jesus having returned from the eastern side. This location is important because both acts of Jesus involve Jewish law. Luke found these stories already joined in Mark, who often set a story within a story. We met this literary arrangement in less dramatic form at 4:31–37 and 5:17–26. The raising of Jairus' daughter is the framing story (vv. 40–42, 49–56), with the healing of the woman with a hemorrhage as the insertion (vv. 43–48). Even though this story within a story was received from Mark, Luke chose to leave the literary form as he received it, and so we have a right to ask Luke why this structure. We can only speculate. One possible answer is historical: this is the order in which they occurred. Another is logical: the inserted story allows time for the sick girl to die. One other possible answer is literary: the inserted story delays the action requested by Jairus, thereby building anticipation and heightening interest.

Whatever the reasons for putting the one story within the

118

other, the two are certainly joined in many ways. In fact, it should be said first that they are in a way joined to the preceding story of the Gerasene demoniac. Jesus has just returned from a ministry among Gentile swine keepers, persons who were "afar off," beyond acceptability. Now Jesus brings God's blessing to two persons who, while certainly within Judaism, are outside because of ceremonial laws. Maybe the double use of the number twelve (the woman was ill twelve years, the girl is twelve years old), symbolic of Israel, is Luke's reminder that it is within Judaism that these two are outsiders. Because the woman has a discharge of blood she is unclean, everything she touches is unclean, and whoever touches her is unclean (Lev. 15:25–30). The law was clear; in her own home, in society, and at the synagogue she was an outsider. The girl, once she dies, defiles those who contact her because of the law concerning a corpse (Num. 19:11–19). Therefore the crowd that welcomes Jesus does so sincerely, but is unaware of the unclean woman, and is interested in Jesus healing a dying girl but not raising a dead one. That the woman crossed the ritual barriers by being in the crowd and by touching Jesus and that Jesus both healed her and gave her a blessing are not at all to be taken as mocking the law; likewise in the instance of Jesus touching the corpse. Jesus, and certainly Luke's Jesus, would not do that. In every society social, medical, and religious distinctions exist, and their justifications are ceaselessly debated. The point here is that with reference to the healing and helping power of God, there are no barriers. To say this is not merely to describe the ministry of Jesus but to remind ourselves of the mandate under which the church lives.

As for the healing of the woman with the discharge, three details in the account deserve our attention. First, that her healing was by a touch is not unusual in the Gospel. Luke said in 6:19, "And all the crowd sought to touch him, for power came forth from him and healed them all." In no sense are we dealing here with the practice of magic. The encounter was personal: Jesus knew he had been touched, that power had gone out from him, and he wanted to meet the one who had received his healing. And the encounter was prompted by faith: "Daughter, your faith has made you well; go in peace" (v. 48). This is the same blessing Jesus gave the sinful woman who anointed him (7:50). Second, this crowd is pushing and shoving to be near him. The crowds in Luke have been favorable to Jesus and have

119

sought his healing power, but here they seem so focused on Jairus' daughter that they are essentially spectators. When Jesus asks who touched him, they deny it, as though he were charging them with some violation. Even Simon Peter (some manuscripts say, "and those with him"; cf. NEB) says, in effect, "There is a large crowd pressing around you; of course someone touched you." However, Jesus distinguishes between simply being present and having faith. And finally, the relationship of the woman to Jesus is not private. True, the crowd did not know she had touched Jesus and been healed, but Jesus would not let it remain a case of one person in a crowd receiving God's blessing and it remaining her own secret. Jesus calls the woman out, in front of all the people she tells what happened, and there before them Jesus affirms her faith and blesses her. She has not only witnessed to the people but now the people have to deal with her story and with her. After the prescribed ritual (Lev. 15:25–30) she will be restored to that community, and now after twelve years they will have to accept her. The people can disbelieve her story, can believe her but only tolerate her in her return to society and to the synagogue, or they can welcome her as they welcomed (v. 40) the one who healed her. Faith is indeed personal, but it certainly is not private.

As for the raising of Jairus' daughter, the scene opens with a synagogue ruler (president, NEB) at the feet of Jesus, the same position of the Gentile demoniac in the prior story (vv. 28, 35). Being a leader in the religious establishment does not exempt him from personal tragedy, but neither does it place him outside Jesus' compassion. Credentials neither admit nor bar: he is desperate, his daughter is dying, and she is his only daughter. This is the second raising of an only child in Luke (7:11–17). The messenger who brought word that the girl had died assumed that death placed her beyond the reach of Jesus' power and suggested they cease pleading with Jesus. Jesus asks the bereaved to put aside fear and to trust in God. The mourners in the house laughed at Jesus. In that culture, families that could afford it hired mourners at such times. These mourners were probably professionals and they knew death and its finality. The girl is dead; now is the time for tears. The raising of the girl is no public display in some attempt to coerce faith; only the parents and Jesus' inner circle (introduced here by Luke for the first time) are present. The miracle does not generate faith but proceeds from faith. The act of raising her involved Jesus' touch

120

and his calling out, apparently in a loud voice (v. 54). The departing and returning of the spirit (v. 55) was a common way to speak of death and life, not only in Judaism (I Kings 17:17–22) but in Greco-Roman culture.

Two details in the record will reappear in Luke's account of God's raising Jesus from the dead. There is the matter of food for the once deceased (24:41–43), and the raising of the dead is not a public spectacle. As in the case of Jesus, so here: those who are already believers experience the act of God giving life to the dead. In fact, in the story before us, Jesus charges the family not to tell what happened. The demoniac of Gerasa was told to broadcast what God had done for him (v. 39), but apparently such proclamation is inappropriate here. Why? Maybe the geographical difference is a factor. Perhaps this event was too closely tied to faith to become the subject for curious minds. Perhaps it is too soon to be talking of being raised from the dead. Maybe Jesus is too close to his own turn toward Jerusalem and death and the act could confuse present and would-be disciples over the uses of Jesus' power in the hour of his own death. The scoffing will come soon enough: "He saved others; let him save himself, if he is the Christ of God, his Chosen One!" (23:35).

The Sending Out of the Twelve (9:1–6)
(Matthew 10:1, 9–11, 14; Mark 6:7–13)

Since the time when they were chosen to be apostles (6:12–16), the Twelve have observed and listened to Jesus. Now the apostles in preparation become apostles ("those sent out") in fact. For their task they are given authority and power without which they can do nothing in the face of demons and disease. Their assignment is threefold: exorcise demons, heal, and preach the reign of God. They will witness to and demonstrate in powerful acts the present and coming kingdom of God. They do not go two by two (Mark 6:7); Luke reserves that for the Seventy (10:1–12). For the itinerary they are to be totally dependent on God and, like the Levites, they could anticipate hospitality and support (Num. 18:31; I Cor. 9:3–14). In New Testament terms, hospitality meant "love of the stranger" as distinguished from "love of brothers and sisters" (Heb. 13:1–2). It was expected in the culture in general and among Christians in particular (Acts 17:7; 21:17; 28:7; Rom. 12:13; 16:23; I Peter 4:9). Whenever it was thought that the stranger was a threat to

121

a community, tests might precede hospitality (II and III John). Jesus pronounced a special blessing on those who were hospitable to his disciples (Matt. 10:40–42). Of the stranger as guest it was expected that offered hospitality would be accepted and offered food eaten. Hence the instruction in verse 4: stay in the house into which you are invited. In other words, do not insult your host by shopping around for the best available accommodations. Inhospitality was to be met not with retaliation but with the simple ritual of judgment (v. 5; Acts 13:51).

As Jesus commissioned them to do, the Twelve go without the trappings of security, "just in case." Had they gone with money and extra provisions, their witness would have been undercut by such an evident lack of faith in God and trust in the hospitality of the people. (How many of the church's sermons are contradicted by budgets and programs of self-protection and security!) They preached and healed *everywhere* (v. 6). We can assume that the villages mentioned were within the territory of Judaism, but Luke does not say that. Luke may use the word "everywhere" because he is thinking of the mission of the church led by these apostles which he will describe in Acts. If the Twelve at this point do go beyond the borders of Judaism, they are but following Jesus who has only recently ministered among both Jews and Gentiles.

Luke 9:7–50
Forebodings and Predictions of the Passion

The brevity of this section should not in any way be taken by the reader as a reflection of its importance in the total movement of Luke's Gospel. Rather than brief, the word describing 9:7–50 is "compressed." Luke has omitted a large body of material that is in Mark 6:45—8:26 (Matt. 14:22—16:12). A careful review of that material would doubtless yield many clear reasons why Luke found it inappropriate to his purpose. Yet whatever his reasons, the effect of the omission is to provide a compact and intense section with unusual thematic unity which moves the reader swiftly from the period of Jesus' very popular Galilean ministry to the turn toward Jerusalem and death (9:51). Contextually, 9:7–50 concludes the Galilean ministry and pre-

122

pares for the journey to Jerusalem. Internally, this section begins by raising the question, Who is Jesus? a question that Jesus then puts to his disciples, answers to which are provided by the subsequent units in this section. We enter, therefore, at 9:7 a major transition in Luke's narrative.

Herod Perplexed About Jesus (9:7–9)
(Matthew 14:1–2; Mark 6:14–16)

Since four Herods make appearances in Luke-Acts, perhaps we should take a moment to get the right Herod before us. This is Herod Antipas, son of Herod the great and tetrarch of Galilee, and the Herod most often mentioned in the Gospels because the ministries of John and Jesus occurred during his rule. Herod's capital was Tiberias on the Sea of Galilee, so it was inevitable that reports about Jesus would reach him. Luke simply says Herod "heard of all that was done" (v. 7); whether that knowledge was sought by him or came along natural channels of news and rumors is unclear. Neither is it clear whether the sending out of the Twelve gave the ministry of Jesus the appearance of a movement and hence to be watched. What is clear is that Jesus was attracting large crowds and that crowds interest political authorities.

That which perplexes Herod is that he gets three different reports about the identity of Jesus. These reports reflect public opinions about Jesus, opinions repeated at 9:18–22, at which point we will examine what they meant and who Jesus was in the eyes of his contemporaries in Galilee. That some thought Jesus to be a resurrected John implies several things: that John was so popular that many could not believe him dead (a common phenomenon among devotees of heroes and heroines); that the circumstances of John's death were sufficiently uncertain and disturbing to fuel a belief in his resurrection; and that the ministries of John and Jesus were similar enough to prompt some to observe Jesus and think, "It is John again!" The reports that Jesus was Elijah returned as one of the prophets of old were, as we will note at verses 18–22, associated with views of the messianic age and the day of the Lord. An astute politician would know that such stories were not merely religious talk of negligible importance. Among the people already restless under foreign rule and heavy taxes, stories that joined Jesus to ancient prophecies about God's future for Israel could become socially and politically inflammatory. Herod was more than ca-

123

sually interested; after all, he had already killed John, a fact to which Luke makes only this one reference (for a full account, see Mark 6:17–29). Herod's curiosity will darken into a desire to kill Jesus (13:31), a desire that will be satisfied through cooperation with Pontius Pilate in Jerusalem (23:6–12). The closing sentence, "And he sought to see him" (v. 9), alerts the reader to anticipate the reappearance of Herod in Luke's narrative.

We should carry forward from the passage at least two very important notes. First, these verses carry a clear prophecy of Jesus' death. This is not the vague anger of religious leaders who discuss with one another "what they might do to Jesus" (6:11). The ministry of Jesus has now reached a center of political power and disturbed a man who has already killed one prophet. Second, Herod asks the question that forms the substantive center of this entire section (vv. 7–50): "Who is this about whom I hear such things?" (v. 9). This question was asked earlier by the disciples following the calming of the storm: "Who then is this?" (8:25). Now the question is on the lips of one who has very different reasons for wanting to know. Soon now Jesus will ask his disciples to answer the question.

Jesus Feeds the Multitude (9:10–17)
(Matthew 14:13–21; Mark 6:30–44; John 6:1–13)

One does not have to search long and hard for reasons why the feeding of the crowds, reported by all four Evangelists, has received so much attention not only in the Gospels but in the church's teaching, preaching, and worship. As a feeding of the people in the wilderness ("a lonely place" in v. 12 is literally "a wilderness place"), it echoes the feeding of the children of Israel in the wilderness in Moses' day and is enriched by that memory. The feeding also highlights Jesus' compassion and especially his concern for the poor and hungry. Also, the church has found in the event a model for ministry: Jesus working through his disciples. A primary reason this story is central in the church's memory is that it prefigures the Lord's Supper (22:19; 24:30), both in the eucharistic language used (v. 16) and on the word translated "broken pieces" which came to be a term for the bread of the Eucharist (*Didache* 9:3–4). And finally, because the story is told eucharistically, it draws the reader's attention to the passion of Jesus, the very heart of the gospel. Like the preceding unit (vv. 7–9), even though in a very different fashion, this

124

passage prepares the reader to hear Jesus speak of his own death which begins in the next paragraph (vv. 18–22).

It is this very prominence of the feeding event that leads to a neglect of its context which, in itself, not only informs the event but also reveals much about Jesus. Only Luke among the Evangelists identifies the place as Bethsaida, the hometown of Peter, Andrew, and Philip, according to John's Gospel (John 1:44). Jesus had received the report of the Twelve concerning their mission (vv. 1–6) and had taken them into a retreat away from the crowds. Perhaps the reason was the same that had prompted his own retreat after busy periods of favorable crowd response: prayer and renewal as well as to deal with the temptations that always lie coiled in the bosom of public praise. Mark says it was a withdrawal to rest (Mark 6:31). Whatever the purpose, a gathering crowd cuts short the interlude. That the crowd interrupts its movement is reflected in the brevity of the account of the apostles' report. Their mission, for which they had been selected and prepared, would surely receive more than a single sentence: "The apostles told him what they had done" (v. 10). But that is all the reader gets. Luke also impresses us with the interruptive nature of the crowd's presence by immediately resuming the story of Jesus' privacy with the Twelve at verse 18. One could read the account by moving from verse 10 to verse 18, omitting verses 11–17, and the continuity would be smooth. What are the Twelve to learn from the interruption? That those who come with pressing needs do not interrupt; that ministry continues, and often is as effective in the break as in the plan. Jesus ministered to the woman with the hemorrhage who "interrupted" Jesus and his followers on their way to the house of Jairus (8:43–48). The weary apostles return from a mission and find themselves in the middle of a mission. Jesus welcomes the crowd (v. 11). The feeding of the crowds takes place during a planned retreat which becomes a full ministry of preaching and healing.

Luke would not have us think of the Twelve as resistant to this ministry when they urge Jesus to send the people to nearby villages for lodging (only in Luke) and food. They are expressing genuine concern for the people within what they regard as the limits of the circumstances. True, they have seen Jesus exorcise demons, heal the sick, and raise the dead, but it is not automatic that they would reason that Jesus' power would transfer to any

125

and all conditions of need. A hungry crowd, in a wilderness, away from home, and with sunset approaching, should be dismissed—that is, if Jesus stopped healing and preaching, they would go home. However, when Jesus acts to feed the people, the apostles are helpful and share in the ministry. Luke's portrait of the Twelve is generally positive; unless we are careful, we may allow Mark's often critical presentation of them to bleed into Luke's story here.

It is important, then, to keep in mind that the feeding of the multitude was an event within and not isolated from a full ministry to a range of human needs. When the church appropriated this story for liturgical use, as bread and fish symbolism and the eucharistic language (took, blessed, broke, gave) indicated it did, the liturgy was not separated from the larger ministry to other needs. The Lord's Supper was joined to a full meal in which those who had shared with those who did not. Apart from feeding the hungry, the Eucharist becomes a ritual detached from life, just as feeding the hungry, apart from the Eucharist, is not fully satisfying. One lives by bread, yes, but not by bread alone. This conviction about responding to human needs physical and spiritual is reflected not only in this story but also in Luke's description of the life of the early church (Acts 2:43–47).

Peter's Confession and the First Prediction of the Passion (9:18–22)
(Matthew 16:13–23; Mark 8:27–33)

Luke, like John (John 6:1–69), joins the feeding and Peter's confession, omitting the material that is in Mark 6:45—8:26. Both Mark and Matthew locate this episode in the area at Caesarea Philippi, but Luke gives no geographical reference. The last place mentioned was Bethsaida (v. 10), with an intervening event occurring in "a lonely place" (v. 12), but Luke seems uninterested in geography here. His concern is to locate this event in the prayer life of Jesus. It would be difficult to overemphasize the central role of prayer in the ministry of Jesus according to Luke. At Jesus' baptism, the experience of God's favor and the empowering of the Holy Spirit came while Jesus was in prayer (3:21). The twelve apostles were chosen after a night of prayer (6:12). Through a life of prayer Jesus was attuned to God's will and empowered to do it. The same will be said of the church in Acts. The expression, "As he was praying alone

126

the disciples were with him" (v. 18) informs us, then, about how Jesus was the instrument of God in word and act, but it also alerts the reader to the critical importance of what is now to take place. The question-and-answer session is no theological discussion, nor is it prompted by curiosity.

The question, Who is Jesus? has been asked twice (8:25; 9:9) but with no answer offered. Now Jesus raises it, and the disciples must respond with a report and a personal acknowledgment. The public opinion is that Jesus is the forerunner of the Messiah. Among those who had not given up hope of the coming of the messianic age opinions differed as to whether the age of God's reign would be preceded by the coming of Elijah himself or another prophet in the spirit of Elijah. The focal text for nourishing this hope (and we must not generalize, as though all Jews looked for a Messiah or even for a reign of God without a Messiah) was Mal. 4:5–6:

> Behold, I will send you Elijah the prophet before the great and terrible day of the LORD comes. And he will turn the hearts of fathers to their children and the hearts of children to their fathers, lest I come and smite the land with a curse.

What is most striking about this public opinion is that the people thought of Jesus in the role we assign to John; that is, he was regarded as a messenger announcing the coming of a Messiah. Perhaps this accounts for some of his popularity: that a Messiah is coming is always an exciting and welcome message. Everyone had a sermon under the title "When the Messiah Comes," a message including every hope, every dream, every ideal condition for which the heart longs. It is no wonder that the church's message that the Messiah has come and he is Jesus has not been as popular. To believe the Messiah *has* come means we can no longer shape him to fit our dreams; he shapes us to fit God's will. That is a difficult adjustment. There is enough misery in the world to make the message that a Messiah *will* come believable; there is enough misery in the world to make the message that a Messiah *has* come unbelievable. The first and major task of a Messiah is to get people to quit looking for one.

When Jesus turns the question of who he is to the disciples, Peter's answer is, in effect, "You are not the forerunner of the Messiah; you *are* the Messiah [Christ]." The confession differs among the Evangelists. Luke's "The Christ of God" is more than a simple elaboration on Mark's "You are the Christ"; the Christ

127

is from God, just as the Holy Spirit is from God. Luke reminds us often that from Adam to eschaton, the story is God's, the purpose is God's, the action is God's. Jesus is, therefore, the Christ *of God* (2:26; 23:35; Acts 4:26), as the apostles were to preach after Pentecost, "God has made him both Lord and Christ, this Jesus whom you crucified" (Acts 2:36). Jesus' responding command to silence is in Luke different from Matthew and Mark for whom the charge to secrecy concerns his identity as Messiah. The teachings about the coming passion are separated from the command to tell no one. For Luke the charge to silence is directly tied to Jesus' prophecy of his suffering, rejection by the religious leaders, death, and resurrection. The participle "saying" joins verses 21 and 22. The subject about which they are to be silent is that Jesus is the Messiah who must suffer. The people cannot—in fact, the disciples cannot—join the term "Messiah" with all the meanings attached to it and the idea of suffering, rejection, and death. That association would take time; it still does. In some Christian circles today, Easter is observed without Good Friday services, and the risen Lord who is to come is preferred over the suffering one who has come.

Unlike Matthew 16:21, Luke does not indicate that the passion of Jesus will occur in Jerusalem, although the rejection by chief priests among others certainly points in that direction. The term "Son of man" (v. 22) is a complicated one and laden with a number of meanings. It can refer to an eschatological figure coming from heaven (Dan. 7:13–14; Matt. 25:31–46), to a prophet like Ezekiel (Ezek. 2:1), or to anyone, as a synonym for human (Ps. 8:4). In its usage here, Son of man is a way of self-referencing and is the equivalent of "I." Matthew has already made this connection for the reader (Matt. 16:21). Noticeably missing from Luke is the sharp exchange between Jesus and Simon Peter, found in both Matthew and Mark. Many students of Luke see in this omission a preservation of a loftier view of Peter and of the Twelve, consistent with Luke's high regard for the apostles as those who are to continue Jesus' mission. This may, in fact, be a proper accounting for the omission, but it should also be said that in Luke the entire occasion is more briefly told, is more subdued, and is wrapped in prayer. Probably it was in his life of prayer that Jesus came to the realization that he must suffer. The "must," here and elsewhere (13:33; 17:25; 22:37; 24:7, 26, 44), points to divine will.

128

There would be no value in speculating as to when the matter and manner of his death first came to the mind of Jesus. Generally speaking, the Bible offers its characters to us through their words and deeds; unexpressed thoughts remain hidden from our view. Of course, the Evangelist, looking back over the whole story, allows death to cast a long shadow over the career of Jesus. When Jesus was six weeks old, Simeon said to Mary, "And a sword will pierce through your own soul also" (2:35). Following Jesus' sermon in Nazareth, there was an attempt on his life (4:29), and angry critics discussed what they might do to him (6:11). More recently, the perplexed curiosity of Herod sends a tremor through the story; he had killed John and now wants to see Jesus (9:9). Naturally these events did not swirl around Jesus without his notice, but we have no word from him on the subject of his death. At 5:35 he said, "The days will come, when the bridegroom is taken away from them, and then they will fast in those days." But who can know when this was said, occurring as it does in a collection of controversy stories? And while the church in reflection understood taking away the bridegroom as his crucifixion, what did Jesus understand by those words? It is enough to know that now Jesus clearly introduces the subject of his own passion. Through prayer he has come to know what he "must" do.

The Demands of Discipleship (9:23–27)
(Matthew 16:24–28; Mark 8:34—9:1)

The literary location of this unit provides a clear occasion to observe how a Gospel was put together. Immediately after Jesus spoke of his own suffering and death was an appropriate time to call upon his followers to participate in the same self-giving. Such a demand would not be for the Twelve alone but for all disciples. However, Jesus is alone with the Twelve, and only they know of his talk of suffering. Historically, then, to speak to "all" (v. 23) about following in his path of suffering would not make sense, because all were not privy to his introduction of the subject of the passion. They would be in the position of having missed the sermon but being present for the closing exhortation. To understand what Luke (and Mark before him) is doing, it is necessary to realize that the Evangelist is addressing the *reader* who has heard Jesus speak to the Twelve about his passion and who is also in a position to hear Jesus speak of following him in self-denial. In fact, the only

129

person able to grasp the meaning of verses 23–27 is the reader. The disciples cannot know about cross bearing, because Jesus has not told them he would die by crucifixion. The "all" cannot know that Jesus is on his way to death, because they do not arrive until verse 23. But the reader knows that Jesus has predicted his own passion, and the reader knows that Jesus died on a cross. Two units, verses 18–22 and verses 23–27, which may have originally been quite separate in time and place, are drawn together to address the reader on the subject of discipleship. Of course, since the cross was a rather common instrument of death used by the Romans, Jesus could have been understood by a Galilean audience, but since his own death, not to mention the manner of it, was still a secret, it is most unlikely. We the readers are the ones being called upon to understand our crosses after the fact of his.

What are our crosses to be borne? Luke alone has the modifier "daily" (v. 23) which shifts the emphasis from martyrdom to sacrificial living. A way of life that could be called cross bearing would have to be a life one had "taken up"; that is, it would be voluntarily chosen. Arthritis, poor grades, an unhappy marriage, or a child on drugs would not qualify, even though these and other difficulties are sometimes called "crosses we have to bear." These and all other human hurts are not beyond the compassion of the one who is touched by the feeling of all our infirmities (Heb. 4:14–16), but they are not crosses as spoken of here. A way of life that could be called cross bearing would have to involve denial of self in the service of God. A cross is not sought or pursued, but it was and still is true that following Jesus in the service of God, which translates into meeting human needs, is on a path along which there are crosses, prices to be paid, pain and hurt to be accepted. We are not speaking of death wish here but obedience to the reign of God. For a definition of reign of God one looks to the ministry of Jesus.

The major part of this unit consists of three parallel sayings, all beginning in the same way (vv. 24–26) and brought together here because they inform cross-bearing discipleship. Each of these sayings has a proverb quality about it and therefore contains a kind of truth drawn from experience and observation that can circulate in any culture as wisdom. Verse 24 carries a general truth: self-centeredness is finally counter-productive and destructive, severing one from the resources that give life. Verse 25 has been and is painfully confirmed in every tragic

130

case of unrestrained greed, regardless of whether it burns in young ambition soon to discover the magnificence of life's promise lost in the poverty of its achievement or in splendid retirement going from resort to resort. Verse 26 reminds us of what we all know very well: the one of whom you are ashamed today may be your judge tomorrow. This is but a variation on the ancient proverb: Whatever you sow you will reap. Yet all three sayings in their present context must be interpreted under the pressure of Jesus' own passion and call to discipleship. Saving life by losing life is not, therefore, a strategy for successful living but is a condition of discipleship: "whoever loses his life *for my sake.*" Or, to seek to gain the whole world as a power move or out of fear of insecurity is a flat contradiction to that life whose power is given by God's Spirit and who is sent into the world without all those "just in case" provisions (vv. 1–6). And if the crucifixion of Jesus is a source of shame and embarrassment to a church that otherwise finds Jesus a fascinating hero, then that church which turns away from the Son of man in suffering (v. 22) must one day face the Son of man in final judgment (v. 26).

The section concludes with a statement (v. 27) that can best be clarified if we observe how Luke differs from both Mark (Mark 9:1) and Matthew (Matt. 16:28). Both Matthew's "Son of man coming in his kingdom" and Mark's "the kingdom of God has come with power" are strongly oriented toward the parousia, that is, the future coming of the Son of man and the final ushering in of the reign of God. Luke does not use the word "coming" but speaks of seeing the kingdom of God. Scholars who have argued that Jesus was speaking of the transfiguration or of the resurrection have done so looking for a special revelatory event but within the lifetime of persons present in Jesus' audience. For Luke, the kingdom is both present in the person and work of Jesus and future in the consummation of God's purpose. Which is his accent here? If the assumption that Luke knew Mark is correct, then Luke has clearly modified Mark in order to reduce the strong futuristic force of the statement. The eschatological quality is not removed but rather put before the listener as a quality or condition of life before God which can be experienced now. The preacher who uses this text to collapse the whole of God's work into the present will have understood Luke only partially; the future fulfillment is never abandoned. Likewise, the preacher who interprets this text to

131

encourage infinite postponement of all responsible engagement in this present age will have read Luke only partially. Was not Jesus' first word in his first recorded sermon in Luke, *"Today* this scripture has been fulfilled" (4:21)?

The Transfiguration of Jesus (9:28–36)
(Matthew 17:1–8; Mark 9:2–8)

Passages on which one has prepared or heard with some frequency sermons or lessons are often the most difficult to read or to hear. The account of Jesus' transfiguration may be such a text. For example, who has not heard interpretations of the transfiguration joined to the following story of a healing that offered a "mountaintop experience" followed by the admonition to "come down into the valley of service"? That there is truth to the analysis that life's rhythm consists of occasions of inspiration in the presence of God followed by occasions of routine and pedestrian duty is not to be contradicted. That pastors need to address with both correction and encouragement those who experience religion as totally one or the other is widely confirmed. However, the text and the context of Jesus' transfiguration vigorously resist such a use of this passage. There are in the Scriptures accounts of experiences of Jesus and of other persons serving the purposes of God for which analogies in our common experiences are not easily found. One reads and studies these accounts, and the experience is one of awe and wonder and worship. The question, What in our lives is a suitable parallel? does not even seem appropriate. Applications and exhortations trivialize. Abraham's offer of his son Isaac—to what shall we compare it? Even Martin Luther would not climb Mount Moriah for homiletical purposes. The baptism of Jesus has inspired and informed millions of baptisms, but not one of them, nor the sum total of them, parallels without remainder Jesus' experience of the heavens splitting, the dove descending, and the voice of God affirming Jesus as both sovereign Son and suffering Servant. Jesus' baptism, say the Evangelists, was an epiphany, a revelation of the divine Son. Now the transfiguration—to what shall we compare it, since it too is an epiphany? Certainly it is not being suggested that texts such as these be avoided. Rather, the preacher or the teacher might be better advised to hold them before the listeners in their full extraordinariness rather than reduce them to fit the contours of our experiences. To be led by a sensitive and thoughtful pastor to the foot of the Mount of Transfiguration, to be helped to sense its significance for Jesus and three apostles, and to be left there for a while in awe of its mystery and power might finally influence life in more ways and in more depth than interpretations that reduce the text to lessons that assume "this is the way life is for us today."

After one has read Luke 9:28–36, reflection on its meaning could well begin by a reading of Ex. 24:12–18. This account of a theophany shares many details with the transfiguration story: the mountain, the cloud, six days (Mark 9:2; Luke has eight; this will be discussed later), Moses, the voice, the glory. In addition, the shining of Moses' face after being in the presence of God (Ex. 34:29–35) surely influenced our text and helps to place the transfiguration in the context of revelatory events. A second step toward interpretation involves attending to the location of this event within Luke's narrative. Luke joins Matthew and Mark in placing this story immediately after the first prediction of the passion, a position that gives the transfiguration a strategic importance parallel to Jesus' baptism (3:21–22). After submitting to the baptism of preparation and before beginning his public ministry, Jesus received heaven's confirmation as Son of God. Here, after speaking of his coming ·passion and before turning toward Jerusalem, Jesus receives heaven's confirmation again. However, on this occasion three apostles hear the voice, a voice that says the talk of death which they have recently heard does not abrogate, does not contradict Jesus' Messiahship. The one who had announced to them that he must suffer, die, and be raised is indeed God's Son and is to be obeyed. We cannot expect that they were able immediately to join suffering and death to the Son of God and Lord, but they now have the two principal ingredients for a faith to proclaim once clarity and power come to them.

Now we are ready to notice the Lukan accents in the story. First, Jesus goes to the mountain to pray and the transfiguration occurs "as he was praying" (v. 29). This statement recalls specifically Jesus' baptism (3:21) and generally his continuing prayer life (5:16; 6:12; 9:18) by which his ministry was sustained in the will of God. Luke says this occurred "about eight days" after the preceding event (v. 28). This could be taken as a connection of the transfiguration to the resurrection which occurred on the eighth day, the day after the Sabbath, or it may signal the use of this story for Christian worship held on the

133

eighth day. The phrase "Behold, two men" (v. 30) ties this story to both the resurrection (24:4) and the ascension (Acts 1:10). The dazzling brightness of the transfigured Jesus will be recalled in the second volume when Luke describes Saul's experience of the risen Jesus appearing in "a light from heaven, brighter than the sun" (Acts 26:13).

Only Luke provides the content of the conversation among Jesus, Moses, and Elijah (vv. 31–33). They spoke of Jesus' approaching death in Jerusalem, or, more literally, of his approaching "exodus," a powerfully symbolic term. That the law (Moses) and the prophets (Elijah) testify to Jesus' suffering, death, and resurrection is an important theme in Luke (24:25–27, 44–46). The three apostles were not privy to that conversation, because they were in a deep sleep. Apparently this experience occurred at night. They wake (the 1971 RSV corrects the erroneous translation "but kept awake" in the 1946 ed.) in time to see the three glorified figures. Peter's spontaneous and not very thoughtful expression of a desire to mark the time and place is interrupted by the coming of the cloud. The cloud frightened the apostles because the cloud was associated with the awesome presence of God (Ex. 24:15–16; Acts 1:9). For Jesus, the transfiguration confirmed who he was and assured that the announced path before him was not only according to the law and the prophets but was the will of God for him. For the apostles, the experience told them that Jesus was God's Son and to be obeyed as he instructed them on the way to Jerusalem and death. For all Luke's insistence on the continuity of Judaism and the Christian community, Jesus is not just another in a line of prophets; he is preeminent. He is to be heard, not over against Moses and the prophets, but as the proper interpreter and fulfillment of what had been preserved in the Scriptures.

Brief and mysterious as it is, Luke's account provides the reader with more information about what happened on the mountain that night than the other nine apostles or anyone else knew "in those days," that is, prior to the resurrection. Peter, James, and John were silent, and properly so; they were not ready to speak of it, and who was ready to hear? As the following episodes will make clear, they are far from understanding. And, of course, we would like very much to penetrate the mystery of this experience, but we cannot. Matthew calls it a vision (Matt. 17:9). One thing is clear: Jesus and his three disciples

134

have an experience of God. Its meaning for Jesus and for them is different, but the only actor in the event is God. Jesus is not acting but is being acted on. The God of Moses and Elijah affirms them in their unity with Jesus but asserts the finality of Jesus. The God who could rescue the Son from suffering confirms for Jesus the way of the cross. This God also tells the disciples, who will soon face conditions that seem to derail if not bring to an end their hope in Jesus, that those very painful conditions do not lie *across* the way but *on* the way to the completion of God's purpose. This is a mountaintop experience but not the kind about which persons write glowingly of sunrises, soft breezes, warm friends, music, and quiet time. On this mountain the subject is death, and the frightening presence of God reduces those present to silence. In due time, after the resurrection, they will remember, understand, and not feel heavy. In fact, they will tell it broadly as good news.

Sketches of the Not-yet-ready Disciples (9:37–50)
(Matthew 17:14–23; 18:1–5; Mark 9:14–41)

It is not the intention of this heading to imply that attention turns temporarily from Jesus or that an unfavorable camera is being turned on the disciples. Luke has consistently high regard for the Twelve. They have been chosen as apostles after a night of prayer (6:12–16), prepared, and sent out with power and authority (9:1–6). But they have been jolted with Jesus' prophecy of his passion and with the demanding word that the path of discipleship is the way of the cross. What effect has it had on them? Are there behavioral or attitudinal changes? In this section they will be seen and heard always in relation to Jesus, for apart from him they are still fishermen. However, as would be true of any of us, being heard and seen in relation to Jesus can accentuate one's flaws and remind us painfully how much in need of grace are the people who not only constitute the church but who also serve as its leaders. In fact, the value of exploring these verses will be radically reduced if the readers fail to identify with the disciples. Sometimes this can be done only with deliberate intent if one is a preacher or a teacher. The tendency among us who share these texts with others is to assume the place of Jesus for ourselves and to place our listeners in the role of the disciples. That is, we speak Jesus' words of correction, reprimand, encouragement, and instruction to others rather than listening to them in the role of disciples.

135

INTERPRETATION

Luke 9:37–50 is a transition section between the introduction of the subject of death and the turn toward Jerusalem at 9:51. The journey itself will be marked by the mounting tension, confusion, and pain attendant upon such a trip and by Jesus' preparation of his disciples by increased time with them in instruction. These verses preview that journey in that both Jesus' passion and teaching the disciples govern all four brief episodes. The four subunits are really four vignettes in which the disciples are revealed as lacking: in power (vv. 37–43a), in understanding (vv. 43b–45), in humility (vv. 46–48), and in sympathy (vv. 49–50). No wonder Luke devotes over nine chapters to the journey to Jerusalem; preparation of the disciples (including the reader) will take time.

The first episode (vv. 37–43a) occurs the day after the transfiguration. The crowd is present, a case of need has been presented to the disciples, they cannot exorcise the demon, Jesus reprimands those involved for a lack of faith, heals the boy (an only child, typical of Luke, 7:12; 8:42), and all are astonished at the greatness of God. The demon possession and the exorcism do not differ from cases previously encountered (cf. the discussion at 4:31–37); the new element is the inability of the disciples. Jesus had given them power and authority over demons and diseases (9:1–6) and they had used that power with effectiveness. Now it is gone. Have they grown arrogant with success and lost their relationship to the source of power? Had they failed to sustain that power through prayer? Has Jesus' announcement of suffering and death robbed them of faith and firm commitment? Or have they been granted failure in order to see that just because Jesus is moving toward death does not mean that his power and authority are diminished? Jesus is not and will not be a victim; he chooses in the power and will of God to go to Jerusalem. His authority over evil spirits has not been withdrawn; the greatness of God is still evident in him.

The second vignette (vv. 43b–45) reveals the disciples' lack of understanding. Their confusion stems from hearing two sharply contrasting voices: one voice is that of the crowd still marveling over the recent demonstration of Jesus' power, and the other is the voice of Jesus predicting again his being delivered into the hands of others. This is to say that the disciples are in the difficult position of having to picture Jesus in two scenes at once: power and powerlessness. Omission of reference to the resurrection serves to emphasize his death. Even though Jesus

136

presses them to pay attention, they have no categories for handling what seems to be a clear contradiction. How or why will one who has power and authority be found in a position of having his life and death determined by others? Will he lose power, or relinquish power, or will his passion be, in some strange, paradoxical way, a powerful act? Whatever views of a Messiah they had held, obviously those views are inadequate for Jesus' words. They cannot grasp what can come only by revelation (Matt. 16:17; I Cor. 2:14; 12:3). In verse 45 there is the mixture, not uncommon in Scripture, of human unbelief and providential concealing. However, the time will come when the risen Christ will open their eyes and minds (24:31, 45).

The third episode (vv. 46–48) exposes in the disciples a lack of humility. The argument among the disciples about greatness is ugly and inappropriate, for it is comparative and competitive destroying their unity, it diverts praise from God to themselves, and it introduces into the circle of Jesus' followers criteria of greatness that are totally foreign to the reign of God. We can only speculate as to the cause of the quarrel: the special experiences reserved for Peter, James, and John; their recent successes when on a mission; locating blame for their failure with the demoniac boy; or perhaps they have now lost the distinction between being called and having credentials. But whatever the cause, this scene helps to clarify why the disciples do not understand talk of suffering. By means of a child, Jesus teaches lowliness of spirit, but notice that his instruction is not to become as a child, a message found in Matt. 18:3. Rather, the humility taught is by means of the practice of hospitality. "Whoever receives one such child in my name" means that whoever welcomes the lowliest has shown humility appropriate to the kingdom. All are anxious to extend hospitality to the great, but disciples of Jesus have the mind to offer hospitality even to a child. In so doing, they welcome Jesus, and in welcoming Jesus they welcome God. In the reign of God there is no selective hospitality.

Finally, in verses 49–50 Luke shows the disciples' failure to have captured Jesus' sympathetic and inclusive spirit. That Jesus had selected twelve to be apostles does not mean that no one else could trust in God as Jesus taught and participate in his ministry. The twelve had been chosen from among many disciples who certainly were not sent home because they were not of the apostolic circle. Exorcisms were performed among the

137

Jews (11:19), and it was inevitable that those drawn to Jesus would call on his name for power over evil spirits. (But Jesus' name was not magic. Luke will tell later about exorcists who invoked the name of "the Jesus whom Paul preaches" and their ritual failed embarrassingly, Acts 19:13–16.) And why not? Who holds the franchise for relieving human suffering? The Twelve, who should have celebrated the fact that the influence of Jesus was spreading, especially in view of their own recent failure (v. 40), manifest a spirit of exclusivism. Apparently that spirit entered the church quite early and it has certainly stayed late. But it is not surprising really; the disciples have shown themselves ambitious and competitive (v. 46). Where leaders compete, it follows that they will also seek to exercise control over the membership of the communities they lead. It is perfectly reasonable, of course, to have standards and guidelines for inclusion in the guild of Christian ministry, but "because he does not follow with us" hardly qualifies as the sole criterion for acceptance or rejection.

PART FOUR

The Journey
to Jerusalem
LUKE 9:51—19:28

In the course of teaching and preaching in the church it is often the case that Scripture is treated unit by unit with attention to individual events or teachings. Contexts in such a method consist primarily of the paragraphs immediately before and after the passage under investigation. Much can be gained by both presenter and listener in such a procedure, especially if one is moving through a biblical book in continuous or semi-continuous readings. However, now and then one comes to a major block of material that demands some consideration as a whole before attention is given to its parts. Such is the nature of the section before us now. "When the days drew near for him to be received up, he set his face to go to Jerusalem" (9:51) is an expression that breaks from what precedes it and that has the quality of setting the tone for what is about to come. One is especially impressed that the narrative is still in chapter 9 and Jesus does not arrive at Jerusalem until 19:29. A first response might be to consider 9:51 as simply an introduction to what immediately follows but as having no thematic connection with the events and sayings lying farther down the rather long road to Jerusalem. Closer examination, however, reveals that this is not the case: Luke repeatedly reminds the reader that what takes place between 9:51 and 19:28 is to be understood as occurring on Jesus' journey to Jerusalem and that the fact of that journey is to influence interpretation of what Jesus says and does (9:51, 53; 13:22, 33; 17:11; 18:31; 19:11, 28).

However, signals within this block of material force the

139

reader to ask, In what sense is this a travel narrative? What kind of journey is involved? Geographical references are puzzling and do not support movement from Galilee to Jerusalem. At 9:51–53 Jesus passes through Samaria; at 10:38–42 (if John 12:1–3 is geographically correct) he seems to be in Bethany, near Jerusalem; he is in Galilee at 13:31, between Galilee and Samaria at 17:11, in Jericho at 18:35—19:10, and near Jerusalem at 19:11. No map of the area permits these markers as evidence of a journey to Jerusalem, especially if Jesus has "set his face to go to Jerusalem" (9:51). Today students of Luke generally conclude that the journey is not geographical but is an editorial structure created by Luke. That Luke found the travel motif helpful for telling the story of Jesus and the church is evident both here and in Acts which is very much occupied not only with the missionary tours of Paul but also with his lengthy journeys to Jerusalem and to Rome. In fact, both of those trips echo the story of Jesus. Just as Jesus saw his going to Jerusalem as the will of God (9:22, 31), so Paul said, "I must also see Rome" (Acts 19:21), and as for Jerusalem, "I am ready not only to be imprisoned but even to die at Jerusalem for the name of the Lord Jesus" (Acts 21:13).

If, then, the journey motif is Luke's construction, what was his organizing principle? Since it was not geographical, what is the journey? Much of the material in this block is peculiar to Luke. Of the entirety of 9:51—19:28, many students of Luke speak of 9:51—18:14 as Luke's special section. The content is a mixture of stories peculiarly Lukan and stories held in common with Matthew, though differently arranged. At 18:15 Luke rejoins Mark's narrative. But the key to Luke's arrangement of the sayings and events is not easy to find. Sometimes the connections seem very loose, even though some units within the whole have clear thematic relationships. In addition, the level of intensity in what Jesus does and says varies greatly. From 9:51–62 one would get the impression that from this moment on there will be no pausing, no relaxing, no tolerated interruptions; the path has been chosen, the die cast, and every step will be toward the cross. Yet within these chapters Jesus will visit friends, be a frequent guest in homes, and do much of his teaching while at the dinner table. Needless to say, many serious students of this Gospel have given up the effort to find Luke's principle of organization and arrangement, being content to say that Luke has provided a frame (the journey) for including

140

a range of situationless episodes available to him in his sources. After all, say some, Jesus is preparing his disciples not only for the crisis at Jerusalem but also for continuing his work, and much of that instruction would have to be improvised as teachable moments occurred.

Two Lukan scholars have provided what they believe to be keys to the structure of 9:51—19:28. Charles Talbert is convinced that this block is built on a literary form familiar in Scripture called a chiasm. A chiastic pattern is one in which a series of ideas or themes is presented and repeated in another series of parallel ideas or themes but in reverse order—for example, ABCD, DCBA. One finds such patterns in briefer form frequently in the New Testament, such as in Paul's statement that Christ was rich (A) but became poor (B), so that by his poverty (B), we might be rich (A) (II Cor. 8:9). Talbert's analysis, for all its detail, covers such an expanse of material that it seems forced and falls under its own weight. For anyone wishing to pursue it further, Talbert has his pattern displayed and explained in *Reading Luke*, pp. 111–113. The other widely debated theory about Luke's structure in the travel narrative is by John Drury. Drury calls this block of material a Christian Deuteronomy, convinced that in the book of Deuteronomy one can find the source for Luke's arrangement. Deuteronomy contains some materials that are connected and some that seem quite random, and according to Drury there is a match with Luke's journey narrative. As Deuteronomy was a guide for a devout Jew, presented as a journey to the promised land with Jerusalem as its center, so Luke here offers a handbook on discipleship in the setting of a journey to Jerusalem (*Tradition and Design in Luke's Gospel*, pp. 138–140). There is no question that in Luke there are genuine echoes of Deuteronomy in language, sequences, and theology. This is not surprising, given Luke's fondness for the Greek Old Testament and his already demonstrated practice of telling stories of Jesus in the manner of Old Testament stories. However, it takes more than Deuteronomy alone to resource this section of Luke, and Drury's proposal is strained and pressed to make the match.

The inability of scholars to come up with the key to the inner logic of 9:51—19:28 is not, of course, fatal for the interpreter and for the church which reads it both for an understanding of Jesus and of its own life in following him. It may be that the pattern will emerge not in a study of a background such as Deuteronomy but in looking ahead to Acts. Or perhaps the real journey Luke has in mind is that of the reader who is being drawn by Luke's presentation of Jesus' journey to Jerusalem into a pilgrimage with Jesus in an unfolding and deepening way, not only to the passion but into the kingdom of God.

Luke 9:51–62
Jesus Establishes the Nature of the Journey

This brief section consists of two units (vv. 51–56 and 57–62), each having its own integrity, but they belong together because verses 51–56 set the tone for the encounter with Jesus in verses 57–62. The unswerving intensity, the destiny-oriented sense of Jesus' move toward Jerusalem, is essential for the reader to grasp the uncompromising demands that Jesus places on would-be followers. This is the same sequence we met earlier (9:18–27): first Jesus prophesies his own suffering and death and then calls his disciples to a life of daily cross bearing.

Passing Through Samaria (9:51–56)

Verse 51 is a statement by the narrator to the reader, and hence the reader knows what those in Jesus' audience did not know. And what do we know from verse 51? First, Jesus knows that his ministry moves swiftly to its close. Second, Jesus is to be "received up," an expression used later by Luke to refer to the ascension (Acts 1:2; also I Tim. 3:16). The ascension implies, of course, the whole drama of crucifixion and resurrection as well as ascension. Finally, verse 51 tells the reader that toward that end Jesus set his face toward Jerusalem. "Set his face" echoes the song of the suffering servant of Isa. 50:7: "Therefore I have set my face like a flint, and I know that I shall not be put to shame; he who vindicates me is near." The statement implies, and therefore leads the reader to anticipate, strong opposition.

The journey to Jerusalem begins with a rejection. Just as Jesus' baptism was followed by rejection in Nazareth, so now the transfiguration, an event parallel to the baptism, is followed by rejection in Samaria. Rejection by the Samaritans on one level testifies to the tension between Jews and Samaritans, but their inhospitality also means they are unwilling to follow one

142

on his way to suffering and death. But more significant is the fact that Jesus has sent two disciples into a Samaritan village to arrange for lodging and food. Jesus was planning to take his ministry among these outsiders, these despised half-Jewish heretics! He has ministered to Jews and Gentiles, to social, ritual, and political outcasts, and now here in Samaria, as far away as one could be and still be in the land. Later, Jesus would say to his disciples, "And you shall be my witnesses in Jerusalem and in all Judea and *Samaria* and to the end of the earth" (Acts 1:8). According to Acts 8:5–25, the Christian mission was successful in Samaria; this was perhaps due in part to the warrant for such a mission in the visit of Jesus to that area (cf. also John 4:1–42).

One can almost appreciate the anger of James and John over the refusal of hospitality to Jesus; they are being protective and do not know how to handle rejection. They bring to mind overzealous evangelists of another generation who extended God's grace to the audience and then tossed balls of hellfire at those who refused the offer. Jesus' disciples remember quite well scriptural precedent for calling down heaven's fire (II Kings 1:9–10), but they have forgotten the recent words of Jesus: when on a mission, accept the hospitality offered you. If none is extended, shake the dust off your feet and move on (9:1–6). Is it not interesting how the mind can grasp and hold those Scriptures which seem to bless our worst behavior and yet cannot retain past the sanctuary door those texts which summon to love, forgiveness, and mercy? Jesus rebukes James and John for an attitude of revenge and retribution, an attitude totally foreign to his ministry and theirs. Some scribes have added an explanatory note to verse 55 (cf. footnote, RSV). The sentiment of this addition is an appropriate one, but the best manuscripts do not contain it. The mission moves on toward Jerusalem.

Accenting the Cost of Discipleship (9:57–62)
(Matthew 8:19–22)

Had Jesus' words "Take up your cross daily" never been spelled out concretely, they could have remained an ethereal ideal having the effect of background organ music or they could have sunk to some meaningless act of self-inflicted pain such as walking to work during Lent with a tack in one's shoe. Here, however, his words are translated into specific circumstances. The threefold pattern, common to storytelling in that culture,

143

is "I will follow," "Follow me," and "I will follow." We do not know whether the three episodes once existed separately; Matt. 8:19–22 has the first two, and in a context prior to any talk of Jesus' passion. The effect, therefore, is quite different in Matthew. Here in Luke, the context provides the commentary. The one who has set his face like a firm stone to go to Jerusalem has no bargains to offer. "I am totally dependent on the hospitality of others; are you willing to be?" he says to the first volunteer. "Loyalty to me takes precedence over a primary filial obligation" he says to the second prospective disciple. "I expect more from you than Elijah asked of Elisha (I Kings 19:19–21)" is his word to the third, also a volunteer. For the preacher of the text to look for loopholes by impugning the motives of the three or by assuming that the father of the second man is not yet dead and may live for years is to trivialize the passage. The radicality of Jesus' words lies in his claim to priority over the best, not the worst, of human relationships. Jesus never said to choose him over the devil but to choose him over the family. And the remarkable thing is that those who have done so have been freed from possession and worship of family and have found the distance necessary to love them.

Luke 10:1–24
The Mission of the Seventy

This report is peculiar to Luke. Both Matthew (Matt. 9:35—10:16) and Mark (Mark 6:7–11) record the sending out of the Twelve, and some of the instructions parallel Luke 10, but there are striking differences. This unit consists of five subunits: instruction of the Seventy, woes upon those who reject the messengers, the return of the Seventy, a prayer of thanks, and a blessing.

The Instruction of the Seventy (10:1–12)

Although Moses' choice of seventy elders to be his helpers (Num. 11:16–25) may be in Luke's mind, more likely the stronger influence is the report of seventy nations in Genesis 10 (seventy in the Hebrew text, seventy-two in the Greek). After all, Luke is anticipating the mission to the nations begun at

Pentecost after Easter when persons gathered "from every nation under heaven" (Acts 2:5). In fact, Gentiles may already be in mind in the instruction, "Eat what is set before you" (v. 8). Food was a critical issue in the spread of the gospel (Acts 11:1–18; Gal. 2:11–21). The practice of sending messengers in teams of two into places where Jesus was to come began when Jesus first turned toward Jerusalem (9:51–52), continues here, and will appear again at Jesus' entry into Jerusalem (19:28–34). Running ahead to announce Christ's coming not only implies preparation but gives to the mission a magisterial or regal tone. But just as strong or even stronger is the eschatological flavor of the passage. Note the analogy of harvest time (end time), the instruction to travel light, and the command to take no time for social amenities (v. 4 may echo II Kings 4:29). Working under the shadow of the eschaton is certainly in keeping with the mood of intense single-mindedness set in 9:51–62.

The missionaries were to depend entirely on the hospitality of their hosts, very likely a practice common among early Christian groups, including missions of Paul and his associates. There was to be no shopping about for the best room and board (v. 7), nor were the missionaries to pronounce doom on those who refused hospitality. Jesus had been rejected in a Samaritan village, but no fire was called down; Jesus moved on to other villages (9:52–56). Rituals of departure were to be brief, leaving such persons to be judged by what they had missed—that is, the kingdom of God had been near (vv. 10–11). There will be a judgment, but that is a word Jesus will speak. Notice that verse 12 is Jesus' word to the missionaries and is not a part of their message. Preachers are not authorized to judge. Notice also that the message to those who accept and to those who reject is the same: "The kingdom of God has come near" (vv. 9, 11). The preachers were not to wait to see how they would be treated before preparing their sermons. Relevance is, of course, important in preaching, but the basic message is not contingent on the response.

Woes on the Impenitent (10:13–16)
(Matthew 11:21–23; 10:40)

The pronouncement of woes on the three cities of Chorazin, Bethsaida, and Capernaum assumes that Jesus and/or his disciples had ministered in them (we have no record of Jesus being in Chorazin, north of Capernaum), that mighty works had

145

been done, and that there was a general failure to repent. We have no reason to question these assumptions, but there is a question about the location of these woes in a commissioning service. Matthew locates them elsewhere. In their location in Luke, the woes can be interpreted as Jesus' prophecy of rejection in those cities, a prophecy placed here because it fits the preceding verses 10–12, or as a Christian reflection, perhaps from the perspective of Acts, on the fate of the gospel in those places. Surprisingly, Galilee seems to have had rather small importance in the spread of the gospel after Pentecost, or at least Luke gives the area very little attention (Acts 9:31). At any rate, the thrust of the woes is quite clear: to whom much is given, of them much is required. These cities had enjoyed a privilege not shared by Gentiles and therefore their punishment would be greater. It is almost frightening to be favored of God. Verse 16 underscores the seriousness of accepting or rejecting the disciples: treatment of them is treatment of Jesus and is treatment of God.

The Return of the Seventy (10:17–20)

The return of the Seventy with reports of success prompts from Jesus a revelatory discourse that continues into the prayer of thanks in verses 21–22. In fact, Luke seems to contrast deliberately the rejoicing of the Seventy and the rejoicing of Jesus; they rejoice in their success, Jesus rejoices in the Holy Spirit (v. 21). Our text, then, seems to lie at the border between concealment (the disciples do not yet understand, but they will when it is revealed to them, 24:16, 31–32, 45) and revelation which Jesus experiences in the Holy Spirit. The report of the Seventy centers entirely on exorcisms even though there is no mention of casting out demons in their instructions (vv. 1–12). The focus, then, is on the evidence of Jesus gaining power over the forces of evil. In response to their report, Jesus shares his revelatory vision which is cast in apocalyptic terms familiar to us from Revelation. That Satan first dwelt in heaven is stated elsewhere (Job 1:6; 2:1; John 12:31; Rev. 12:7), and Luke's description of his fall is probably based on Isa. 14:12–15. Psalm 91:13 lies back of the promise that the righteous shall be immune to and will triumph over evil and antagonistic forces.

146   However, a central question is whether Jesus' vision is descriptive of what has happened in this successful mission or of what will happen when the disciples have their eyes opened

(24:31), receive the Holy Spirit which now resides in Jesus (Acts 1:5, 8), and move Jesus' mission into the whole world (Acts 1:8). No doubt, the successful mission of the Seventy prompts this reply of Jesus, but it is not a reply confined to their mission. Notice the mixing of tenses: "The demons *are* subject to us" (present); "I *saw* [literally, was seeing] Satan fall" (continuing past); and "Nothing *shall* hurt you" (future). That which has been and is taking place in Jesus' ministry and theirs will move to its completion in the future. As he so often does, Luke is undoubtedly here thinking of the mission of the church following the empowering of the Holy Spirit. There was exorcising of demons (Acts 8:7), the rooting out of Satan's work within the membership (Acts 5:3), the power of the Spirit over Simon the magician (Acts 8:18–24), the punishment of Herod Agrippa who laid violent hands on the church (Acts 12:20–24), the defeat of the false prophet Elymas by Paul (Acts 13:4–12), and even an immunity to the strike of a serpent (Acts 28:3–6). Jesus' vision does not, therefore, make too much or too little of the success of the Seventy but rather sets it into the larger frame of God's reign.

However, Jesus does warn the Seventy that triumphalism is an inappropriate spirit among disciples. Our chief joy should be, not that we have certain gifts and powers, but that God has received and accepted us, that our names are "written in heaven" (Dan. 12:1; Phil. 4:3; Rev. 3:5; 13:8; 20:15). This sobering reminder recalls Jesus' word reported in Matthew: "On that day many will say to me, 'Lord, Lord, did we not prophesy in your name, and cast out demons in your name, and do many mighty works in your name?' And then I will declare to them, 'I never knew you; depart from me, you evildoers'" (Matt. 7:22–23).

A Prayer of Thanks and a Blessing (10:21–24)
(Matthew 11:25–27; 13:16–17)

We will look at these two subunits together even though they probably existed separately in Luke's source (as in Matthew) and even though the prayer and the blessing have different audiences. Thanksgiving and blessing belong together in worship, and it could well be that we have here two pieces from an early Christian liturgy. Consider the movement of the entire unit (10:1–24): seventy messengers are instructed and sent out; they return with the joy of success; Jesus shares with them his

147

vision of the final victory now begun; Jesus cautions against triumphalism and self-congratulation; Jesus breaks into inspired speech in gratitude to God; and Jesus turns to his disciples with a blessing that reminds them of God's favor on them. If they were in position to hear Jesus' words in verses 13–15, then they should also understand the burden of that favor.

We learned in chapters 1—2 in the inspired songs of Zechariah, Mary, Simeon, and Anna that for Luke one of the primary manifestations of the presence of the Holy Spirit is in words. The Holy Spirit "says." Jesus is prompted by the Spirit to thank God for "these things" which have been revealed to babes (v. 21). In this context Luke probably means by "these things" the evidence of God's reign over evil spirits as reported by the Seventy, meaning that Jesus' journey to Jerusalem is wrapped in power, not resignation, and his being "received up" (9:51) will mean final enthronement, not defeat. To the extent that the disciples were beginning to grasp the meaning of what was really going on, they too were participating in revelation. The fuller revelation will come after the resurrection (24:31–32, 45). The "wise and understanding" do not grasp such things, because true spiritual discernment does not come by observation (Matt. 16:17) but by revelation of the Spirit (I Cor. 2:14–16; 12:3). This prayer, therefore, participates in the reversal we have already met frequently in Luke, here expressed as "concealed from the wise, revealed to babes."

The Christology of verse 22 is patterned on the ancient image of Sophia, or Wisdom, or its masculine form, Logos. Wisdom personified was an intermediary between God and the world, being God's agent for creating, sustaining, and bringing messages to the world (Job 28:12–28; Prov. 8:22–36; Ecclus. 24:1–24). Even a casual reader can see how early Christians saw in Jesus the embodiment of God's eternal Wisdom. Paul says it in I Cor. 1:20, 26–29, but the New Testament's principal subscriber to this perspective is John (John 1:18; 6:35–59; 7:25–30). Luke 10:22 (and Matt. 11:27) is so similar to a number of texts in John's Gospel that the German scholar K. A. von Hase has called the passage "a meteorite from the Johannine heaven." Whatever its source, Luke's use of it in this location provides, along with the benediction in verses 23–24, a beautiful doxological conclusion to a service of commissioning and receiving kingdom messengers.

148

Luke 10:25–42
Two Stories About Hearing and Not Hearing

Having blessed his disciples for seeing and hearing (vv. 23–24), Jesus now encounters two persons who do not at all get the point of what he is about or what the reign of God means. One is a lawyer, that is, an expert in the law of Moses, and the other is a woman named Martha. Their situations, the obstacles to their hearing, and Jesus' responses to them are quite different, but they are being considered together for what might be the same reason Luke placed them together: contrasting needs and remedies. One is to "go and do"; the other is to "sit down and listen." Jesus' word is not the same to everyone in every situation of need. That Jesus wrote prescriptions rather than offer patent medicine should caution teachers and preachers about hasty generalizations and uncritical transfers of Jesus' words to new situations.

Jesus and the Lawyer (10:25–37)
(Matthew 22:34–40; Mark 12:28–31)

Jesus has said the wise and prudent miss what babes understand. This story illustrates the truth of that word (v. 21). The parallels in Matthew and Mark are only partial. Both set the event in Jerusalem, in the closing days of Jesus' ministry, and in a series of controversies. In Luke, the question concerns eternal life and not the greatest commandment, and in Luke, Jesus has the lawyer answer his own question. Luke alone has the parable, or perhaps more precisely, the example story, of the helpful Samaritan. The Samaritan story is carefully woven into the conversation between Jesus and the lawyer so as to create symmetry in the telling. In the first part of the text (vv. 25–28), the lawyer asks a question and so does Jesus; the lawyer gives an answer and so does Jesus. In the second part (vv. 29–37), the lawyer asks a question and after the intervening story so does Jesus; the lawyer answers and so does Jesus. The questions and the answers are most impor-

149

tant. The lawyer knew the answers to his own questions, and in both cases Jesus expressed full agreement.

Then what is wrong with this conversation? We have two good questions, two good answers, and two men who agree. What else could one ask? All kinds of things are wrong. Asking questions for the purpose of gaining an advantage over another is not a kingdom exercise. Neither is asking questions with no intention of implementing the answers. The goal of witnessing or of theological conversation is not to outwit another, and the preacher will want to avoid handling this text so as to show how clever Jesus was. Having right answers does not mean one knows God. Students can make a four-point in Bible and miss the point. Jesus did not say to the lawyer, "Great answer! You are my best pupil." Rather, Jesus said, "Go and do."

It is now generally understood that the joining of the commands to love God (Deut. 6:5) and to love neighbor (Lev. 19:18) had already occurred prior to Jesus, and the lawyer rather than Jesus giving the answer (contra Matthew and Mark) supports that view. It is the matter of love of neighbor, however, which is the single focus of the remainder of the text. This is not reductionistic: twice Paul wrote that the whole of the law is summed up in love of neighbor (Rom. 13:8–9; Gal. 5:14). Jesus did not, however, regard the lawyer's framing of the question about love of neighbor as the proper one. To ask, Who is my neighbor? could imply selectivity, that some are neighbors and some are not, and therefore, Who are the ones I am to love? After the story, Jesus rephrases the question: Who proved to be a neighbor? This shift does not necessarily mean that Jesus altered the function of a parable that originally was told for a different purpose.

Quite possibly the parable did come from Luke's sources and may have been a story Jesus heard in his culture. It certainly assumes that listeners know about priests, Levites (temple assistants), Samaritans, and the bitter tension between Jews and Samaritans (John 4:9). Samaritans were descendants of a mixed population occupying the land following the conquest by Assyria in 722 B.C.E. They opposed rebuilding the temple and Jerusalem (Ezra 4:2–5; Neh. 2:19) and constructed their own place of worship on Mount Gerizim. Ceremonially unclean, socially outcast, and religiously a heretic, the Samaritan is the very opposite of the lawyer as well as the priest and the Levite. The story must have been a shocking one to its first audience, shattering their categories of who are and who are not the people of God. In its present usage in Luke, the story offers an example of acting in love which is without preference or partiality and which expects nothing in return.

A word to the preacher. The story of the helpful Samaritan is certainly extractable (vv. 30–35) and portable to other settings. It may be used as a parable if the situation and the audience would justify employing the kind of dynamic which parables generate (review the discussion of the parable at 8:4–8). Some settings diseased by social, religious, economic, or racial barriers could properly justify such a use of the story, perhaps jarring the listeners into a new perspective on love of neighbor. In other situations, this story can well function as Luke employs it, to give an example of what is really involved in being a neighbor. In either case, two suggestions might be in order. First, painting unnecessarily unattractive portraits of the priest and the Levite greatly weakens the story. The force of the parable depends very much on its realism and its ability to invite people to identify with characters within it. If the priest and the Levite are presented as ethically dead and totally void of human caring, then no listener will say, "I too behave that way." While their behavior was certainly not commendable, neither was it without reason. The body on the roadside could have been a plant by robbers to trap a traveler. And certainly contact with a corpse would have defiled the priest and the Levite and disqualified them from their temple responsibilities. When they saw the victim, theirs was a choice between duty and duty. So understood, many listeners will recall similar situations. Second, great care should be given to the search in our culture for analogies to the Samaritan. Often poor analogies trivialize a text. Remember that this man who delayed his own journey, expended great energy, risked danger to himself, spent two days' wages with the assurance of more, and promised to follow up on his activity was ceremonially unclean, socially an outcast, and religiously a heretic. That is a profile not easily matched.

Jesus, Martha, and Mary (10:38–42)

Jesus has just met a man skilled in Scripture who has trouble hearing the word of God, and Jesus offers him an example, a Samaritan. Now Jesus visits with a woman so busy serving she does not hear the word, and Jesus offers her an example, her

151

sister. To the man, Jesus said to go and do; to the woman, Jesus said to sit down, listen, and learn.

Only Luke relates this episode, but John joins him in knowing Martha and Mary. John knows them as sisters of Lazarus and locates their home in Bethany near Jerusalem (John 11:1; 12:1–3). In both stories that John tells, the behavior of the two corresponds to Luke's description: Martha goes out to meet Jesus, while Mary sits in the house (John 11:20), and at dinner Martha serves and Mary anoints the feet of Jesus (John 12:1–3). In Luke, it is Martha's house, she receives Jesus into the home, and the story centers on her and Jesus. Her sister Mary is described, but she never speaks or otherwise enters the action. The radicality of the story should not be missed: Jesus is received into a woman's home (no mention is made of a brother) and he teaches a woman. Rabbis did not allow women to "sit at their feet," that is, to be disciples. However, this story accords well with 8:1–3; Luke has no problem with women being numbered among the disciples.

Martha has extended hospitality and is in line for the blessings that go to those who receive Jesus or his disciples (9:48). Her complaint is reasonable, but Jesus' response to her anxiety is not fully clear. Manuscripts differ on verse 42: Some read, "One thing is needful"; others read, "Few things are needful, or only one." Is Jesus saying that Martha is preparing too many dishes; only a few, in fact, only one is needed? The specific words are cloudy, but the symbolism seems clear enough. The word of God and not food is the one thing needful, for we do not live by bread alone but by every word that comes from the mouth of the Lord (Deut. 8:3; Luke 4:4; John 6:27). This is the portion or dish Mary has chosen. But we must not cartoon the scene: Martha to her eyeballs in soapsuds, Mary pensively on a stool in the den, and Jesus giving scriptural warrant for letting dishes pile high in the sink. If we censure Martha too harshly, she may abandon serving altogether, and if we commend Mary too profusely, she may sit there forever. There is a time to go and do; there is a time to listen and reflect. Knowing which and when is a matter of spiritual discernment. If we were to ask Jesus which example applies to us, the Samaritan or Mary, his answer would probably be Yes.

Luke 11:1–13
Teachings on Prayer

There is no reason for the reader to assume that Jesus said all these things on one occasion. To assemble materials into compatible sections on miracles, controversies, parables, prayer, and other themes or forms is common in the Gospels. That these sayings originally had different settings is supported by the fact that Matthew parallels Luke 11:2–4 at Matt. 6:9–13 and Luke 11:9–13 at Matt. 7:7–11. Luke's parable of the friend at midnight (vv. 5–8) is found nowhere else. To the whole, Luke provides an introduction in two parts: the example of Jesus and a disciple's request (v. 1). Jesus at prayer is a frequent and very important image in this Gospel: at baptism (3:21), before choosing the Twelve (6:12), before the first prophecy of his passion (9:18), and at his transfiguration (9:28), among other occasions. Jesus' prayer life has now prompted a request from a disciple. Perhaps John had given to his disciples a form of prayer that was an identifying mark of the group. We know his disciples fasted and prayed (5:33). It was not unusual for rabbis to teach specific prayers. Notice that the text treats prayer as a learned experience, not simply as a release of feelings. Discipline is clearly implied.

The clear breaks in the passage yield three distinct units: verses 2–4, 5–8, and 9–13. Luke's form of the Lord's Prayer (vv. 2–4) is briefer than the more familiar and liturgically extended version in Matt. 6:9–13. It consists of two brief petitions of praise and three petitions for those praying. The prayer is that of a community (us, we), not of a private individual, and the community's primary desire is for the coming of God's kingdom, God's reign. It is therefore an eschatological prayer, a quality underlined by the short phrases such as "Thy kingdom come." Verse 3 contains an obscure word that may mean bread "for today" or "for tomorrow." If it is properly "bread for tomorrow," then the petition probably refers to bread from heaven at the final coming of the kingdom. However, the present tense of "give us," meaning "continue or keep on giving to us," coupled with the phrase "day by day" argue in favor of a petition for provi-

153

sion of daily food. After all, disciples go on missionary tours with no extra rations (10:4–7) and depend on the hospitality of others. That the petitioner asks God to forgive *sins* as we forgive everyone their *debts* to us may possibly reflect Luke's concern that possessions not hinder community fellowship (6:30; Acts 4:32; 5:1–11). The final petition is probably eschatological: do not lead us into trial, that is, the final thrashing about and agony of evil before the end.

The parable of the friend at midnight (vv. 5–7; v. 8 is commentary) is awkward and difficult for several reasons. It is one long question with many clauses joined with conjunctions in Semitic fashion. In addition, the opening "Which of you?" asks the reader to identify with someone going at midnight to ask a friend for bread, but the attention shifts totally to the friend in bed who finally gets up. And finally, parables beginning with the question, "Which one of you?" as a general rule have as the expected answer, "No one." Because of these unusual features, one suspects that this parable, maybe in a more extended form, once had a context dealing with the end time, as does Matthew's parable of the bridegroom coming at midnight (Matt. 25:1–13). In its present setting, however, the message is about prayer. But that message does not lie in comparing God to a friend who responds only under pressure. Rather, the point is that if our friends answer importunate (shameless, NEB) appeals, how much more will God who desires to give us the kingdom (12:32).

The concluding unit (vv. 9–13) extends further the reasoning from lesser to greater, or "how much more" will God respond to you. The analogy moves from friends to parents: if parents give good gifts, how much more so will God. Luke has egg and scorpion instead of Matthew's loaf and stone (Matt. 7:9) but with no difference in meaning. Prayer is to be continual asking, seeking, knocking (present imperatives), but even so, this persistence is within a parent-child relationship which assures good gifts. In Luke, it is the Holy Spirit (Matthew has "good things") which is the gift of God. The gift of the Holy Spirit is central in Luke for understanding both Jesus (3:21) and the church (24:49; Acts 1:4, 5, 8; 2:38). The Holy Spirit leads and empowers Jesus, and when the Holy Spirit comes to Jesus' followers (Acts 1:8) they will be led and empowered to continue what Jesus began to do and to teach before he was received up. Without the Holy Spirit there was not, there is not, a church.

154

Luke 11:14—12:1
Conflicts and Controversies

Obviously a common feature of Luke's style as a narrator is to put sharply contrasting materials back to back. The story of Jesus being anointed by a sinful woman is followed immediately with the record of women participating in Jesus' ministry (7:38—8:3); Jesus' lesson to a lawyer about being a good neighbor is followed by the contrasting lesson to Martha (10:25–42). Now Luke turns from the promised gift of the Holy Spirit (v. 13) to this section launched by the exorcism of a mute spirit. Luke brings together materials some of which are variously located in Matthew and Mark. The reader finds this section a bit difficult to follow because the thematic center is not evident. The mood is almost totally that of conflict and controversy, but there are a few positive moments, although quite brief. Upon closer examination, however, the substance of the whole is revealed at the outset in verses 14–16. Jesus performs an exorcism and three responses follow: the crowd marvels, some critics question the source of Jesus' power, and others call for a sign as proof. Although they are not in this order, Jesus will respond to all three attitudes toward his work, his answers being woven into the pattern of the narrative. And the whole of the encounter will serve as ground for a rather lengthy exposé of the hypocrisy and errors of Jesus' critics. We will try to be fair to the entire content by considering it in three units: verses 14–28, 29–36, and 37—12:1.

Concerning Jesus' Power to Exorcise Demons (11:14–28)
(Matthew 12:22–30; Mark 3:22–27)

In verse 14 Luke does not give us a full description of an exorcism but rather a summary report, as though to say, "All that will follow below was triggered by the exorcism of a mute spirit." After an equally summarized report of the responses—the crowd marveled, some sought a sign from heaven, others questioned his source of power—Luke takes up the responses, beginning with the charge that Jesus worked by the power of Satan. To understand the encounter, it is not enough to charge

155

Jesus' critics with that irrational anger which rises when one's opponent does something, even if it is a good and helpful act. No one denies that the man has been freed from the mute demon; the evidence is clear. The question is, by what power did Jesus do it? Even though it may appear strange to us, the fact that good has been done (a man healed) does not, in the biblical world, automatically mean that God has acted. In fact, that the man was mute does not automatically mean an evil spirit was at work. Recall that Zechariah was mute but it was God's doing (1:20); this man is mute and it is due to a demon. There are powers and there are powers. The magicians in Egypt matched Moses miracle for miracle for several rounds. Luke is very aware of the presence of magicians, and Christians who worked in the power of the Holy Spirit often encountered them. For example, in Samaria was a man who so amazed the people that they said of him, "This man is that power of God which is called Great" (Acts 8:9–13). Were the missionaries also magicians? Was Jesus a magician? As irreverent as such questions may seem to us, to those present the answers were not obvious. Modern minds ponder such unusual events and ask, Did it really happen? Luke's audience pondered such unusual events and asked, Who did it?

The charge against Jesus is that he is using the power of Beelzebul ("Baal the prince"; the Greek text does not say Beelzebub, "Lord of the flies," II Kings 1:2). Jesus answers the charge in three ways: with logic (Satan would not work against himself); with a comparison (By what power do exorcists among you work?); and with a challenge (If I work by the finger of God, Ex. 8:19, then the kingdom has come). The fact is, says Jesus, Satan is strong, but now he is being overthrown by a stronger power (vv. 21–22; recall 10:17–18). Jesus is saying that his work and that of his disciples is the beginning of the end for the forces of evil. There have been and will be continuing clashes; good news for the people always has strongly entrenched opponents, but Jesus and his followers are encouraged by his vision: "I saw Satan fall like lightning from heaven" (10:18). However, Jesus offers no other "proofs." His hearers have seen and heard; now they must choose. The Holy Spirit and spirits that hurt, maim, and alienate do not walk together; the one "who is not with me is against me" (v. 23). Discipleship calls for decision, to be sure, but this encounter reminds us that it also calls for discerning the spirits to see whether they are of God.

In fact, one should not set too high a premium on ousting evil spirits, says Jesus (vv. 24–26; Matt. 12:43–45). Unless the removal of the evil is followed by filling the life with good, even more evil will return and the last condition is worse than the first. An empty life, like an empty house, invites intruders. Even small boys, intending no wrong to anyone, can hardly resist a rock through the window of a house without occupants. The gravest danger to those who remove but do not replenish is a false sense of security, or maybe even an arrogance. Paul charged a group in the church at Colossae with false piety and self-worship in the slogan, "Do not handle, Do not taste, Do not touch" (Col. 2:21). Such persons are almost welcoming back the exorcised demon who will return with seven friends uglier than he.

Luke stated at verse 14 that some response to Jesus was favorable. The outburst by a woman in the crowd registers that favor (vv. 27–28). It may be that this blessing of Jesus' mother was placed here by Luke under the influence of Mark who locates the coming of Jesus' mother and brothers after the Beelzebul controversy (Mark 3:20–35). The response of Jesus is the same as given in Luke's earlier account of the arrival of Jesus' mother and brothers (8:19–21): For Mary and for all, hearing and doing bring blessedness.

Concerning the Search for Signs (11:29–36)
(Matthew 12:38–42; 5:15; 6:22–23; Mark 8:11–12)

At the beginning of this section (v. 16) Luke stated as one response to Jesus the demand for a sign from heaven. Jesus now answers that demand even though it is a general answer not necessarily related to the exorcism and apparently addressed to a large crowd. In the setting of the exorcism the demand was for a sign from heaven, that is, not simply proof of Jesus' power but evidence that it was from God, not from Satan. Even here we should not think solely in terms of proof as convincing evidence of a miracle. That is involved, to be sure; and then, as now, the search for such proof was never finally convincing. Faith is more than response to evidence, and to the one who will not trust, final proof is never quite enough. However, the question broader than proof of this or that event is the desire to be persuaded that God is involved, that this is God's doing, that what Jesus is doing is what God wills and does in the world and in the lives of people.

157

INTERPRETATION

How could such a desire be satisfied, and even if it were, would not such a sign from heaven be coercing and therefore destroy the possibility of faith which can come only from free decision? Jesus says the search for signs is therefore the quest of persons who are "evil," that is, disobedient and rebellious. For this reason, miracles seldom generate faith; rather, they spawn curiosity, argument, and an increased appetite for signs. Luke does not, like Matthew, confine this response to scribes and Pharisees. Although Mark says no sign will be given (Mark 8:12), Luke and Matthew agree that the only sign is the sign of Jonah. However, for Matthew, Jonah's three days and nights in the whale was a sign of Jesus' death and resurrection (Matt. 12:40), but for Luke, Jonah's preaching was the sign. The Ninevites received Jonah with repentance; the queen of the South received wisdom from Solomon. Therefore the people of Nineveh and the queen of the South will judge Jesus' audience, for they do not receive a prophet greater than Jonah, a man wiser than Solomon. The book of Acts will unfold the story of an increasing embrace of the gospel by Gentiles as Israel becomes less hospitable.

The unit concludes by Luke's joining three separate and elsewhere unrelated (cf. Matthew) sayings (vv. 33, 34–35, 36) under the general image of "light." Apparently what is being said is that Jesus' message is clear enough and able to give God's light to persons of integrity and openness (of a sound eye). But those who will not see cannot see.

Jesus Counters His Critics (11:37—12:1)
(Matthew 23:1–36)

Matthew places much of this material, and in a different order, at the close of Jesus' ministry during the intense debates and interrogations in Jerusalem. By placing it earlier, Luke pulls these confrontations back from the edge of death, even though verses 53–54 bring the fate of Jesus back into the mind of the reader. In addition, Luke places these clashes in the home of a Pharisee where Jesus is a dinner guest (v. 37). This does not so much soften the conflict as it reminds us that Jesus and Pharisees had much in common. They worshiped together every Sabbath at the synagogue; Jesus often was a dinner guest with Pharisees (7:36; 14:1); and it was Pharisees who warned Jesus about Herod's desire to kill him (13:31). In other words, Jesus is not an outsider firing broadside at institutionalized religion.

Rather, he is sharply critical of religion that has become self-perpetuating, that has hardened principles given for life into regulations that suffocate and condemn, that has quantified piety and lost its heart, that has, in sum, lost its capacity for self-criticism. Without continual self-evaluation and correction, all structures of religion decay into idolatry. And there is no reason to suppose that Luke preserves this material purely out of historical interest or out of some perverted pride in dancing over the grave of an opponent. Were not the church of Luke's time already falling victim to these ancient errors, there would have been little reason to report Jesus' mealtime conversation with Pharisees and lawyers.

The woes against these Pharisees center on three issues: giving meticulous care to legal details and neglecting God's justice and love; coveting attention and pride of place; and being hidden contaminators of the nation's life, like buried graves. The three woes against the lawyers have to do with burdening others while claiming personal exemption; honoring dead prophets while consenting to and participating in the very causes of their deaths; and confusing the people by the gross incongruities between their lives and their teachings. By the inclusion of apostles in verse 49, Luke is evidently thinking about the church and not solely about Jesus and his audience. The expression "Wisdom of God" in verse 49, although seeming to be a reference to some written document, undoubtedly refers to Jesus himself. Matthew 23:34 makes this identification directly (cf. I Cor. 1:24; also see the discussion at 10:21–22). Verse 50, "It shall be required of this generation," may be a prophecy of the fall of the nation and of Jerusalem (21:20–24).

Luke concludes the section with two comments. The one is a summary statement to the effect that the scribes and the Pharisees who felt convicted by Jesus' words continued to press him, to provoke him to say something self-incriminating, and to set for him verbal ambushes. But in this report there is no surprise; Jesus is on his way to Jerusalem. The other comment is a warning of Jesus to his disciples concerning the harmful influence of hypocritical Pharisees. Increasing crowds (12:1) can turn the head and rob one of the powers of discernment.

Luke 12:2—13:9
Exhortations and Warnings

Luke gathers these teachings in his favorite context: his disciples surrounded by a large crowd (literally, ten thousand in the Greek). This double audience was present for Luke's Sermon on the Plain (6:17–49) and Matthew's Sermon on the Mount (chs. 5—7). These words are for disciples, but they are not secret words, nor is the circle of discipleship closed. All can listen in, learn what it means to be a disciple, and take a place at the feet of Jesus if they so desire. As with the Sermon on the Plain, we can anticipate here a collection of teachings on a range of subjects. If the reader is to expect a difference between these words of Jesus and those in the sermon of chapter 6, it will most likely be in the greater urgency in words spoken on the way to Jerusalem.

A Call for Open Confession (12:2–12)
(Matthew 10:26–33; 12:32; 10:19;
cf. also Mark 4:22; 8:38; 3:28–29)

Luke has drawn together and arranged sayings found in a variety of settings in Matthew and in Mark. Apparently these teachings were prompted by the final word in 12:1, hypocrisy. We tend to think that hypocrisy (acting, as onstage; wearing a mask) is one type: pretending to be a believer when one is not, pretending to be a disciple when the heart and the mind are set on other values. However, under certain circumstances the reverse form of hypocrisy might be the problem: pretending not to be a disciple when in reality one has made a commitment to follow Jesus. When and why would a disciple pretend not to be? Under strong pressure, under persecution, when put in a fear-producing situation. Simon Peter pretended not to be a disciple at the trial of Jesus and denied him three times (22:54–62). So here in verses 2–12 Jesus talks of that hypocrisy which does not pretend to be but pretends not to be. It is apparent from verses 11–12 that all these sayings pertain to behavior under the fire of persecution and therefore are worded to fit the circumstances of the church as much as that of Jesus' followers

160

during his lifetime. In fact, these words are more fitted to the church after Jesus' resurrection than to the immediate disciples, because these sayings both imply and openly state the gift of the Holy Spirit to them. In Luke's understanding, the Holy Spirit was promised by Jesus and granted after his ascension (24:49; Acts 1:4–5, 8; 2:1–4, 38). Luke will elaborate further on confession and witnessing under persecution in the apocalyptic speech of Jesus in chapter 21.

This unit, then, participates in both present and future and contains both warning and promise. In the eschaton all secrets and mysteries will be revealed (a verb form of "apocalypse"). However, since the eschatological age has already begun and the reign of God ushered in by Jesus, all who follow Jesus must themselves be open rather than secretive about their confession of faith and the word of witness. There will be occasions of threat and trial, to be sure, but disciples are not to be intimidated into silence. Those who have power to kill the body do not compare to the one who holds their eternal destiny. The word "hell" (v. 5) translates Gehenna, the name of a valley near Jerusalem with repulsive associations. In ancient times children were sacrificed here to the god Molech (Jer. 7:31–32), which may have prompted the conversion of the place into a desolate trash and garbage heap (II Kings 23:10). It therefore easily qualified as a symbol for God's punishment (Mark 9:43–48; Rev. 14:7–13; cf. the article on Gehenna in *Harper's Bible Dictionary*). It is God, not man, who is to be feared finally. But on the positive side, the opposite of fear is trust. The God who knows even the number of hairs on your head, and who is mindful even of the sparrow, can be trusted to care for Jesus' own disciples. In the court of heaven (Job 1:6; Isa. 40:1; Zech. 3), final acknowledgment or denial will already have been determined on earth.

In verse 10 is Luke's version of the sin that will not be forgiven (Matt. 12:32; Mark 3:29). For both Matthew and Mark, this sin against the Holy Spirit is in the context of the controversy in which Jesus is charged with working by the spirit of Satan. Apparently the meaning there is that attributing the work of the Holy Spirit to Satan, charging the Spirit of God with association with evil, calling a blessing a curse, was blasphemy against the Holy Spirit. Some early Christians, as reported in the *Didache, the Teaching of the Twelve Apostles,* believed that blasphemy against the Holy Spirit was rejecting the inspired

161

speech of a Christian prophet. One can understand therefore why the churches took great care in distinguishing between true prophets and false prophets. Here, however, Luke places the saying in the context of faithful witnessing under persecution. Since words and acts against Jesus were done in ignorance (23:34; Acts 3:17; 17:30) because it was not understood that in Jesus God was visiting the people (19:41–44), those words and deeds will be forgiven. However, when the Holy Spirit is given to the church and that Holy Spirit provides what to say and the power to say it (vv. 11–12; 24:49; Acts 1:8), any ridiculing or denouncing or profaning that Spirit will be fatal for the church. The Spirit of God is the hallmark of the church; by God's Spirit the church lives, worships, and witnesses. If, therefore, the church capitulates to pressure and persecution to the point of blaspheming its own life-giving Spirit, no alternative for life is available.

Concerning Possessions (12:13–34)
(Matthew 6:25–33; 6:19–21)

It is no giant step to move from the fear and intimidation which produce silence and denial to the larger arena of anxiety and fear which produce greed and a grasping after things as a means of securing one's future. Whether Luke consciously made such a transition is, of course, uncertain, but in a broad collection of teachings the reader looks for connections and governing themes. Verses 13–34 have an inner unity around the subject of material goods, with three subjects being treated: covetousness (vv. 13–21), anxiety (vv. 22–32), and a call to simplicity of life (vv. 33–34).

Only Luke among the canonical Gospels gives the report of quarreling brothers and the response of Jesus with both direct instruction and the parable of the rich fool. There is, however, a noncanonical Gospel, the *Gospel of Thomas,* which has the conversation of Luke's verses 13–14, though without context or elaboration (Saying 72), and separately the parable of the rich fool, though in simpler form (Saying 63). The subject of coveting arises in Luke because of an interrupting request by someone in the crowd. Apparently this person had detected in Jesus a fairness of spirit that would qualify him to settle a dispute over an inheritance. There were regulations for such cases (Num. 27:1–11; Deut. 21:15–17), but at least in the opinion of the one who is obviously the younger brother, those laws were not being followed. The ugly dispute is all too familiar: haggling over furniture, dishes, silverware, house, land, and savings account left by the deceased. Jesus is asked to be a referee and he refuses; after all, who can judge whose greed is right? Rather than act as judge, Jesus states a proverbial truth (v. 15*b*) and elaborates with a parable (vv. 16–20), verse 21 being a commentary on the parable. The parable is not inextricably joined to the context and therefore, like most parables, is portable to other contexts. However, verses 13–15 do influence the way the parable is heard (For a discussion of a parable as such, see the commentary at 8:4–8.)

The parable calls covetousness folly. It could also have said it was a violation of the law of Moses (Ex. 20:17) and of the teachings of the prophets (Micah 2:2). Even so, it seems to have been a widespread problem in the church (Rom. 1:29; Mark 7:22; Col. 3:5; Eph. 5:5; I Tim. 6:10). This craving to hoard not only puts goods in the place of God (in Pauline theology, covetousness is idolatry, Rom. 1:25; Col. 3:5) but is an act of total disregard for the needs of others. The preacher will want to be careful not to caricature the farmer and thus rob the story of the power of its realism. There is nothing here of graft or theft; there is no mistreatment of workers or any criminal act. Sun, soil, and rain join to make him wealthy. He is careful and conservative. If he is not unjust, then what is he? He is a fool, says the parable. He lives completely for himself, he talks to himself, he plans for himself, he congratulates himself. His sudden death proves him to have lived as a fool. "For what does it profit a man if he gains the whole world and loses or forfeits himself?" (9:25).

We have known since Mary sang of the reversal of fortunes of the full and the empty (1:53) that Luke would again and again raise the seductive and difficult subject of possessions. He will hold up as the standard for disciples the voluntary sharing of one's goods. This, says Luke, was the message of John the Baptist (3:10–14) and of Jesus (6:30; 16:19–31) and was the practice of early Christians (Acts 4:34–37).

The second theme in this unit on possessions concerns anxiety (vv. 22–32). The injunction against anxiety is not a general one; in the New Testament anxiety sometimes refers to a form of care that is positively regarded, such as Paul's anxiety for the churches (II Cor. 11:28) and Timothy's anxiety for the welfare of the Philippians (Phil. 2:20). Here the issue is preoccupation with material things. Everyone, of course, protests that he or

163

she only wants enough, but no one knows how much is enough until one has too much. The fact is, says Jesus, that this anxiety reflects a lack of trust in God, a lack of interest in the kingdom, and a lack of generosity toward those in need. And such anxiety is not productive: it cannot add one whit (18 inches) to one's life (stature? cf. footnote, RSV). This expression may echo Ps. 39:5, a cubit meaning one more step to life's walk. Anxious grasping is the pursuit of all those who live in the darkness of not knowing that God is aware of them and their needs. Birds and flowers can be our teachers when it comes to depending on God. Those who put kingdom matters first will not only have their needs met but will have the kingdom as well. Seek God's kingdom, yes, but do not add the kingdom to the list of things about which to be anxious. That is counterproductive and an exercise in unbelief. Rather, seek the kingdom in the firm belief that it is God's desire to give it to you (v. 32).

The discussion of possessions closes on a positive note in verses 33–34. Turning from grave warnings about covetousness and anxiety, Jesus calls for a liberation from both in acts of generosity. Almsgiving was, along with prayer and fasting, the foundation of Jewish piety, and the Christian community continued this responsibility toward the needy, sometimes in acts of radical unselfishness (16:9; 18:22; 19:8; Acts 2:44–45; 4:32–37; 9:36; 11:27–30). In both Jewish and Gentile Christianity, concern for the poor was a priority (Gal. 2:10) and totally consistent with the value system in which disciples of Jesus lived. And it makes no sense really for those who traveled light on missionary tours (10:4) to be burdened with surpluses when at home. It is striking that churches timid and tentative on the subject of money have taught and preached the reverse of verse 34, making appeals for the listeners' hearts on the assumption that where the heart is, there the treasure will be. After reaping a harvest of hearts but very little support for the budget, some have come to acknowledge the realism of Jesus' words: where the possessions are, there the heart will be.

Concerning Preparedness and Fidelity (12:35–48)
(Matthew 24:43–51)

This unit consists of two parts: words addressed to all disciples (vv. 35–40) and words for Christian leaders (vv. 41–48). The reader here not only is mindful of the fact that Jesus is on his way to Jerusalem but is also anticipating the Lord's return. Both of these prospects give solemnity and urgency to the teachings.

The words addressed to all center around two images and two parables. The two images are girded loins (the loose outer garments gathered up at the waist to facilitate work or travel) and burning lamps. These images speak of being prepared and being awake. The first parable concerns a master returning from a marriage feast, a parable that recalls Matt. 25:1–13. This parable is a very positive one: servants are prepared and awake, even if the master does not return until the third watch (the Jewish night had three watches). The implication is that the master (the Lord) had not yet returned, even in Luke's day, but the preparedness and the watchfulness are not relaxed. After all, calculating the Lord's return is inadequate and inappropriate motivation for Christian behavior. Servants prepared and awake not only are blessed by the master (vv. 37, 38) but are treated to a most extraordinary reward: the master serves them at table. The second parable has to do with a householder and a thief (vv. 39–40). The night thief was a common motif for impressing on listeners the uncertainty of a disruptive event (I Thess. 5:2–11; II Peter 3:10; Rev. 3:3). Of course, the householder does not know when a thief will come; of course, the householder cannot stay awake all the time. However, one can be prepared, if not always awake. The Son of man will come, and will come unexpectedly. Not only will it be a surprise as to time but it will be disruptive, as would be the coming of a night thief (the description of its disruptive nature will appear at ch. 21). But readiness is possible, for it consists of continuing faithfulness at one's duties. When that is the case, uncertainties are no cause for alarm or anxiety.

The second part of this unit (vv. 41–48) is addressed to leaders, those who are "set over" the master's possessions and servants and who "know the master's will." The question of Simon Peter launches these teachings of Jesus, all carried by the image of a master, his servant in charge (church leaders), and the management of the household. Places of leadership offer unusual temptations to the abuse of others and misuses of power, and leadership positions in the church are not exempt. The New Testament is broadly aware of the problems (Acts 20:28–33; Rom. 16:17–18, II Cor. 11:19–20; I Tim. 4:12–16; I Peter 5:1–6; II Peter 2:1–2). The leader whose behavior is based

165

on faithfulness and not on calculations as to the Lord's return will be blessed. The unfaithful and arrogant in power will be punished according to the nature of their behavior, their knowledge of the Lord's will, and the level of power and privilege enjoyed. The Jewish law distinguished between intentional and nonintentional wrongs (Num. 15:27–31; Deut. 17:12). Apparently in these warnings degrees of punishment differ according to knowledge and power, ranging from being cut to pieces (v. 46) to a light beating. Accountability to God is in balance with levels of leadership and influence. The closing proverb (v. 48) is true in every arena of life together.

Concerning the Crisis Created by Jesus' Ministry (12:49–59) (Matthew 10:34–36; 16:2–3; 5:25–26; Mark 10:38)

As the scattered parallels in Matthew indicate, verses 49–53, 54–56, and 57–59 were probably to be found in different contexts originally, but they are joined here in two ways. First, the context of Jesus going to his passion in Jerusalem makes these urgent sayings appropriate to a single setting. Second, the critical presence of Jesus, causing the rise and fall of many (2:34), separating fear and faith and hence dividing many families, is the governing consideration in all three subunits. As the Gospel of John expressed it, Jesus is the crisis of the world (John 12:31). Crisis does not mean emergency but that moment or occasion of truth and decision about life. An adequate image is that of the gable of a house. Two raindrops strike the gable and that moment could conclude with their being oceans apart. To be placed in the situation of decision is critical, for to turn toward one person or goal or value means turning away from another. According to these sayings, God is so acting toward the world in Jesus of Nazareth that a crisis is created, that is to say, Jesus is "making a difference," even within families. Peace in the sense of status quo is now disrupted. Historically this has been proven true, and it will be finally true in the eschaton.

In verses 49–53 there are two governing images: baptism, a reference to the passion into which Jesus will soon be plunged (Mark 10:38), and fire, which symbolizes judgment, purification (Mal. 3:2–3), and the Spirit of God (3:16; Acts 2:1–4). Until his passion and the subsequent sending of the Spirit, Jesus is constrained and pushing against all restraints. Verses 54–56 are addressed to the crowds and not, as customarily in Matthew (Matt. 16:1–3), only to religious leaders. The people, says Jesus,

166

are quite clever in reading weather signs but are blind to the sign from God: the ministry of Jesus among them. In fact, the time of God is now and is so urgent with meaning and importance that common wisdom dictates that everyone attend immediately to his or her relation to God. Wise people settle accounts before they reach court and the jurisdiction of the magistrate; once the judge takes charge of the case, it is too late for any other recourse (vv. 57–59). In other words, give attention to your life before God now, because if delayed until the eschaton, all that remains is the sentencing. It is interesting that Matthew (Matt. 5:25–26) applies this same image of a case going to court to urge reconciliation now with an offended brother (or sister). The difference between Luke and Matthew may not be so great as it seems at first. Attending to one's relation to God and to a fellow member of the community are often experientially the same. Jesus has already joined love of God and love of neighbor so as never again to be unjoined (10:25–37).

The Call to Repentance (13:1–9)

This passage is not only characteristically Lukan but it has no parallel in the other Gospels. To say it is Lukan is to speak of its content and its context. The subject matter is repentance, a theme more frequent in Luke than in other New Testament writers. In fact, for Luke the gospel is the offer of repentance and forgiveness of sins (24:47). As to context, two observations are in order. First, Luke follows the immediately preceding image of judgment with this call to repentance, and he follows the call to repentance (vv. 1–5) with a parable of divine patience (vv. 6–9). This placing of contrasting ideas back to back is typically Lukan, the contrasting units forming the paradox of the Gospel. For example, in 12:57—13:9 the reader has to ponder this: God is the judge of our behavior and yet God offers to all of us opportunity for repentance; attending to one's relation to God is a matter of most urgent business now and yet God is patient with a fig tree that may yet bear fruit. Luke does not destroy severity by infusing grace, nor does he destroy grace by infusing severity. As a theologian he knows that any mixing of severity and grace or any attempt to average them will result in that which is neither severity nor grace. Not all preachers of Luke have learned that. The second observation about context 167 is that it is typically Lukan to provide at the beginning of a parable rather than at the end (though occasionally in both places) clues to its interpretation. In addition to the present text, examples can be found at 10:29; 12:15; 15:1–2; and 18:1, 9.

This passage has two distinct but related parts, verses 1–5 and 6–9. The first part recalls two tragic events to which we have no other historical access: a bloody vengeful act by Pontius Pilate against Galileans at worship in Jerusalem and the collapse of a tower near the pool of Siloam. Curious and concerned as we may be to know more of these two tragedies, enough is stated here to prompt the two statements of Jesus, each of which ends with the pronouncement, "But unless you repent you will all likewise perish" (vv. 3, 5). Surely it is not coincidental that the tragedies affected both Galileans and Jerusalemites and that the one is an act of human evil, the other what we term natural evil. Jesus is as inclusive in his comments as the problem is universal: Why did this tragedy happen to these people?

The question is as old as the human race, finding classic expression in Job, Psalm 37, and Psalm 73. According to John 9:2, disciples of Jesus asked him, "Rabbi, who sinned, this man or his parents, that he was born blind?" The question assumes a direct correlation between suffering and sin, a correlation that in some cases is unmistakably evident. However, is the connection of such a general nature that one can say the good are prosperous and healthy while the evil sink into poverty and illness? Some biblical writers say yes—for example, the composer of Psalm 1. Many have agreed. So influential has been this notion that many have looked upon their own lack of success or experiences of loss as divine punishment. In fact, some have argued against acts of charity toward such persons because such acts would interfere with God's punishment! On the other hand, Jesus announced God's favor on the poor, the maimed, the blind, the crippled. That in itself should have broken any insistence that one's financial, social, or physical condition is always a direct reflection of one's spiritual state. The common observation that sometimes the evil prosper and sometimes saints suffer should have shattered the ancient dogmas. In fact, that Jesus of Nazareth, Lord and Christ of God, suffered at the hands of lawless men should have buried forever the connection that argues that those who suffer are the worst sinners. But it has not. Perhaps no one has explored and exposed easy answers to the question "Why?" more poignantly than Thornton Wilder in his short novel *The Bridge of San Luis Rey*.

168

And so they come to Jesus and want to know if violence and suffering are random or according to divine law. Jesus rejects such attempts at calculation, not only because they are futile but also because they deflect attention from the primary issue: the obligation of every person to live in penitence and trust before God, and that penitent trust is not to be linked to life's sorrows or life's joys. Life in the kingdom is not an elevated game of gaining favors and avoiding losses. Without repentance, all is lost anyway.

Luke's parable of the barren fig tree may be a recasting of the story of the cursing of the fig tree (Matt. 21:18–19; Mark 11:12–14; or perhaps Matthew and Mark recast the parable). Luke's story leaves open the possibility of fruitfulness. The delay of God's judgment because of a prophet's intercession is not uncommon in the Old Testament, nor is God's restrained judgment in recognition of repentance (Jonah). According to II Peter 3:8–9, God has delayed the day of the Lord in order to give more people opportunity to repent and to avoid that final terror. This parable speaks in a similar vein: there is yet time. God's mercy is still in serious conversation with God's judgment.

Luke 13:10–35
Tensions and Forebodings of the Passion

The approaching passion in Jerusalem casts its shadow over this material. This brief section opens with a controversy in a synagogue, Luke's last reference to Jesus teaching in a synagogue. It closes with a reappearance of Herod Antipas, his perplexed curiosity about Jesus (9:7–9) having soured into thoughts of executing him. Midway in this section Luke says, "He went on his way through towns and villages, teaching, and journeying toward Jerusalem" (v. 22). As stated earlier, geographical references are either so irregular or so lacking altogether that attempts to reconstruct the journey should be abandoned. The journey is theological and pedagogical in its arrangement; the disciples are being prepared for Jerusalem and for events beyond Jerusalem. So is the reader; especially the reader.

Controversy Over a Sabbath Healing (13:10–17)

This story, appearing in Luke alone, recalls the similar incident at 6:6–11 and, even earlier, the tension in the synagogue

169

at Nazareth (4:16–30). It might be helpful to review comments on those two texts to refresh the memory about the synagogue, its leadership, and its services. To be in the synagogue on the Sabbath day, as was Jesus' custom (4:16), was to be at the heart of Judaism in its most prevalent and in many ways its strongest form. In Luke's own day, Jerusalem and the temple had been destroyed, but there were synagogues in every city (Acts 15:21). The stooped woman apparently had come to worship, although the synagogue ruler spoke to the crowd about coming on the Sabbath to be healed (v. 14). At any rate, the woman does not approach Jesus, makes no request of him, and nothing is said of her faith. Once healed, she praises God (v. 13). In this regard, the story is similar to healings reported in the Gospel of John in which Jesus takes the initiative and the healing becomes a witness to or a sign of a larger truth (John 5:1–18; ch. 9).

The synagogue ruler, indignant over a healing on the Sabbath, makes his appeal to the people: there are six other days in the week for healing, but not on the Sabbath. His words are an indirect attack on Jesus and a strong reprimand of the people as accessories because they came on the Sabbath for healing. Jesus does not disguise his response by the indirection of speaking to the people; rather, he speaks directly to the ruler, the plural "hypocrites" likewise indicting all of the ruler's colleagues in this conflict. The controversy plays on the words "bound" and "loose." Jesus loosed the woman from the infirmity in which Satan had bound her. If their law permitted the loosing of a bound (tethered) animal for watering on the Sabbath, should it not be permitted that this woman, not an animal but a freeborn daughter of Abraham, not tethered for a few hours but bound for eighteen years, be loosed from Satan's bond on the Sabbath? Jesus' argument, from the lesser to the greater, is incontrovertible. The house is divided: his adversaries are put to shame, all the people rejoice. Such is the effect of the presence of Jesus and of a sign of the in-breaking of God's reign over the forces of Satan. The event dramatizes 12:49–53: the peace of the way things have always been is shattered by the word and deed of Jesus. If helping a stooped woman creates a crisis, then crisis it has to be.

170 Parables of the Kingdom (13:18–21)
(Matthew 13:31–33; Mark 4:30–32)

Again we have in the case of these two parables an excellent example of interpretation by location, a method that preachers and teachers could well learn from Luke. Mark has the parable of the mustard seed, Matthew has both, but both Matthew and Mark place them in a collection of parables. As with any parables, residing in a collection has the positive effect of exhibiting the independent quality of this literary genre; that is, parables have their own integrity and tend to carry their meanings in themselves. A specific context is not essential for meaning, although context affects meaning. The negative effect of being placed in a list is that parables become more secretive, for without a context a parable tends to mean so many different things, there being no curb or guide for the reader, that the reader may be so occupied with discerning the secret that the word of God is not heard. Luke has placed these parables in the tension-filled journey to Jerusalem, immediately after a Sabbath healing and controversy and immediately before Jesus is asked, "Lord, will those who are saved be few?" (v. 23). Therefore, even though we cannot retrieve the context in Jesus' life in which these parables were told, we can ascertain what Luke says by his use of them.

The two parables draw upon two very common experiences: a man plants a mustard seed ("in his garden" seems very non-Palestinian and may reflect Luke's context) and a woman puts leaven in flour. Both men and women feel at home in the images. Both perform small acts that have expansive consequences. This, says Jesus, is the way the kingdom of God is. A woman bound by Satan has just been loosed; not a major, earth-shaking event, but in that single act is the beginning of the reign of God in the world and the beginning of the end of Satan's destructive power. Do not therefore be discouraged over what seems to be a lack of success. God is at work; just as seed and leaven carry their futures within them, so discern the act and do not be depressed by the opposition or by the immensity of the task. It is true that Jerusalem and death lie ahead, but God is at work. Think of the mustard seed and the leaven and be hopeful, for you have participated in small acts that will affect lives far beyond this time and place.

Strict Requirements for the Kingdom (13:22–30)

Luke senses that it is time again to remind the reader: "He went on his way through towns and villages, teaching, and journeying toward Jerusalem" (v. 22). The reminder hardly seems necessary; the words of Jesus in their gravity and urgency have implied as much. However, the comment, along with the

171

question of someone in the crowd, "Lord, will those who are saved be few?" (v. 23), provides Luke with the opportunity to gather up in summary fashion the demands for access to the kingdom. That Luke gathers these teachings is indicated by the fact that the parallels in Matthew are in six different locations. That this unit can be called a summary is evident in that what Jesus says here has already been said, even if in different images.

Someone among the listeners asking a question is a familiar method of launching materials in Luke (11:1; 12:13; 12:41; 13:1). The question is not that person's alone, unless that person has been following Jesus since 9:51. More realistically, it is the question of the reader who has felt the cumulative weight of Jesus' teachings since Jesus first turned toward Jerusalem. The composite answer to the question, "Lord, will those who are saved be few?" is clearly evident in the internal disjunctures and shifts. For example, verse 24 speaks of the narrow door, an image of the necessity of discipline in order to enter (Matt. 7:14 is the more familiar form of this saying). However, in the next verse, "door" conveys a very different message. Here it is a closed door, that eschatological moment when the time of opportunity is ended (vv. 25–27 echo Matt. 25:1–13). The next shift of thought is that of a large ingathering into the kingdom consisting of the faithful in Israel and of outsiders, that is, Gentiles. Finally, verse 30 is a floating saying found at the close of many collections of teachings (Mark 10:31; Matt. 19:30; 20:16).

Is it possible, then, to put verses 22–30 into focus without violating any individual saying? Perhaps the following will help. The question to Jesus is, Will only a few be saved? Jesus answers by saying that the invitation is open but the way into the kingdom is narrow and demands more than casual interest. And, in fact, the door of opportunity will not remain forever open. God's purpose moves toward the eschaton, and when the door is closed it is closed. The door will certainly not be reopened for persons whose only claim is that Jesus once visited their town or preached in their streets or that they once saw Jesus in a crowd or knew members of his family. These appeals are not only futile but also self-incriminating because their opportunities carried obligations. ("To whom much is given.") And added to the pain of sitting before a closed door will be the sight of large numbers who are admitted, not only the expected ones among Israel's ancient faithful but also the unexpected Gentiles who heard and believed. This summary provides Israel, Luke's

172

reader, and us opportunity to assess where we stand in relation to the reign of God.

A Warning About Herod and a Lament (13:31–35) (Matthew 23:37–39)

From a literary point of view, a warning and a lament are of quite different textures, but they are here joined by the word "Jerusalem" which closes the warning and opens the lament. Thematically the two are harmonious in that the death which Herod threatens is the death which Jerusalem will provide. Having noticed Luke's reasons for the location and arrangement of these two pieces of the tradition, we now separate them for further examination.

Verses 31–33 are found in Luke alone. The reappearance of Herod Antipas, tetrarch of Galilee, provides for Luke's narrative continuity, progression, and anticipation. Herod had beheaded John, and upon hearing about Jesus amid reports that he was John resurrected, Herod was perplexed and curious to the point of wanting to see Jesus (9:7–9). Now Herod wishes to cure his perplexity and be done with these disturbing prophets by killing Jesus also. The reader senses in the expression "Herod wants to kill you" that we have not heard the last of him, and we have not (23:6–12). However, a question arises that further holds the reader in anticipation: How can Herod be involved in Jesus' death if Jesus dies in Jerusalem which is outside Herod's jurisdiction? And there is no reason to suspect that here the Pharisees are party to some plan of entrapment. Some Pharisees differed strongly with Jesus on interpretations of the law, but some also seemed open to Jesus (7:36; 11:37; 14:1). Luke certainly gives no totally unfavorable portrait of them. A Pharisee was a moderating voice in the Jewish council when it was dealing with the early church (Acts 5:34), and some of the members of the church were Pharisees (Acts 15:5). In fact, according to Luke, Paul himself acknowledged near the close of his ministry, not "I *was* a Pharisee" but "I *am* a Pharisee" (Acts 23:6). Luke provides preachers and teachers with an opportunity to correct the very generalized and often uninformed prejudice against Pharisees which exists in some churches.

Jesus' response to Herod as "that fox" is unclear in its implication. In the Old Testament the fox is destructive; in Greek literature, clever. In any case, Jesus is neither intimidated nor deterred by the threat, because he works under the divine

173

imperative: "I must go on my way" (v. 33). The expression "The third day I finish my course" (v. 32) speaks directly of a brief limited time for completion of his ministry and indirectly of Jesus' death and resurrection which are, in God's purpose, the finish of his course (cf. John 5:36; 17:4; 19:28; Heb. 2:10). It is the will of God that these things take place in Jerusalem. For Luke, Jerusalem is central for both the Gospel and Acts. Luke refers to Jerusalem ninety times; the entire remainder of the New Testament, forty-nine. Very likely the mention of Jerusalem at verse 33 serves in part as the occasion for the lament over Jerusalem at verses 34–35.

However, literary reasons for Luke's location of the lament do not satisfy the chronological question it raises. "How often would I have gathered," "you would not," and "your house is forsaken" are expressions implying a ministry of Jesus in Jerusalem, but he has yet to go there. How is this to be understood? Matthew places the saying near the end of Jesus' ministry in Jerusalem (23:37–39), a natural place for it. Hence, when in Matthew Jesus says, "You will not see me," there is the additional "again," referring to the final coming of the Son of man. In Luke, however, Jesus is on his way to the city and so there is no "You will not see me *again*" but "You will not see me *until.*" The reference is clearly to his approaching entry into the city when the people shout, "Blessed is the King who comes in the name of the Lord!" (19:38), almost the exact words of 13:35. Such is the apparent incongruity in Luke: the lament assumes that Jesus has ministered and been rejected in Jerusalem, and it also assumes that he will soon be entering the city. The interpreter has several avenues available. One can simply say that from Luke's standpoint the ministry and the rejection in Jerusalem are accomplished facts and can be so described in advance, just as Luke treats Jesus' death and resurrection as accomplished facts prior to their occurrence. Or, Jesus is here prophesying with a certainty which is reflected in the use of past tense verbs. Another possibility is that Jesus had an earlier Jerusalem ministry about which Luke does not write but which he here implies. In the Fourth Gospel most of Jesus' ministry is in Jerusalem and its environs. A fourth interpretation is that Jesus is not referring to himself but to God in the lament which was originally God's lament over the city. In II Esdras 1:28–30 God says to Israel, I was to you as a father to sons, as a mother to daughters, as a hen gathering her brood under her wings.

174

Finally, and this fifth possibility has much in its favor: by this "premature" location of the lament, Luke is saying there is yet time to repent, to receive pardon for sin, and to welcome the reign of God. That offer, in fact, will continue to be made following Jesus' death, resurrection, and ascension, an offer not only to Jerusalem but to the entire world (24:47; Acts 1:8).

Luke 14:1-24
Table Talk

Luke here gathers four disparate units of material by means of the context of a meal. These four stories do not depend on each other for meaning, but it is important that they all occur "at table." Table talk was not only a fairly common literary device for gathering and disseminating discussions on a range of topics, but banquets did, in fact, provide occasions for philosophers and teachers to impart their wisdom. However, for Judaism, for Jesus, and for the early church, table fellowship was laden with very important meanings, religious, social, and economic. Comments on table fellowship were made at 5:29–32 and 7:31–35 and there may be profit in reviewing those discussions now. What is important at this point is that the reader not regard 14:1–24 as a break in the action or as a casual interlude in the heavily sober journey to Jerusalem begun at 9:51. That journey is still in the minds of Luke and the reader, and events or teachings that occur at table in no way detract from its unrelenting progress or its divine imperative. Nothing can be for Luke more serious than a dining table. Both the Eucharist and revelations of the risen Christ occur there (24:28–32). It was while eating together (literally, "sharing the salt") that Christ gave his disciples the promise of the Holy Spirit and their commission (Acts 1:4–8), and it was by table fellowship that Jews and Gentiles were able to be the church (Acts 10:9–16; 11:1–18).

Dispute Over a Sabbath Healing (14:1–6)

Verse 1 provides the setting for this event and for the teachings in verses 7–11, 12–14, and 15–24. The reader of Luke is not at this point surprised that Jesus is dining as guest of a Pharisee; he has done so previously. Jesus did not find it necessary to

175

exclude the religious in order to include publicans and sinners; his spirit is inclusive in the broadest possible sense. Neither is it surprising that Jesus is being watched; tensions have developed, some of them have been charged with hypocrisy, Jesus has been charged with breaches of the law, and differences of interpretation are not inconsequential. And, in fact, the dispute over Sabbath healing recalls very similar occurrences at 6:6–11 and 13:10–17. Only the argument in support of the healing, legal concessions to emergencies, differs. One has to ask, therefore, what reason Luke might have for telling controversy stories that differ so little from each other. Perhaps the frequency of such stories reflects the critical role of Sabbath observance in Judaism and the continuing tension not only between church and synagogue over the matter but also between Jewish and Gentile groups within the church. It is significant that following the Jerusalem conference, which Luke reports in Acts 15, the Gentile churches are asked to show deference to Judaism only in matters of idolatry, unchastity, and foods (Acts 15:20). No mention is made of the Sabbath. Either that matter had already been settled, or it was not a critical issue, or it was left to the convictions of different Christian communities to observe or not observe the Sabbath. One suspects, however, in Luke's time and place, that if not between Christian groups, then between church and synagogue, Sabbath observance still generated a great deal of tension.

A Lesson for Guests (14:7–11)

According to verse 1, Jesus is at dinner in the home of a Pharisee and, while there, observes the social behavior of both guests and host. The everyday activity of home and marketplace, farm and fishing boat provided Jesus not only revelations of the true character of his listeners but also opportunities to reveal the way life is in the reign of God. Plutarch once observed that it is in the small, apparently trivial act that character is most accurately reflected. The observations of Jesus support that statement. And if the incarnation teaches us anything, it is that the frequent and familiar are not to be overlooked in defining life in the presence of God. Therefore those commentators who treat lightly verses 7–11 and 12–14 as a bit of social commentary by Jesus have missed the real nature of "kingdom talk." In fact, Luke gives ample evidence that the subject here is the kingdom of God. He says in verse 7 that what follows is

176

a parable, a clue to the reader that more than etiquette is involved, just as more than sowing was involved in the parable of the sower (8:4–8). And Jesus closes at verse 11 with a pronouncement, the same one used to conclude the parable of the two men going to prayer (18:14) and to warn the hearers against self-serving pride (Matt. 23:12).

The preacher and the teacher will want to realize how easily Jesus' lesson to guests can be wasted. The human ego is quite clever and, upon hearing that taking a low seat may not only avoid embarrassment but lead to elevation to the head table, may convert the instruction about humility into a new strategy for self-exaltation. Jesus does not offer a divinely approved way for a person to get what he or she wants. Taking the low seat because one is humble is one thing; taking the low seat as a way to move up is another. This entire message becomes a cartoon if there is a mad, competitive rush for the lowest place, with ears cocked toward the host, waiting for the call to ascend.

A Lesson for Hosts (14:12–14)

Being a host carries with it many pleasant and positive connotations, such as friendliness, generosity, graciousness, and concern for the comfort of others, and in many cases these terms are appropriate descriptions. However, Jesus observed an occasion, and certainly not an isolated one, on which hosting was an act by which one person gained power over others and put them in his debt. All of us know the ugly face of generosity which binds and the demonic character of gifts with strings attached. A host who expects a return on his or her behavior will not offer service or food to those who cannot repay, and so guest lists consist of persons who are able to return the favor. However, in the kingdom God is the host, and who can repay God? Jesus is therefore calling for kingdom behavior, that is, inviting to table those with neither property nor place in society. Since God is host of us all, we as hosts are really behaving as guests, making no claims, setting no conditions, expecting no return. Luke's fourfold list of the poor, the maimed, the lame, and the blind (v. 13) is no surprise to the reader; we have known since Mary's song (1:46–55) and Jesus' inaugural sermon (4:16–30) that these were kingdom people.

177

The radicality of the text should not be missed. Both the synagogue and the church are constitutionally committed to the care of the poor and the disabled. Some courses of action are not options, and this is one of them. Here, however, Jesus is not calling on Christians to provide for the needs of the poor and the disabled; he says to invite them to dinner. This is the New Testament's understanding of hospitality. The word translated "hospitality" means, literally, "love of a stranger." Recall Heb. 13:1–2: "Let love of brother and sister continue; do not forget love of the stranger" (trans. mine). Hospitality, then, is not having each other over on Friday evenings but welcoming those who are in no position to host us in return. Nor does the text speak of sending food to anyone; rather, the host and the guest sit at table together. The clear sign of acceptance, of recognizing others as one's equals, of cementing fellowship, is breaking bread together. In the Christian community no one is a "project." Do you suppose Jesus was serious about opening church halls and homes in this way?

The Parable of the Banquet (14:15–24)
(Matthew 22:1–14)

The parable repeats and enlarges the concept of hospitality introduced in verses 12–14. It may have been the mention of a resurrection (v. 14) which prompts the remark of a guest (v. 15) which, in turn, occasions the parable. This parable is the fourth and last unit set at table in the home of a Pharisee (v. 1). Matthew's form of this parable (Matt. 22:1–14) is more dramatic, enlarged, and allegorized, and is placed within the disputes between Jesus and religious leaders in the final days in Jerusalem. Here in Luke, Jesus is on his way to Jerusalem. A version of this parable is also to be found in the *Gospel of Thomas* (Saying 64), and a knowledge of that record of it may also be helpful to the preacher (the *Gospel of Thomas* is available in several English translations; the article on this non-canonical Gospel in *Harper's Bible Dictionary* is also recommended).

Unlike Matthew's version, Luke's parable is simple and life-size. A man gives a banquet and invites many. The parable assumes the social custom of an invitation in advance and an invitation at the time of the meal to those who had accepted the first. However, between the first and the second invitation the circumstances of the guests have changed. The anger of the preacher and the teacher should not be unleashed against these persons as though their excuses were thin and empty. They

178

were not. Those who say no are not clutching at any notion that might get them out of a commitment toward which no loyalty is felt. We are not here listening to worn-out stories about faulty alarm clocks, heavy traffic, noisy neighbors hindering sleep, misplaced calendars, or tardy car pools. The economic pressures felt by the first two and the recent wedding of a third (the threefold pattern was common in storytelling, although there is a fourth rejection in the *Gospel of Thomas*) were excuses honored in most societies. In fact, marriage exempted one from military duty in Israel (Deut. 20:7; 24:5). The forces against which God's offer contends are reasonable and well argued, but God's offer has priority not simply over our worst but also over our best agendas. Those who attend do so not because there was nothing else to do but because the banquet was the best among attractive alternatives.

There is no reason any of the listeners would have been shocked by Jesus' story up to the point of inviting persons to replace the original guests. Everything is as usual, even though regrettable, about planning a dinner party, preparing, and inviting, only to have guests not show. Such is the nature of a parable; it is drawn from nature or common life (cf. comments at 8:4–8). But, like many parables, this one has a jolt in an unexpected turn: rather than inviting others from the same social circle as the original guests, the host turns to the streets of the city, bringing in the poor, the maimed, the lame, and the blind (v. 21; same as above, v. 13), and then to transients on public roads (v. 23). That these last would have to be compelled or urged was congenial to the vigorous extension of hospitality to passing strangers who would be reluctant before such a surprising invitation. The two disciples at Emmaus "constrained" the stranger (Jesus) to accept their hospitality (24:29). The final scene of a banquet table filled with new guests must have been a very surprising one to the fellow whose pious comment launched the parable: "Blessed is he who shall eat bread in the kingdom of God!" (v. 15). Apparently the man was not only enjoying the banquet before him but felt confident of a reserved seat at the messianic banquet in God's kingdom. When he looks over the guests at table in Jesus' story, he sees neither himself nor anyone from his circle of friends.

How is this story to be heard? Parables by their very nature are heard in a number of ways, even by the same person at different times. Interpretation depends in part on where the

179

parable itself ends. If at verse 21, then Luke's familiar use of the reversal to announce the gospel is the format here: insiders are out and outsiders are in. If the parable proper extends through verse 23, then it is almost inevitable that one think of God's offer first to the rejected and the marginal in Israel (on the streets of the city) and then to Gentiles (strangers on the outskirts of the city). Perhaps it is now too late for those who were invited first but who said no. Verse 24 is clearly not part of the parable: the speaker is no longer the host of the banquet but Jesus, and the one addressed is no longer the servant (the "you" is plural) but everyone. The parable can be heard historically: prophets gave the first invitation; Jesus calls those invited; they refuse; the unacceptable in Israel and Gentiles are invited. The parable can also be heard polemically, as a defense and justification of the church whose membership included persons who would have been or were rejected in most circles. Or the parable may be heard as a prophetic word of Jesus to a church rapidly becoming "the establishment," uttering pious phrases (v. 15), comfortable in a false confidence of its own salvation, and no longer inviting to God's table the poor, the maimed, the lame, and the blind. In any case, the first task of the preacher or the teacher is not to interpret the parable for others but to hear it, personally and as a member of the community of disciples.

Luke 14:25–35
Teachings Concerning Discipleship

Sections of material such as this offer a real challenge to the preacher and the teacher, and for a number of reasons. Some of the teachings here repeat messages found earlier in Luke. There is also an apparent lack of internal unity in the passage, and, in fact, parallels in Matthew and Mark are found distributed in other contexts. In addition, this section shifts abruptly from the audience and content of the immediately preceding section (vv. 1–24). Since some of the teachings here have their own integrity and do not depend on context for meaning, they may safely be extracted and treated without fear of violation. However, the first duty of the interpreter is to

180

search for clues within the section which may not only aid in understanding Luke's arrangement but also provide the guidelines for dealing with the passage as a whole.

At verse 25 Luke alerts the reader that what follows will be spoken to an audience different from that in verses 1–24. From semiprivate conversations in a home Jesus returns to the public arena. We are given no geographical reference, but again large crowds gather. It is evident that Jesus is not facing reluctance but enthusiasm, similar to that which he met at 9:57. These people come to him (v. 26), he is not calling them out to a life of discipleship. One is to read what follows, therefore, as the response of Jesus to the enthusiasm of persons who seem totally unaware that he is going to Jerusalem and to the cross. After the transitional verse 25, verses 26–33 have a kind of literary unity in that they are built on a refrain: "Whoever does not . . . cannot be my disciple." This refrain appears at verses 26, 27, and 33. This format of opening and closing a body of material with the same expression (called an inclusio) serves as a literary device for gathering sayings that otherwise would not belong together, and it certainly cannot be assumed that all these teachings were given on a single occasion. As we will notice later, verses 34–35, seemingly quite detached (parallels are at Matt. 5:13 and Mark 9:50), may have been brought to this location by Luke as a final caution to unreflective enthusiasm.

Jesus is on his way to Jerusalem, but what is the nature of the journey? Is it a funeral procession? Apparently only Jesus has seriously faced the issue of his death; the Twelve certainly have not yet grasped it. Is it a march? Very likely some think so, investing a good deal of emotion in imagining the projected clash: Galilee versus Jerusalem, peasants versus power, laity versus clergy, Jews versus Romans, Jesus versus the establishment. Is it a parade? Obviously this crowd thinks so, oblivious to any conflict, any price to pay, any cross to bear. The crowds swell; everybody loves a parade. What does Jesus have to say to hasty volunteers? In sum, his word is, Think about what you are doing and decide if you are willing to stay with me all the way.

To the call to cross bearing, heard earlier at 9:23, is joined the almost frightening demand to hate one's family and one's own life (v. 26). To hate is a Semitic expression meaning to turn away from, to detach oneself from. There is nothing of that emotion we experience in the expression "I hate you." Were that the case, then verse 26 alone would cancel all the calls to

181

love, to care, to nourish, especially one's own family (I Tim. 5:8), found throughout both Testaments. And to hate one's own life is not a call for self-loathing, to regard oneself as a worm, to toss oneself on the trash heap of the world. We have not been given any right to judge ourselves. Paul considered valueless "rigor of devotion and self-abasement and severity to the body" (Col. 2:23). What is demanded of disciples, however, is that in the network of many loyalties in which all of us live, the claim of Christ and the gospel not only takes precedence but, in fact, redefines the others. This can and will necessarily involve some detaching, some turning away.

The two parables embedded in this passage (vv. 28–32) say in their own way what Jesus is saying in the preceding verses: Are you sure you wish to follow me? Is the price more than you are willing to pay? The first parable is drawn from rural life and involves building a tower in a vineyard from which the farmer can stand watch against thieves and foraging animals. The second pictures the royal house where great issues of war and peace are settled. But rich and poor alike, royalty and peasants alike, have essentially the same decision to make when faced with a major expenditure of time, property, and life itself: Does this cost more than I am able or willing to pay? The decision is no different when one is facing the call to discipleship: the enthusiasm for beginning is there, but do I possess the resources to carry through to completion? In the undisciplined idealism of the 1960s many dreams soured and noble enterprises fell short of action, but one practice (among many) was begun that for the church seemed appropriate and healthy. In many churches, when persons presented themselves for membership, the question was asked, "Do you know what you are doing? Do you realize what this means?" A period of instruction followed, not solely on matters of doctrine but of the costs of discipleship, after which the persons, having counted the costs, were given the opportunity to say yes or no. The procedure recognized the difficulty of being a Christian in a culture that assumed that everyone was in a situation where, as Luke says, "there was a great multitude." Regrettably, in churches with declining memberships and budgets, many feel that recitals of cost or anything else possibly discouraging to prospective members should be delayed, if not eliminated altogether.

182

Upon a first reading, the saying about salt in verses 34–35 seems detached and out of place. Why did Luke place it here?

Perha'ps in the analogy Jesus continues to address the enthusiastic but uninformed multitude. Just as salt can lose its savor, so can an initial commitment, however sincere, fade in the course of time. Even with attention and with the nourishment of prayer, reflection, fellowship, and activity, commitments will be severely tested once Jerusalem is no longer a distant goal but a very present and painful reality. Enthusiasm that placed Jesus before all other commitments cools before the question, "Are you one of his disciples?" and suddenly those other commitments to job and station and family beg again to come first. Under pressures both open and subtle, pressures all of us know, salt does not decide to become pepper; it just gradually loses its savor. The process can be so gradual, in fact, that no one really notices. Well, almost no one.

Luke 15:1–32
Three Parables of Joy

We are now entering that part of Luke's Gospel which is so heavily sprinkled with parables, most of them without parallels in Matthew and Mark. Even though Luke does share with Matthew and Mark some parables drawn from nature, most of those peculiar to Luke are more related to human activity and relationships and are more narrative in style. Since before us now are three parables, the interpreter may wish first to review either the brief essay on parables at 8:4–8 or refer to some of the reading cited there. The three parables of chapter 15 are a trilogy in that all three speak of the joy of finding that which was lost. This trilogy is not surprising, since offering material in triplets is not uncommon in Luke (9:57–62; 11:42–52; 14:18–20; 20:10–12). The first two of the three are so similar in length, form, content, and closing comment that they can be treated together fairly. The ending to each refers to "one sinner who repents," an expression that seems more to anticipate the third parable than to fit either the lost sheep or the lost coin. Perhaps the function of the phrase is to set up the final parable of the loving father in which there is the return of a penitent. Only the first, the parable of the lost sheep, has a parallel (Matt. 18:12–14); the others are in Luke alone.

183

In a manner typical of Luke, the reader is prepared to hear the parables by an introduction which is, in a way of speaking, an interpretive context in the ministry of Jesus. Again, no geographical reference is given; the setting consists rather of three statements: Jesus attracts tax collectors and sinners (v. 1), the Pharisees and the scribes criticize his receiving and eating with such persons (v. 2), and Jesus responds with a parable (v. 3). The reader is therefore to hear what follows as the response of Jesus, and hence the response of the church, to critics who find in the presence of tax collectors and sinners around Jesus something contradictory, or inappropriate, or unsavory, or repulsive, or socially disruptive, or in violation of the nature and purpose of true religion. More correctly, it should be said that these people are not simply in Jesus' presence; he "receives" (RSV) or "welcomes (NEB) them, a term that could mean Jesus is host to them as guests. The issue, then, is table fellowship, breaking bread together being the sign and seal of full acceptance. We remember the charge which by now has become almost a refrain of rejection: "Behold, a glutton and a drunkard, a friend of tax collectors and sinners!" (7:34). As to what was so offensive about tax collectors and sinners, and what was so vitally important about table fellowship, a review of comments at 5:29–32 and 7:31–35 might be helpful.

Before moving to the parables themselves, the reader will want to take a moment to consider where he or she is sitting while receiving the stories. Is it beside Jesus, as though joining Jesus in addressing these parables to critics, or is it among those being addressed by Jesus? In texts in which Jesus is facing opponents, we who deal with these texts can so easily, but certainly not intentionally, preach and teach them as the voice of Jesus rather than as those who need to hear the voice of Jesus. This does not mean we must label ourselves Pharisees and scribes, but it does mean we realize that these texts were written not simply out of historical interest in the religious community surrounding Jesus but primarily because these texts addressed a church with the problems herein associated with Pharisees and scribes. There is no room to say, "Lord, I thank thee I am not as they were." In addition, locating ourselves in the stories will tend to make us more understanding of those who disagreed with Jesus. Their position reflects a warning firmly stated in the Old Testament (Prov. 1:15; Ps. 1; Isa. 52:11) about associating with evil persons, a warning Paul found useful in dealing with

184

moral issues in the Corinthian church (II Cor. 6:14–18). And what parent has not said to a teenaged son or daughter, "Birds of a feather flock together"? The Pharisees are not alone in believing that the separation of good and bad people preserves a community's sense of righteousness and is essential for the moral instruction of the young. Jesus' failure to observe such distinctions seemed to some dangerous to the moral and religious fiber of the community and disturbingly radical. It still is so regarded by some, even within the church. Perhaps the most fitting location for us, then, is not with Jesus or with the Pharisees but among tax collectors and sinners, who find ourselves welcomed and forgiven in his presence.

The Parables of the Found Sheep and the Found Coin (15:4–10)

By the use of the conjunction "or" at verse 8 Luke joins these two parables which are obviously twins: "What man," "What woman." Matthew sets the story of the sheep that was found in the context of instructions to church leaders to restore the erring (18:1–14). Matthew's sheep "goes astray," is sought, and *if it is found* (18:13), there is rejoicing. In Luke the sheep is lost, as are the sinners who come to hear Jesus, and it is sought *until it is found* (v. 4). Back of Luke's image of the tender shepherd lie Ezek. 34:12; Isa. 40:11; and 49:22, passages in which God is portrayed as the shepherd who seeks and gently restores the lost sheep. So strong is the love for the lost sheep that the ninety-nine are left in the wilderness (desert) while the search goes on. It is in an old gospel song, not in Luke, that the ninety-nine safely lay sheltered in the fold. If the ninety-nine are safe in a fold, then the search for one lost sheep is but an act of frugality, an exercise of common sense. It is foolish not to act when there is a possible gain with no possibility of loss. But how is one to assess the search by a shepherd who leaves ninety-nine in the wilderness? Either the shepherd is foolish or the shepherd loves the lost sheep and will risk everything, including his own life, until he finds it.

That Luke parallels the parable of a man with one about a woman is not surprising; we have met his inclusiveness many times before. The woman's ten silver coins (drachmas) represented about ten days' wages and many months of saving. Like the shepherd, she seeks "until she finds it" (v. 8); there is no giving up in either story. The joy of finding is so abundant that

185

it cannot be contained; one person alone cannot adequately celebrate it; there must be a party to which others are invited. Jesus invites even his critics to join him and all of heaven in celebration of finding the lost. This joy, elaborated more fully in the party for the returned son in the next parable, is the heart of the gospel. Finding and restoring the lost gives pleasure to God as well as to all who are about God's business. But this joy is also the offense of the gospel. Celebrating the recovery of a lost sheep? Yes. Celebrating the recovery of a lost coin? Yes. But throwing a party for a prodigal? Would it not be better for him, a better witness to the neighbors, and a better demonstration of the righteousness of God if he were taught a lesson he would never forget?

The Parable of the Loving Father (15:11–32)

Easily the most familiar of all Jesus' parables, this story has been embraced by many persons who have not felt the full impact of the offense of grace that it dramatically conveys. The focus of the parable is the father: "There was a man who had two sons," but it is most often called the parable of the prodigal son. This way of identifying it says more about its use in the preaching of the church than it does of its own message. In fact, it is interesting that all three parables in this chapter are popularly known by their negative rather than positive features: the *lost* sheep, not the found sheep; the *lost* coin, not the found coin; and the *prodigal* son, not the loving father. And all this in spite of the fact that all three end in celebrations of joy. A great deal of preaching, especially in American churches, has devoted an inordinate amount of time on the conditions addressed by the gospel rather than on the gospel itself. While it is true that a dark-velvet background helps bring out the beauty of the diamond cast against it, one almost gets the impression that some preachers enjoy the dark background more than the diamond. The parable is of love and forgiveness and joy.

This parable is extraordinary in its composition, developing its plot in an economy of words, using only the necessary characters, with no more than two onstage at one time, and arriving at a resolution that requires the reader's consent to be satisfactory. The reader who expected (or wanted) the father to give the party for the son who stayed home and worked hard feels a jolt which the parable does not relieve with its simple declaration, "It was fitting to make merry and be glad." Grace seems

186

to abrogate justice, and the parable, with the restraint vital to a parable, leaves the reader to struggle with the tension. The parable is consistent in its own frame of values: twice it is said that the younger son was dead and is alive again, was lost and is found (vv. 24, 32). The reader might have expected, on the literary principle of end stress, that the final phrase would have been "was dead, is alive" on the assumption that no condition is worse than death, no condition is better than life. But such is not the climax in this parable's scale of values. There is a condition worse than death, to be lost; there is a condition better than life, to be found. As to whether we have in verses 11–32 a union of two parables (vv. 11–24, 25–32), as some scholars have argued, such a judgment misses on two counts. First, the opening "There was a man who had two sons" makes the father's relation to each of the sons ingredient to the story. This is not a parable of a younger son and a parable of an older son, but a parable of a father. Only if one thinks of it as a story of the prodigal son does the scene with the older son seem added on. Second, the apparent conclusion at verse 24, found again at verse 32, does not mark out two stories, for repetition of lines is not uncommon in parables (e.g., Matt. 25:14–30).

As in the treatment of all parables, the teacher and the preacher would do well not to try to explain it; let it stand alone and do its work on and in the hearer. Like an explained joke, an explained parable violates the listener. One will want, of course, to remove any obstacles to hearing that hinder audiences beyond the time and place of the first hearers. Bits of helpful information can therefore set the parable free to work again. For example, according to Jewish custom, a younger son received one third of the inheritance which was usually received at the father's death but which had been divided earlier (I Kings 1—2). To eat swine was to become as a Gentile and outside the covenant (Lev. 11:7; Isa. 65:4; 66:17). The pods referred to (v. 16) were the long pods of the carob tree, eaten by animals and, at times, by the extremely poor. Otherwise, terms, actions, and relationships belong to the human story and are clear to a modern audience.

Without question, this parable was offensive to the Pharisees and the scribes who first heard it, and time has not removed that offense. If anything has dulled the edge of the story, it is its frequent use, or more correctly, its partial use. One hears too often of the fun-loving boy who had to get out of the

187

house or of the older son who is cartooned as a hard-hearted miser who never learned to dance. If one's listeners have been treated to numerous casual partial tellings of this story, but with no real sense of the way grace offends a sense of fairness or how forgiveness comes across as condoning, then it might be well to underscore two elements in the story that often get neglected. One is the party. It was the music and dancing that offended the older son. Of course, let the younger son return home. Judaism and Christianity have clear provisions for the restoration of the penitent returnee, but where does it say that such provisions include a banquet with music and dancing? Yes, let the prodigal return, but to bread and water, not fatted calf; in sackcloth, not a new robe; wearing ashes, not a new ring; in tears, not in merriment; kneeling, not dancing. Has the party canceled the seriousness of sin and repentance? We might even ponder whether, had we lived next door, we would have attended that party. The second element often overlooked is that the father not only had two sons but loved two sons, went out to two sons (vv. 20, 28), and was generous to two sons (vv. 12, 22, 31). Perhaps it is because of the competitive rather than cooperative spirit of our society, but the common thought is that there must be losers if there are winners. Hence, even in religion, it is very difficult not to think Jews *or* Gentiles, poor *or* rich, saint *or* sinner, publican *or* Pharisee, older son *or* younger son. But God's love is both/and, not either/or. The embrace of the younger son did not mean the rejection of the older; the love of tax collectors and sinners does not at all negate love of Pharisees and scribes. Such is God's love, but we find it difficult not to be offended by God's grace toward another, especially if we have serious questions about that person's conduct and character.

Luke 16:1–31
Teachings Concerning Wealth

If the journey to Jerusalem is understood as Luke's context for Jesus preparing his followers (including the reader) not only for Jesus' passion but for discipleship to and beyond the events in Jerusalem, then we could say that a body of teaching on the subject of possessions was not only expected but inevitable. No subject is of more concern to Luke when he is drawing together the teachings of Jesus for disciples. This is not to say that other New Testament writers neglect the matter; by no means, but we have met the issues of wealth and poverty in Luke with the frequency of a refrain. Luke has used practically every literary vehicle available to him to put the subject before the reader: the song of Mary (1:46–55), the sermons of John the Baptist (3:10–14), the prophecy of Isa. 61:1–2 (4:16–30), blessings and woes (6:20–25), the parable of the rich fool (12:13–21), warnings about anxiety (12:22–31), advice to guests and hosts (14:7–14), and now the two parables of chapter 16. But it is not in literary forms alone that Luke's word about possessions contains variety; the message itself is not always the same. Woes are pronounced on the rich and yet the rich are saved (19:1–10). Missionaries on their itineraries are to take no provisions, and yet those who have the means to give food and lodging to them are blessed. Beatitudes are spoken to the poor, and yet possessions can be used for good (8:1–3; 10:29–37; 12:32–34). In the early church, those who had shared voluntarily with those who did not, and the ministry of Paul included receiving and delivering offerings for the famine-stricken poor in Judea (Acts 2:44–45; 4:32–35; 11:27–30). In fact, the two parables now before us represent a positive and a negative use of material things. Clearly, Luke understood as well as we that the issues of wealth and poverty are complex, that anxiety about money is a disease among both those who have it and those who do not, and that a generous sharing of one's goods can free one from the danger to the soul which lies coiled in the possession of things. Overall, Luke understands that prosperity casts a shadow over human life and it is the poor who are the objects of God's special concern. Nowhere is that conviction more evident than in the story of the rich man and Lazarus, the second of the parables now before us.

The discussion in chapter 16 is in two parts, verses 1–13 and 14–31. Each part has as its centerpiece a parable, and each parable begins "There was a rich man." The first part is addressed to disciples (v. 1) and speaks of a constructive use of money; the second is addressed to Pharisees (v. 14) and points to a use of money that is spiritually fatal. In the first part, only verse 13 has a parallel (Matt. 6:24); in the second, verses 16–18 have parallels at Matt. 11:12, 13; 5:18; 5:32; 19:9; and Mark

10:11–12. These scattered parallels to what Luke has joined in one brief space alert us to the need to search for Luke's principle of composition in order to understand his abrupt shifts and discontinuities. We might console ourselves in advance with the knowledge that to most Lukan scholars the location of the content in verses 16–18 within the larger discussion of wealth remains very much a mystery.

The Parable of the Shrewd Steward (16:1–13)

This parable is addressed to the disciples, but here as elsewhere the Evangelist offers not only the parable but also interpretive comments. Luke is doing what all preachers do, that is, interpreting the Jesus tradition for a new audience in a new situation. In order to understand Luke's interpretation of the parable it is necessary to distinguish between the parable itself and Luke's comments. Making this distinction is not for us (though it is for some researchers) a way of getting "back of the Gospels to Jesus," nor is it for the purpose of discerning levels of authority in a text; that is, words of Jesus are more authoritative than words of Luke. We deal with the entire text as we receive it as Scripture, but this is Luke's Gospel and we are trying to hear his message about and from Jesus. We ask, then, where does the parable end and commentary begin? The opening of verse 9, "And I tell you," is clearly a saying of the Lord and therefore offered by Luke as Jesus' own interpretation of the parable. If that is the case, then verse 9 interprets the parable to mean that disciples are to handle material things ("mammon" is a Semitic word for money) so as to secure heaven and the future. This is to say, how one handles property has eternal consequences. Verse 9, therefore, underscores what Jesus said at 12:33: "Sell your possessions, and give alms; provide yourselves with purses that do not grow old, with a treasure in the heavens that does not fail." However, verse 8b also seems to be an interpretive generalization on the parable. According to 8b, therefore, the parable admonishes the children of light (I Thess. 5:4–5) to learn from the people of this world. And what is the lesson? Like the steward in the parable, use possessions so as to gain, not lose, one's future. If, then, the parable ends at verse 8a, the steward is commended for prudence, for his astuteness (NEB).

190

Many Christians have been offended by this parable, and on two grounds. First, some find it a bit disturbing that Jesus would find anything commendable in a person who has acted dishonestly. Why that should prove offensive is not fully clear, for everyone is a mixed bag of the commendable and the less commendable. Love of family, generosity, and loyalty are traits to be praised in persons with some unsavory ways. It is enough that Jesus did not commend the dishonesty, a quality in the man that should not discolor everything else about him. Some commentators have tried to clean up the steward by saying that his reduction of the various bills due his master was simply the subtraction of the steward's commission, a temporary loss he was willing to sustain in exchange for future favorable treatment by these customers of his master. This is an interesting view, but were it the case, the steward would not have been dishonest. The more likely interpretation is that he falsified the amounts owed his master to gain the favor of those who would later offer him hospitality in the time of his unemployment (v. 4). The second and related offense in this parable is the use of words such as "shrewd" and "clever" to describe people of the kingdom ("children of light"). The words have so commonly been associated with self-serving behavior, if not ethically questionable behavior, that it is difficult to speak of a "shrewd saint." Of course, part of the problem lies in the anticerebral bias in the church and the unwillingness, if not inability, of many to conceive of thinking as a kingdom activity. Apparently, to be childlike is taken to mean naive, even though Jesus is said, according to Matt. 10:16, to have alerted his disciples to be "wise as serpents and innocent as doves."

In summary, therefore, the parable of the clever steward and its attending interpretations say to Jesus' disciples that for all the dangers in possessions, it is possible to manage goods in ways appropriate to life in the kingdom of God. However, as with the subject of prayer at 11:1–13, Luke uses this parable as the occasion to gather other sayings of Jesus on the subject of material goods. Each of the sayings in verses 10–13 states a proverbial truth which in no way depends on the parable for its meaning. Verses 10–12 contain sayings all of which are framed on what logicians call an argument a fortiori, that is, an argument from the lesser to the greater. The life of a disciple is one of faithful attention to the frequent and familiar tasks of each day, however small and insignificant they may seem. The one faithful in today's nickels and dimes is the one to be trusted with the big account, but it is easy to be indifferent toward small

191

obligations while quite sincerely believing oneself fully trust-
worthy in major matters. The realism of these sayings is simply
that life consists of a series of seemingly small opportunities.
Most of us will not this week christen a ship, write a book, end
a war, appoint a cabinet, dine with the queen, convert a nation,
or be burned at the stake. More likely the week will present no
more than a chance to give a cup of water, write a note, visit
a nursing home, vote for a county commissioner, teach a Sunday
school class, share a meal, tell a child a story, go to choir practice, and feed the neighbor's cat. "Whoever is faithful in a very
little is faithful also in much" (v. 10). Verse 13 makes an abrupt
shift in literary form, the "lesser to greater" of verses 10–12
giving way to an "all or nothing" pronouncement. No servant
can pledge allegiance to two masters at once; whoever tries to
do so discovers in time that in actuality to only one is love and
loyalty given.

The Parable of the Rich Man and Lazarus (16:14–31)

The first parable of this chapter (vv. 1–8*a*) was followed by
comments on the parable and the subject of possessions generally (vv. 8*b*–13). By contrast, the second parable is preceded by
comments that bear upon the parable (vv. 14–18), although in
ways not explicit or clear to the reader. The audience is no
longer disciples but Pharisees, who are here portrayed as lovers
of money who make fun of Jesus' position on money (v. 14). It
is not necessary to picture these men as godless materialists
whose religion is only a facade, even though our culture has
come to suspect that money madness prompts holding up a
Bible and talking easily of faith in God. The Pharisees love
money within a theological framework that justifies their position (v. 15). Jesus has separated God and mammon (v. 13), and
they scoff at his view. This apparently means that theirs is a
theology in which God and mammon are comfortably joined.
Such a theology is often called Deuteronomic, because in that
book (and others of that tradition) the word is clear: obey God
and you will be blessed in war, in the marketplace, in the field,
and at home (Deut. 28). Godliness is in league with riches;
prosperity is the clear sign of God's favor. This debate within
the Bible and among Christians today was discussed at 13:1–5
and need not be repeated here. It is enough here to say that
Jesus and these Pharisees differed on their theological interpretations of wealth and poverty. If the Pharisees further justified

192

their position by alms and acts of charity out of their abundance, Jesus says that God perceives what is really going on, and God's assessment of our endeavors is frequently a reversal of our own.

The shift of audience from disciples to Pharisees seems abrupt, but the sudden shift is softened by the fact that the subject remains unchanged: money. However, verses 16–18 present the reader with real problems of contextual continuity. A number of theories have been offered as explanation for what seems to be a strange insertion. Some scholars hold that Luke found these sayings together in his source (called Q, a designation for material held in common by Matthew and Luke) and that he simply left them as they were. Those who find in Deuteronomy the primary source for Luke's literary format (cf. the discussion at 9:51) handle the difficulty here by pointing to similar literary discontinuities in that book. For example, verse 18 introduces into the discussion words of Jesus on marriage and divorce. In Deuteronomy 24 marriage and divorce are discussed in a context in which possessions and financial obligations are the major topic. Other commentators, of a more practical and pastoral mind, do not regard a statement on divorce out of order at all in a discussion of material goods; the two subjects are universally joined. Experience has confirmed the truth of the familiar line in Gustave Flaubert's novel, *Madame Bovary:* "Of all the winds that blow on love, the demand for money is the coldest and most destructive." Perhaps the most ingenious, and somewhat persuasive, treatment of these verses is by E. Earle Ellis (*The Gospel of Luke,* p. 201), who sees them as introducing the parable of the rich man and Lazarus (vv. 19–31). As we shall see shortly, this parable seems to fall into two parts: verses 19–26, which tell of the rich man and Lazarus and their fates, and verses 27–31, which speak of not believing the law and the prophets and therefore not believing the gospel. Ellis holds that verses 14–15 introduce the first part of the parable and verses 16–18, concerned as they are with the law and the prophets, introduce the second part. This theory may be a bit too intricate to satisfy the reader of Luke. However, if the Pharisees misread the law and the prophets in justifying a love of wealth, and if the rich man in the parable interpreted his and Lazarus' conditions as evidence of God's favor and disfavor according to a certain reading of the law and the prophets, then both the Pharisees and the rich man are judged by the very Scriptures they had used to justify their

193

life-styles. Thus verse 31 would conclude what is introduced not at verse 19 but at verse 14. We will walk through these verses assuming such continuity but not for a moment unaware of the difficulties that beset every approach.

The Pharisees found in Deuteronomy and other selected texts a gospel of wealth. There can be no denying it: Scriptures can be found that support the position that the righteous prosper and the wicked suffer (cf. comments at 13:1–5). Jesus, who blessed the poor and urged a free sharing of one's goods with those in need, regarded the Pharisees' view as a gross misinterpretation of the Old Testament. Even though the gospel of the kingdom has been preached since John and multitudes are storming the door (v. 16), this does not mean that the law and the prophets have been canceled. Jesus' contention with Pharisees is not a case of the new superseding the old; by no means. His contention is over a proper reading of the old. Not one dot (a decorative scribal marking on the text) of the law was void (v. 17); what Jesus is saying and doing is according to the law rightly understood. For example, Deut. 24:1–4 was interpreted by some of the Pharisees to get out of one marriage and into another, but, says Jesus, marriage is sacred and a life covenant, the breaking of which is a sin (v. 18). It is difficult to see any reason for verse 18 here except as an example of proper versus improper use of the law. Both Matthew (Matt. 19:3–12) and Mark (Mark 10:2–12) deal at some length with issues of marriage and divorce and provide a context for the discussion (cf. also I Cor. 7:10–16). The subject in Luke 16:14–31 is not marriage and divorce but correct interpretation of the law and the prophets. Jesus now provides a story that vividly dramatizes to the Pharisees a gross misreading of the Scriptures and the consequences of it.

We have been referring to the story of the rich man and Lazarus as a parable, as it is so designated in much of the literature. We are aware, however, that this is the only "parable" of Jesus in which proper names occur: Lazarus and Abraham (in the Latin Vulgate "rich man" is translated "Dives," but that is not the man's name). In addition, the use of the name Lazarus and the mention of raising him from the dead naturally prompt questions about the relationship between Luke's story and the account of the raising of Lazarus in John 11. There seems to be more than coincidence here, but speculations about sources and influences will not advance our discussion of verses 19–31.

194

And finally, on the issues of whether this story is a parable is the question of its unity: Is it one story or one story with an addition, or two stories? Every reader notices that verses 19–26 have one focus and verses 27–31 another. It has rather generally been referred to by students of parables as a "double-edged" parable. In the remarks that follow, it will be assumed that verses 27–31 are essential to the parable in that they return the reader to the reason for the parable in the first place. The story is addressed to Pharisees not simply on the issue of wealth and poverty but on a justification of their view on the basis of the law and the prophets. That matter is not fully addressed until verse 31. Apparently Luke has taken a popular and familiar story and developed it into a strong polemic on the proper interpretation of Scripture.

The first part of the parable (vv. 19–26) is a much-traveled story, forms of it being found in several cultures. Some scholars trace its origin to Egypt, where stories of the dead and of messages being brought from the dead are in abundance. At least seven versions are to be found in the rabbis. In one version the characters are a rich merchant and a poor teacher; in another, a rich and haughty woman and her servile husband. The story in Luke is, of course, Jewish in orientation (Father Abraham), appropriate to an audience of Pharisees and to the point that Luke is making. Theologically it is most congenial to Luke, not only in its perspectives on rich and poor but also in the reversal of the fortunes of the rich man and Lazarus. An eschatological reversal is central in Luke's understanding of the final coming of the reign of God. The parable reflects popular beliefs about the hereafter and the state of the dead. The preacher will want to avoid getting reduced into using the descriptions of the fates of the two men as providing revealed truth on the state of the dead. In other words, this is not a text for a sermon on "Five Minutes After Death." Details are rich and sharp. For the rich man, life is a daily banquet at a bounteous table, his abundance spilling over onto his person, draped as he is in robes of royalty over fine Egyptian undergarments. Nothing about him even hints of need. The poor man, clothed in running sores, squats (lies) among the dogs, gaunt, hollow-eyed, and famished, his face turned toward the rich man's house in the museum stare of the dying. Both die, but only the rich man has a burial (v. 22). Now their roles are reversed. Lazarus is an honored guest at the messianic banquet, while the rich man lies in anguish in the

195

flames of Hades (Old Testament: Sheol). Their conditions are now unalterably final.

Let us pause to remind ourselves that whatever this story meant in other contexts, it is here used by Luke to address Pharisees who loved wealth and scoffed at Jesus' position on the subject (v. 14). As Pharisees whose religion was of the Book, their love of wealth found its confirmation in the law and the prophets, as pointed out at verses 14–15 above. Whoever is careful to obey the commands of God shall be highly favored: "Blessed shall you be in the city, and blessed shall you be in the field. Blessed shall be the fruit of your body, and the fruit of your ground, and the fruit of your beasts, the increase of your cattle, and the young of your flock" (Deut. 28:3–4). The equations are quite clear to them: wealth = blessed of God = obedience to God's commandments. If, then, the parable is to address them, the rich man cannot be an exaggeration of godless materialism but a realistic portrait of a man whose wealth was taken as evidence of God's favor, a man with whom the Pharisees can identify. Otherwise the story has interest but no power. And as for the poor man, is not his condition the punishment of God on a life unknown to us but known to God? It is true that Luke reveals nothing directly about the characters of these two men, and some have faulted the story for its apparent economic prejudice: the rich go to hell, the poor go to heaven. But there is a theology assumed in the parable that Luke is attacking, a theology that says of the one who delights in God's law, "In all that he does, he prospers," but "the wicked are not so" (Ps. 1:3–4). In fact, and may this thought self-destruct immediately, the rich man could have defended his not helping Lazarus with the argument that one should not interfere when God is punishing a person Such has been the reasoning of some church people in this country who have refused to minister to the hungry and the homeless.

This portrait of the rich man has been drawn to fit the Pharisees before whom he is placed. Whatever confirmation and support the rich man and the Pharisees found in the Scriptures for their love of wealth, it is a fact that the situation presented in the parable is a clear violation of those same Scriptures. The law of Moses specifically required that the harvest be shared with the poor and the transient (Lev. 19:9–10), and the law spelled out other ways to carry out the fundamental injunction, "You shall open wide your hand to your brother, to the

196

needy and to the poor, in the land" (Deut. 15:7–11). And the prophets offered no release from the law:

> Is not this the fast that I choose:
>   to loose the bonds of wickedness,
>   to undo the thongs of the yoke,
> to let the oppressed go free,
>   and to break every yoke?
> Is it not to share your bread with the hungry,
>   and bring the homeless poor into your house;
> when you see the naked, to cover him,
>   and not to hide yourself from your own flesh?
>   Isaiah 58:6–7

Neither did Jesus: "But it is easier for heaven and earth to pass away, than for one dot of the law to become void" (v. 17). It is because of this point about the law and the prophets that for Luke the parable must continue, even though stopping at verse 26 would have already made a point vital not only for Luke but for all disciples of Jesus: wherever some eat and others do not eat, there the kingdom does not exist, quote whatever Scripture you will.

In verses 27–32, the rich man wants a message sent to his five brothers so they can avoid the torment of Hades. Abraham tells him that they already have in the law and the prophets the adequate and sufficient message, just as the rich man did. The rich man knows that just as he missed the word of God to him in the Scriptures, so might his brothers. Something more extraordinary is needed, such as someone rising from the dead. Not only is Abraham's word true in principle, that the Scriptures are sufficient for faith and for a life in the will of God, but it was also, in Luke's view, true historically: the rejection of the risen Christ had its root in the misunderstanding of the true meaning of the law and the prophets. According to Luke, it is not only on the subject of wealth and poverty that Jesus and not the Pharisees properly interprets Scripture; Luke has been careful to show, from the birth narratives on, that what Jesus says and does is according to Scripture. Later, Luke will point out that the risen Christ taught his disciples to understand Moses, the prophets, and the writings (24:25–27, 44–47). And even later, in Acts, Luke will present the early church's message about Jesus as being true to the Jewish Scriptures (Acts 2:16–36). Luke does not, as many preachers after him have,

197

handle the tensions with Judaism by easily speaking of the Old superseded by the New. Jesus and the church lived within that tradition and worked at an interpretation of that tradition which opened the way for the full reign of God. The meaning of Scripture and the will of God concerning material goods, wealth, and poverty was a vital subject in the debate between Jesus and some of the Pharisees. The debate continues, but now it is between Jesus and some of his followers.

Luke 17:1–10
On Sin, Forgiveness, Faith, and Duty

The audience shifts again to the disciples to whom Jesus addresses four independent sayings (vv. 1–2, 3–4, 5–6, 7–10). Some of the sayings of Jesus are like proverbs, and because they carry their meanings intrinsically rather than contextually, they are quite portable. The teacher and the preacher would not violate any one of the teachings, therefore, by lifting it from its present location and listening to it separately. However, Luke has woven these four teachings into what is almost a narrative which might be considered in this way: On two subjects Jesus gives very demanding instructions, sinning against a brother or sister (vv. 1–2) and treatment of one who sins against you (vv. 3–4). So difficult seem the teachings that the disciples ask for greater faith, in response to which Jesus calls out and affirms the faith they have (vv. 5–6). However, warns Jesus, you will never, even with increased faith, move above the role of servant whose obedience is co-extensive with life itself; there is no such thing as above and beyond service and duty (vv. 7–10). With this movement in mind we will walk through the four instructions.

Both the first and the second teaching have to do with living together in the community of faith. In the Christian fellowship, two kinds of difficulty will arise often, threatening the harmony of the community. One difficulty grows out of the fact that not all members are at the same level of maturity; there are always "little ones," that is, brothers and sisters newly baptized. The speech and behavior of more mature members could cause one of these new to the faith to stumble and fall. "Being the cause of stumbling" more accurately translates the matter at issue than do "temptations to sin" (v. 1) and "cause to sin" (v. 2). Both Matthew (Matt. 18:6–7) and Mark (Mark 9:42) have parallels here, but it is Paul who corresponds with congregations struggling with this issue in concrete ways who helps us to see the complexity of the matter (I Cor. 8; Rom. 14:13–21). Disciples are free, responsible to their Lord; are the needs and problems of the new members of the community to curb and reduce that freedom? Paul states what Luke 17:1–2 implies: there is a law higher than the law of freedom and that is the law of love. In the fellowship of believers, disciples are to be responsibly considerate of one another.

The second kind of difficulty that threatens the fellowship comes with those occasions when disciples sin against one another (vv. 3–4). This teaching is very realistic; members of the community violate one another. However, that same sense of responsible love called for in verses 1–2 prevails here. The shape of this love is to rebuke in order to correct, and to forgive, even if it is repeated seven times in one day. Matthew elaborates the dynamic here into a procedure for discipline within the fellowship (Matt. 18:15, 18–22). But even in the brief form that Luke gives, the instruction proceeds on assumptions, some of which need to be discussed openly to determine whether they any longer prevail. For example, verses 3–4 assume the following: the relationships among disciples of Jesus are based on ethical standards, the violation of which is sin; what brothers and sisters do is not their business alone but affects the community; responsible love can both give and receive a rebuke; relationships in the Christian community can, with pain to be sure, generate and deal with repentance; words of forgiveness can be spoken and heard with no one seeming superior or trying to play God. These assumptions need to be discussed, claimed, modified, or replaced; it is difficult to imagine a faith community being formed and sustained in silence on these matters.

It is no wonder that the apostles, upon hearing the instructions in verses 1–4, say to Jesus, "Increase our faith!" (v. 5). Notice the terms "apostles" and "the Lord"; Luke clearly has in mind not only Jesus and his immediate followers but also the risen Lord of the church and the apostles as leaders of that church. In verse 5 they are feeling the burden, the heavy burden, of that leadership. Jesus' response to them (variant forms are in Matt. 17:20; 21:21 and Mark 11:22–23) calls for a close examination, especially the expression, "If you had faith . . . ."

199

INTERPRETATION

The Greek language has basically two types of "if" clauses: those which express a condition contrary to the fact ("if I were you") and those which express a condition according to fact ("if Jesus is our Lord"). The conditional clause in verse 6 is of this second type; one could translate it "If you had faith [and you do]." Jesus' response, then, is not a reprimand for an absence of faith but an affirmation of the faith they have and an invitation to live out the full possibilities of that faith. Even the small faith they already have cancels out words such as "impossible" (a tree being uprooted) and "absurd" (planting a tree in the sea) and puts them in touch with the power of God. That Luke has "sycamine tree" (a kind of mulberry) instead of "mountain" as in Matthew and Mark in no way alters the message: faith lays hold of God with whom nothing is impossible, and it is God who empowers the life of discipleship.

The fourth and final teaching (vv. 7–10) is in the form of a parable and is without a parallel in Matthew and Mark. It opens in a manner common to a number of Lukan parables: "Will any one of you?" or "Which one of you?" (11:5–7; 14:23, 31; 15:4, 8). The assumed answer is always no or no one. The parable is built around the slave–master relationship, rather common in New Testament parables but without a clear analogy in our culture. The preacher will have to make an interpretive move to bring the story forward—an uncritical transfer of the relationship to, for example, employees–employers would be misleading. The slave in the story does double duty, in the field and in the house, but the slave understands that his time and labor belong to the master. Even after a period of obedient service, there is no ground for boasting (Rom. 3:27), no period of fulfilled duty beyond which merits begin to accumulate. Jesus came among us as one who serves, and so are his followers servants. There is no place or time, therefore, at which the disciple can say, "I have completed my service; now I want to be served." If this parable was prompted by the remark of the apostles at verse 5, then two things can be said. First, the lesson is especially applicable to leaders of the church who can easily forget that they are "servants of the servants of God." Because many people work out their relationship to God in the ways they relate to the minister, special treatment, both positive and negative, can contribute to that forgetfulness. Second, the request for increase of faith (v. 5) must not seduce the apostles or any leaders to assume that with the increase comes elevation in position so

200

that the period of serving ends. Apostles and all leaders of the faithful come under the instructions for all disciples. In the field or in the house, a servant is a servant.

Luke 17:11—18:30
Teachings Leading to the Final Prediction of the Passion

Before we move to the individual units in this section, we need to consider three statements. First, this section is bordered by comments about the journey to Jerusalem. At 17:11, "on the way to Jerusalem" is a reminder to the reader that Jesus is moving toward his passion, and that fact washes over the words and events of this section. It has been a long journey since 9:51 at which point Jesus set his face to go to Jerusalem, and, as with any long journey, travelers experience so much along the way that they may forget the destination and its purpose. Most who lose their way do so not by wrong decisions but by drifting. At 17:11 Luke can almost see Jerusalem in the distance and he points it out to the reader. This section will end at 18:30, because at 18:31, "Behold, we are going up to Jerusalem," Jesus will not leave the meaning of the journey to the disciples' memory of 9:18–22 or 9:43–45; he will prophesy for the third and final time his passion in the city. At 9:51; 13:22; and 17:11 the reader, not the disciples, is told that Jesus is on his way to Jerusalem. However, at 18:31 the disciples will be told again directly as they approach the city what will soon take place. The interpreter of Luke will want to notice that in the narrative the journey to Jerusalem is occurring at two levels: Jesus is taking his disciples and talks to them about it, conversations we are permitted now and then to overhear; the narrator is taking the reader to Jerusalem, and in addition to overhearing Jesus speak with his disciples, the reader is occasionally informed directly about the journey. Such is the difference between 17:11 (to the reader) and 18:31 (to the disciples).

The second comment about this section is that most of the material within it is peculiar to Luke. A few statements by Jesus have parallels in Matthew or Mark but in different sequences

201

and locations. Those who study Luke by giving attention to the ways he and the other Evangelists agree and differ will be for most of this section without that aid in their study method. But at 18:15, and this is the third and final comment, Luke will rejoin the narrative order of Mark, an order followed also by Matthew. Generally speaking, Mark will be followed until the resurrection narratives. This comment is for those whose habit it is to read Luke in a Gospel parallel and is not intended to urge that procedure on everyone. Our eyes are on Luke, and the glances we give to the others are not for the purposes of correcting, supplementing, or harmonizing. The principal effect thus far, and it will likely continue to be so, is to add to our appreciation of Luke as a narrator of the story of Jesus, not only of his artistry but also of his freedom in the use of his sources, one of which most likely was Mark.

The Grateful Leper (17:11–19)

We learned early in the journey to Jerusalem that references to places cannot be lined up on a route from Galilee to Judea. Geography is sometimes literary, sometimes theological, and sometimes physical. Here the border between Galilee and Samaria is a fitting location for a story involving both Jews and a Samaritan (v. 16). As for lepers, a review of the comments at 5:12–16, an earlier report of Jesus healing a leper, may be helpful. What Luke says here corresponds with what we know of lepers. They kept distant from non-lepers (v. 12; Lev. 13:45–46; Num. 5:2), they formed their own colonies (II Kings 7:3), and they positioned themselves near trafficways in order to make appeals for charity. Showing themselves to a priest after healing was according to the law (Lev. 14:2–32). However, when treated as a single story, verses 11–19 give some problems to the reader. Was the Samaritan, who lived outside the requirements of Judaism, included in the command to go to a priest? Also, why reproach the nine for not returning (vv. 17–18) when they had been told to go show themselves to a priest for a confirmation of their cure and a release from the status of uncleanness? In fact, their healing occurred in their going, that is, in their obedience (v. 14). And finally, the statement of Jesus to the Samaritan who returned, "Your faith has made you well," seems unusual, since all of them were healed.

202

Some of the difficulties are removed when we understand this as a two-part story: verses 11–14 and 15–19. The first part is a healing story with the usual elements: a cry for help; Jesus responds; the healing occurs, here in the act of obedience rather than prior to their obedience, as at 5:12–16. That is, Jesus treats the lepers as already healed, and in their act of obedient faith their healing takes place. The second part is the story of the salvation of a foreigner. It is the foreigner who returns, who praises God, and who expresses gratitude to Jesus. When Jesus says, "Your faith has made you well" (RSV), the blessing certainly refers to some benefit other than that which all, including the other nine, had received earlier. The verb translated "made well" is the same word often translated "to be saved." For example, at 19:9, 10 this is the word used to say that "salvation" has come to Zacchaeus because Jesus came to seek and "to save" the lost. What we have, then, is a story of ten being healed and one being saved.

That it was a foreigner with two counts against him who received salvation by faith is not surprising in Luke who treats favorably the marginalized. The man is a Samaritan and hence a social outcast and a religious heretic, and he has leprosy. But in leper colonies, the common problem renders Jew/Gentile distinctions unimportant. And not only in leper colonies; also in the presence of Jesus. However, only the foreigner receives the full blessing of Jesus' ministry. That is regrettable, because the nine had been received and healed. The story anticipates what is yet to come in Acts: a growing blindness in Israel, a receptivity among Gentiles. Why was this the case? Israel's special place in God's plan for the world had turned in upon itself, duty had become privilege, and frequent favors had settled into blinding familiarity. The reasons are many, are deep, and are complex, but this story does not give license to point the finger. It is often the stranger in the church who sings heartily the hymns we have long left to the choir, who expresses gratitude for blessings we had not noticed, who listens attentively to the sermon we think we have already heard, who gets excited about our old Bible, and who becomes actively involved in acts of service to which we send small donations. Must it always be so?

This perspective on a story that is really two, one of healing and one of salvation, echoes II Kings 5:1–14. We have seen how Luke enjoys telling Jesus stories on the pattern of Old Testament stories (7:11–15 is an example). So he does here: Naaman was a foreigner who was healed of leprosy by Elisha; Naaman

203

was then converted to Israel's faith. Luke has already shown us his fondness for this story (4:27).

Concerning the Kingdom and the Coming Son of Man (17:20–37)

In chapter 21 Luke records the apocalyptic discourse of Jesus which is prompted by questions about the destruction of the temple. In that discourse the end of the temple and the destruction of Jerusalem are historical events to which the discussion of the end of history and the coming of the Son of man is tied (Matt. 24; Mark 13). Here, however, Luke separates the parousia (coming of the Son of man) from the fate of Jerusalem. This discourse is also free of references to cosmic convulsions and other signs of a final travail. The questions and issues here have to do with the coming of the kingdom and the sudden parousia of the Son of man.

The discussion in verses 20–37 has a double audience: the Pharisees ask Jesus when the kingdom of God is coming (vv. 20–21) and Jesus speaks to his disciples about the coming of the Son of man (vv. 22–37). The two parts of the discussion are related in vocabulary (both contain the expressions "Lo, here!" and "Lo, there!") and in the issue of the relation of the present to the future. It is no surprise that the Pharisees asked Jesus about the kingdom (reign) of God. All pious Jews, whether or not their beliefs included a Messiah, longed for the coming full reign of God. The reign of God meant different things to different people, but generally it conjured up images of peace, freedom, and prosperity. To ask when God's reign would come was to miss on two counts. First, human calculations about God's activity are futile, if not arrogant and irreverent. The subject is the reign *of God;* the when, where, and how are tucked away in God's own wisdom. Only human endeavors, which have such pleasing results as to be called the kingdom of God, can submit to human calendarizing. But the kingdom is not of human construction: "Fear not, little flock, for it is your Father's good pleasure to give you the kingdom" (12:32). The answer to the question of when is the same as that given by Jesus to his disciples when they asked if he would now restore the kingdom to Israel: "It is not for you to know times or seasons which the Father has fixed by his own authority" (Acts 1:6–7). Yet even an answer that clear, and by Jesus himself, has not prevented the continuing conversion of the Bible into an almanac and every news magazine into a gold mine of clues as to when. Predictions are made, some people are persuaded, tragedy and disappointment follow.

The second reason the question asked by the Pharisees misses the mark is that they seek signs of the kingdom's arrival while rejecting the only real signs available. Jesus had earlier said to them, "You know how to interpret the appearance of earth and sky; but why do you not know how to interpret the present time?" (12:56). The presence of Jesus is the presence of the kingdom. And the signs of it? The deaf hear, the lame walk, the dead are raised, and the poor have the good news preached to them. These conditions mark the presence of God's reign in the world. The kingdom, said Jesus, "is in the midst of you" (v. 21). The phrase can be translated "within you," but two factors persuade against it: the "you" is plural and the persons addressed have opposed rather than embraced the message of Jesus. The popularity of the translation "The kingdom of God is within you" is not related to the issue of a correct rendering of the text but rather to the preferences of a culture heavily psychologized whose premiums are on self-realization and the therapeutic values of religion. Extreme individualism and the subjective captivity of the gospel are conditions so prevailing in the churches as well as in society that the reader of these comments will undoubtedly already have thoughts on the matter that run far ahead of these sentences.

Jesus turns immediately to his disciples, Luke's arrangement of the material giving the impression that the disciples had overheard Jesus' response to the Pharisees. It is not sufficient to account for the location of these words (vv. 22–37) by the simple fact of some words in common with verses 20–21: "Lo, here!" and "Lo, there!" One gets the impression that Jesus realized his disciples could easily have misunderstood his words to the Pharisees. If the kingdom of God is in our midst, then is here and now all there is? Granted, some marvelous experiences have been made possible by the presence of Jesus: the poor, the maimed, the crippled, and the blind have found relief, but this has been but a beginning, the front edge, as it were, of the reign of God. So much pain, oppression, poverty, and grinding hardship remain; surely we will see its final eradication. Is there not to be a final consummation which has long been

205

associated with the coming of the Son of man? The Son of man was a heavenly figure in late apocalyptic Judaism who was to come in a final redemptive role (Dan. 7:13-14; cf. the article "Son of man" in *Harper's Bible Dictionary*). Perhaps the disciples are thinking that Jesus' answer to the Pharisees' question eliminates a future eschaton, a full arrival of that which we have experienced in Jesus as a foretaste.

In theological terms, the issue is called realized eschatology; that is, the kingdom of God is realized here and now. And, of course, there is genuine truth in this perspective. Jesus' words here at verse 21 say so. Both Paul and John speak often of the present benefits of life in Christ: we have been raised with Christ; we have passed out of death into life; whoever has the Son has eternal life; life eternal is to know God and to believe in the one whom God has sent. To fail to claim these present benefits is to sit among those who, whether out of sincerity, apathy, or irresponsibility, consider the kingdom postponed. These are the ones who say over every problem, every injustice, every scene of oppression, every case of human misery, "But when the Lord comes," or "But in heaven," or "In the sweet by and by." There is comfort here, to be sure, but there is also the unrealized abundance of life now, and, even more tragic, no initiatives are taken to alter the conditions in which misery and oppression continue. Just as believers can be overly invested in the future, they can also be too confined to the present in what some refer to as overrealized eschatology. Some New Testament scholars believe this latter position to have been widespread in the early church, including Luke's audience (Talbert, *Reading Luke*, pp. 167-169). Be that as it may, either view that denies the other breaks apart the kingdom formula: already and not yet, in our midst and still to come, has come and will come. Jesus' words to the Pharisees (vv. 20-21) and his words to his disciples (vv. 22-37) join to teach the reader the complete formula.

Yes, says Jesus, the Son of man will come, but it will not be when you first long for "one of the days of the Son of man," that is, the days of the Messiah, the last days, the messianic age. And the early Christians did long for that day; suffering ostracism, misunderstanding, false rumors, and physical abuse, they prayed "Maranatha!" ("Our Lord, come!" I Cor. 16:22). Jesus goes on to say, "You will not see it" (v. 22); that is, you will experience a delay of the parousia, a longer than expected wait for the coming of the Son of man. Needless to say, this delay would be especially painful to those who expected it immediately (19:11), and in time produced in some a flagging of zeal, discouragement, a collapse of morals, and an appetite for appealing heresies. The word of Jesus to his disciples, therefore, is a word of certainty about the parousia, but uncertainty as to when. In their anxious expectation they are not to be fooled by the calculators (v. 23). In fact, one event will certainly precede all others: the Son of man, here identified as Jesus, must first suffer and be rejected (v. 25). That very real fact must flavor all messianic expectation; as there can be no Easter without Good Friday, there can be no "second coming" without the first. To invest in the return of the Messiah while avoiding his journey to the cross is to choose a dazzling triumphalism that has nothing to do with the kingdom of God.

When will that day be? It will come with the suddenness of lightning and at a time when life seems to be proceeding normally, as in the days of Noah and of Lot. When it does come, one is to give oneself fully to it, not attempting to save life or property. Such attempts are self-defeating. After all, that event will be so decisive and final that it will separate two in bed or two at work (notice that some later manuscripts insert a v. 36, clearly a borrowing from Matt. 24:40).

And where will this take place (v. 37)? To the curious, the answer is no more satisfying than the answer to the question, When? Jesus responds with a proverb that echoes Job 39:26–30. Both the where and the when of the parousia will be known after it occurs, not before. It is after a prey is dead that one sees the gathering of vultures.

Two Parables on Prayer (18:1–14)

Before we move to consider these two parables, a few reminders to ourselves as interpreters are in order. First, the material before us is in parable form and therefore carries its own force to stir and provide the hearer to arrive at an interpretation. While some parables teach or confirm a teaching, others break up the soil of previous teaching and prepare for a new perspective. Therefore, as we saw in the discussion at 8:4–8, much of the meaning of a parable depends on the listener whose mind is teased into active thought. Just as these two parables probably existed separately and in other contexts, so a teacher or a preacher may extract the parables again and set

207

them in new contexts in order to hear them anew. For example, verses 2–5 and 10–13 are the parables proper, have their own integrity, and, when apart from the present context, can speak forcefully to a hearer. However, and as a second reminder to ourselves, we are, when interpreting Luke, obligated to pursue his understanding and use of the parables. This is to say that both immediate and larger contexts are key factors in our present consideration of these stories. A third and final reminder is that the proven literary artistry of Luke should predispose us to discern patterns in the location and arrangement of units within the Gospel, patterns that are themselves factors in interpretation. The reader owes this to Luke, even when units are placed side by side that on the surface seem unrelated to each other, the possibility of "reading in" what is not there notwithstanding.

One could say that Luke has joined these two parables because they both deal with the subject of prayer. This observation is true but insufficient. Upon a closer reading, it is evident that both parables are about God's vindication, that is, God's upholding, justifying, exonerating, and confirming. That this is the subject of both is somewhat concealed in the RSV which translates the same word "vindicate" in the first parable (vv. 3, 5, 7, 8) and "justify" in the second (v. 14). According to the first story, God will soon vindicate the saints, but in the second, it is not those who think of themselves as saints who are vindicated but those who confess they are sinners. This placing of seemingly contrasting stories back to back (vindication of saints/ vindication of sinners) recalls such an arrangement earlier in Luke. Two examples: in chapter 7 Luke moved directly from a story about Jesus and "a woman of the city" to a report about Jesus and women who participated in his ministry (8:1–3). In chapter 10 Luke joined two stories, one saying in effect "Go and do likewise" (the helpful Samaritan) and the other, "Sit still and listen" (Martha and Mary).

A final way of seeing the inner unity of verses 1–14 is contextual. In 17:22–37 Jesus had spoken of the coming of the Son of man and the longing of his disciples for that day (v. 22), a day that would bring final deliverance from the oppressive conditions under which they lived out their faith. How long will the Lord delay? In 18:1–8 that longing and its continuing disappointment are answered. However, a warning is issued to disciples who await the great eschatological reversal when rich and

208

poor, powerful and powerless, oppressor and oppressed switch places: be careful lest you yourselves become victims of that reversal. After all, the reversal will also include the self-righteous and sinners. This warning comes in verses 9–14. Such is the pattern and the movement of thought in 17:22—18:14.

As for the parables themselves, both are in Luke alone, and with both Luke provides introductory statements of purpose (vv. 1, 9) and closing commentary (vv. 6–8, 14). The first parable assumes an audience that has been taught to pray "Thy kingdom come" but has been experiencing persecution and hardship and as a result begins to "lose heart." By Luke's day, several generations had passed since Jesus had taught his disciples to pray, and enthusiasm and faithfulness can be eroded by time alone, as well as by suffering and abuse (Heb. 6:11–12; II Peter 3:11–14; Rev. 21:7). In this respect the disciples seemed not to have moved at all past the lament of their forebears:

> For thy sake we are slain all the day long,
>   and accounted as sheep for the slaughter.
> Rouse thyself! Why sleepest thou, O Lord?
> Awake! Do not cast us off for ever!
> Why dost thou hide thy face?
> Why dost thou forget our affliction and oppression?
>   Psalm 44:22–24

By means of the parable of the judge and the widow (an image of helplessness in that culture, easily victimized by the powerful), Jesus assures his followers that God "will vindicate them speedily" (v. 8). As in the parable of the steward caught cheating, the lesson here comes in a story involving a person not of commendable character. It is important therefore not to allow the interpretation to get trapped in a simple equation: the unjust judge = God. Rather, the movement of the parable is from the lesser to the greater: if a cruel judge will give way to the unrelenting pressure of the widow, how much more will God listen to the prayers of the saints? In this respect the parable here is quite similar to the parable of the friend at midnight (11:5–8). That having been said, it remains the unavoidable truth that both stories present prayer as continual and persistent, hurling its petitions against long periods of silence. The human experience is one of delay and honestly says as much, even while acknowledging the mystery of God's ways. Is the petitioner being hammered through long days and nights of

209

prayer into a vessel that will be able to hold the answer when it comes? We do not know. All we know in the life of prayer is asking, seeking, knocking, and waiting, trust sometimes fainting, sometimes growing angry. Persons of such a prayer life can only wonder at those who speak of prayer with the smiling facility of someone drawing answers from a hat. In a large gathering of persons concerned about certain unfair and oppressive conditions in our society, an elderly black minister read this parable and gave a one-sentence interpretation: "Until you have stood for years knocking at a locked door, your knuckles bleeding, you do not really know what prayer is." His and our encouragement comes not only in this parable but also in Jesus' own prayer life. Luke says Jesus sometimes prayed all night (6:12), and some ancient texts say of his praying on the night of his arrest: "And being in an agony he prayed more earnestly; and his sweat became like great drops of blood falling down upon the ground" (22:44).

Following the parable, Jesus poses his own question to disciples who have been asking him When? and Where? concerning the coming of the Son of man. When the Son of man does come, will he find faith still alive among us? It is those who endure who will rejoice at his coming; for others, it will be a day of darkness, not of light.

We have already noted how the parable of the Pharisee and the publican follows reasonably that of the judge and the widow and serves as an elaborated word of caution. It remains for us now to listen to it a bit more intently. Theologically, verses 9–14 present in parabolic form the central doctrine of God's justification of sinners and the ultimate failure of self-righteousness. This doctrine is most often associated with Pauline theology, but in fact, it is as old as the Garden of Eden, the tower of Babel, and Jonah's mission to Nineveh. In Luke's narrative, the essential thrust of this parable has been carried by the criticism of certain Pharisees that Jesus receives and eats with tax collectors and sinners (5:30; 7:29–30; 15:2). Here, however, the message is conveyed not by direct debate but by a favorite vehicle of Luke's, the reversal motif (1:51; 6:20–26; 16:19–31). While the not justified/justified verdict pertains to the present state of the two men, tones of the eschatological reversal can be clearly heard in the closing aphorism: The exalted will be humbled, the humble will be exalted (v. 14).

210

Without any question the parable was a shock to its first

listeners. If anyone within the community of Judaism would not go home from the temple justified, it would be a tax collector. Working for a foreign government collecting taxes from his own people, a participant in a cruel and corrupt system, politically a traitor, religiously unclean (cf. comments at 5:29–32), a publican was a reprehensible character. While his prayer is in the spirit of Psalm 51, his life is offensive. As for the Pharisee, his recitation of his performance is that of one exceeding the law's demands. His prayer of thanksgiving is a modification of a common rabbinic prayer ("I thank thee that I am not . . .") joined to the spirit and content of Ps. 17:3–5. He strikes us as arrogant, to be sure, but no one can doubt his disciplined adherence to the moral and ethical code of his faith. He is the faithful, dependable, tithing type who pay the salaries of ministers so they can preach on the parable of the Pharisee and the publican! For this parable to continue to speak with power, the preacher will need to find in our culture analogous characters. The Pharisee is not a venomous villain and the publican is not generous Joe the bartender or Goldie the good-hearted hooker. Such portrayals belong in cheap novels. If the Pharisee is pictured as a villain and the tax collector as a hero, then each gets what he deserves, there is no surprise of grace and the parable is robbed. In Jesus' story, what both receive is "in spite of," not "because of." When the two men are viewed in terms of character and community expectations, without labels or prejudice, the parable is still a shock, still carrying the power both to offend and to bless. But perhaps most important, the interpreter of this parable does not want to depict the characters in such a way that the congregation leaves the sanctuary saying, "God, I thank thee that I am not like the Pharisee." It is possible that the reversal could be reversed.

Children and the Kingdom (18:15–17)
(Matthew 19:13–15; Mark 10:13–16)

Those who are studying Luke using a synopsis such as *Gospel Parallels* will have noticed that at 18:15 Luke rejoins the order of the Markan narrative. However, Mark preceded this unit with Jesus' teaching on marriage and divorce, giving that Gospel a block of material on marriage, children, and possessions (the next unit). Luke's presentation of Jesus and the children immediately follows the parable of the Pharisee and the tax collector with its closing aphorism, "Every one who exalts

211

himself will be humbled, but he who humbles himself will be exalted" (v. 14). This unit about children and the kingdom, therefore, flows directly out of that aphorism. In fact, verses 15–17 could easily have begun with the words "For instance." This single purpose accounts for the way Luke has edited his Markan source. Luke has no need for the actual blessing of the children or for Jesus' indignation toward the disciples, elements of the story quite appropriate in Mark. Luke has found in the pronouncement at verse 17 the point he wishes to make and with it concludes his report: "Truly, I say to you, whoever does not receive the kingdom of God like a child shall not enter it." Verse 17 is another way of saying verse 14.

Those who brought the children to Jesus so that he might touch them had observed not only the blessing of his touch to others but also a quality in him that assured them of his love and care for children. Jesus' disciples either had not seen this quality in Jesus or perhaps did not think the time and place appropriate for such a ministry. Jerusalem lay ahead, controversies were afoot, Herod Antipas had threatened, and in the minds of the disciples the kingdom was very near (19:11). These are momentous days, tensions mount, and God's business is being conducted; therefore, remove the children. Investing time and attention on them brings no immediate dividend; children underfoot can delay the kingdom. Such may have been the kind of thinking that prompted the disciples to rebuke the parents. Yet whatever their thoughts, the rebuke itself reveals how far the disciples are from understanding the nature of the kingdom and the truth of 18:14 and 17. Merit and achievement, two words not applicable to small children, are apparently very much in the disciples' minds as they think about God's kingdom. Luke's account dramatically accents Jesus' lesson about the kingdom and that one receives it without claim or boast, without recitals of deeds or gifts, by saying that the children brought to Jesus were infants. The minister will therefore be careful not to commit the common error of saying we are to become as children (the text does not say that) and then cataloging all the beautiful qualities of children which we should emulate. These are infants! And beyond that, if children possessed all the qualities that pertain to the kingdom (humility, dependence, trust, love, etc.), then they would *merit* the kingdom, which totally contradicts the point Jesus is making. Infants come with nothing and thus receive; to hear that and to say that is enough.

212

The Rich and the Kingdom (18:18–30)
(Matthew 19:16–30; Mark 10:17–31)

In this unit Luke continues the commentary on verse 14, the exalted will be humbled and the humble exalted. This is now Luke's third lesson on that text: those proud by reason of their association with Jesus are taught by Jesus' embrace of the infants; now those proud by reason of wealth are about to be taught. All three Synoptics say the man was rich; Matthew says he was young; Luke says he was a ruler (perhaps of a synagogue): hence the composite, "a rich young ruler."

We do not know what prompted the ruler's question. There is no attempt at entrapment; that he called Jesus "good," a designation Jesus rejects, need not be taken as ingratiating flattery to disarm Jesus. Mark says the man knelt, having run to come to Jesus (Mark 10:17), prompting many to comment about the man's desperate state and the emptiness of riches in the life of one still searching for a satisfied and peaceful heart. There is nothing of that here. Luke says that the man became sad upon learning that he could not have both his money and eternal life (v. 23). He may have come merely for confirmation that eternal life was his, especially if his theology was of the type that took prosperity to be evidence of God's favor (cf. comments at 16: 14–31). But whatever the motivation, the man's problems become evident at two points. First, his question is flawed. He asks, "What shall I do to inherit eternal life?" (v. 18). Notice the combination of "do" and "inherit"; they are contradictory. One "does" in order to earn, not to inherit. Already there appears in him a mind-set contrary to Jesus' words in verses 14 and 17. Second, while there is no reason to doubt that the ruler had kept from his youth the commandments Jesus recites, it soon is clear that there is one he has not kept, the first and foundation command in the Decalogue: "You shall have no other gods before me" (Ex. 20:3). The ruler belongs to a tradition that had been told that life and blessing in the land would be theirs if they loved God and obeyed God's commands. However, if they worshiped other gods, theirs would not be life but death, not blessing but a curse (Deut. 30:15–20).

Jesus knows the condition of the man and writes the prescription for life, a prescription we have met frequently in Luke, perhaps most forcefully at 12:33. The ruler is invited to trust God completely, but he cannot or, rather, will not. He is no longer in the position of being bedazzled and enticed by the

213

prospect of wealth; he has lain too long in silken ease, fared too well at banquet tables, rested too comfortably on the security of his surplus, moved too far from the cries of the hungry, enjoyed too obviously the envy of those less prosperous, assumed too much that he could buy everything he needed. He depends on his money. In short, he is an idolater. His encounter with Jesus ends sadly, because, upon the realization that he cannot serve God and mammon, he has chosen mammon. It is most likely not the case that there was ever a time or place when he said to himself, "I choose mammon over God"; experience and observation teach us that his condition is one to which people awaken after years of the creeping spread of materialism. Earlier he might have extricated himself, but now he is "very rich."

Luke does not say the man went away (Mark 10:22) but only that Jesus enlarged upon the sad case before him and said, not solely to him but to those nearby who could overhear, "How hard it is for the rich." The statement sounds more like an observation than a regulation. A camel going through the eye of a needle (v. 25) is a proverb about the humanly impossible and not a description of a camel, stripped of his burden, crawling through a small gate. The question from bystanders is a proper one: How can anyone be saved, since all of us participate to a lesser or a greater extent in the love of money which afflicts this ruler? The answer is the same one given to Abraham and Sarah when they were told that they would have a child, the same one given to the Virgin Mary as she stood in awe and bewilderment: nothing is impossible with God. Only God can save, whatever one's condition.

The disciples are not uninterested in this discussion, to put it mildly. They have invested a great deal in this venture with Jesus, and Peter says so in a statement that is half question, half reminder (v. 28). Jesus answers Peter and all who will hear that anyone who detaches himself or herself from life's primary relations for the sake of God's kingdom will find abundantly more attachments (possibly a reference to the community of believers) in this life as well as life eternal in the new age. It is important to note that in Luke there is no mention of houses and lands in the rewards of this life. Both Mark and Matthew include houses and lands a hundredfold (Mark 10:30; Matt. 19 :29). For Luke, the abundant and multiplied blessings for the dedicated disciple are all in terms of relationships (v. 29), and

214

the history of the church as the family of God confirms the fulfillment of this promise. Those who have interpreted the Christian life as a materialist success story find no support in the Gospel of Luke.

Luke 18:31—19:28
From the Final Prediction of the Passion Until the Entry Into Jerusalem

Prior to his account of Jesus' entry into Jerusalem, Luke will relate four events in the ministry of Jesus: the final prediction of the passion (18:31–34), healing a blind man near Jericho (18:35–43), dining with Zacchaeus at Jericho (19:1–10), and telling the parable of the pounds to those who thought arrival at Jerusalem meant the arrival of the kingdom (19:11–28). This section begins and ends with the expression "going up to Jerusalem." We are again given a geographical marker, Jericho, but this time it really does give us a clue to the progress of the journey. Jericho was the last town of significance before one left the Jordan Valley to make the ascent to Jerusalem. Since Jesus is moving toward the city in a large crowd of pilgrims (18:36; 19:3), one needs little imagination to sense the expectations, the arguments over the nature of the kingdom, the confusion, the rumors, and the predictions of what will happen once they arrive in the Holy City.

The Final Prediction of the Passion (18:31–34)
(Matthew 20:17–19; Mark 10:32–34)

To the Twelve, Jesus says that the journey signaled at 9:51, already having been discussed by Jesus with Moses and Elijah on the mountain (9:31), is near completion. In this final prophecy of his passion, details are added. That Jesus' death and resurrection were according to the law and the prophets was dramatized in the conversation with Moses and Elijah at the transfiguration and stated repeatedly in both the Gospel and Acts (24:25, 27, 44; Acts 3:18; 8:32–35; 13:27; 26:23). In addition to specifics of Jesus' shameful treatment, Luke for the first time implicates the Gentiles. In fact, no reference is made here to

215

religious authorities. No doubt, Luke is looking back on the event, with the conspiring of Herod Antipas and Pontius Pilate and the participation by both Jews and Gentiles in Jesus' death. Following Pentecost, the Christian preachers will announce that even the details of Jesus' death fulfilled what the Holy Spirit said through David:

> Why did the Gentiles rage,
> and the peoples imagine vain things? . . .
> And the rulers were gathered together,
> against the Lord and against his Anointed.
> Psalm 2:1–2 as quoted
> in Acts 4:25–26

As for these details of the passion, notice that there are six statements of mistreatment, suffering, and death, and only one about the resurrection. This apparent imbalance is not due to a love of the tragic but rather to a recognition that the suffering and death of Jesus constituted the major faith problem for Jesus' followers and the major theological problem in the proclamation that Jesus of Nazareth was God's Messiah. If there is a tendency toward denial in every death, this was especially so in the case of Jesus. Whole theologies were built around denials of his death: Simon of Cyrene was mistakenly crucified instead of Jesus; the vinegar offered to Jesus contained a drug and he only appeared to be dead; and so the stories went. Modern denials take the form of huge Easter services without acknowledgment of Good Friday. In the ancient church, the denials were answered by a return to the insistence of texts like Luke 18:31–34 in the Apostles' Creed: "Suffered under Pontius Pilate, was crucified, dead, and buried."

One final note about 18:31–34: Luke says not only that "they understood none of these things" but also that "this saying was hid from them." The combination recalls the similar mixture in Exodus: "Pharaoh hardened his heart" and "God hardened Pharaoh's heart." Logic breaks down in the Bible's struggle to relate human failure and divine purpose. Luke is not reticent to see God's hand in both not seeing and seeing by the disciples. At 9:45 and 24:16 similar statements are made. In Luke's theology, what is really going on in Jesus' death and resurrection is not grasped by human intelligence but comes by revelation. That revelation must now wait until after the resurrection. At that time the risen Christ will open the eyes and

216

minds of the disciples, not only to who he is but to the fact that his passion fulfills the Scriptures (24:16, 25–27, 31–32, 44–45).

Healing the Blind Man Near Jericho (18:35–43)
(Matthew 20:29–34; Mark 10:46–52)

Luke follows "But they understood none of these things; this saying was hid from them, and they did not grasp what was said" (v. 34) with a story that demonstrates Jesus' power to open the eyes of the blind. There is no reason to take this story as a rebuke of the Twelve; rather, it is prophecy and promise of what Jesus will do for them (24:31–32, 44–45). Jesus had begun his ministry with an announcement that he would give sight to the blind (4:18), and the fact of such a ministry was offered to John the Baptist as partial evidence on which to make a judgment as to whether Jesus was the Messiah (7:22). It is striking that in the story before us, Jesus opens the eyes of a man who can already see. The blind beggar calls Jesus "Son of David," that is, Messiah. In this sense he can see what the crowd cannot, for the crowd, in its rebuke of him (v. 39), revealed its own blindness. In that this account speaks of the blind seeing and those with sight being blind, there is a kinship to John's story of Jesus healing a blind man (John 9).

The reader recognizes, of course, that more is going on there than simply Jesus enabling a blind beggar to see flowers and trees and the faces of family and friends, remarkable as that is. On another level Jesus opens the eyes of the blind. Jesus is hailed as Messiah; the beggar is declared to be "well" (v. 42; recall that the word also means "saved," 17:11–19, and will be so used in the next story, 19:1–10); the beggar becomes a disciple, following Jesus to Jerusalem; the beggar glorifies God (again, recall 17:11–19). Luke 18:35–43 is thus both a healing and a salvation story. In addition, the event anticipates the entry into Jerusalem. This is evident not only in the proximity of Jericho to Jerusalem but also in the swelling crowds both in front of and behind Jesus, in the hailing of Jesus as Messiah, and in glorifying and praising God.

By way of anticipation, the reader might well hold the title "Son of David" in solution, for it is both true and problematic for Jesus. We will, at 20:41–44, discuss this issue, because Jesus himself raises the question, "How can they say that the Christ is David's son?" However, at this point we should keep in mind that the blind beggar's words "Jesus, Son of David" are not

217

unambiguously positive. On one hand, Luke is clear that Jesus is of the house and lineage of David (2:4). Luke affirms this both in the birth story and in the inspired songs prior to Jesus' birth (1:32, 69). But on the other hand, the image of Jesus as being like David and sitting on David's throne can stir hopes political and military and give to the confession "Jesus is the Messiah" meanings quite at odds both with the nature of Jesus' ministry and with the fact of his crucifixion. For Luke to say or to confirm that Jesus is the son of David is one thing; for a crowd of Galilean pilgrims or for a gathering of political activists to say it is quite another. What words mean is tied to who says them and under what circumstances. Consider, for example, the words, "His blood be on us and on our children!" (Matt. 27:25). Hear those words as those of an angry crowd willing to assume responsibility for Jesus' death, and then hear them as a prayer of penitent sinners. The difference is as great as the difference between "Jesus, Son of David" and "Jesus, Son of David."

Salvation Brought to Zacchaeus (19:1–10)

We have come so far with Luke that his stories echo in our memories previous stories. The account of Jesus and Zacchaeus in Jericho, found only in Luke, recalls the immediately preceding story of the blind beggar. Though one is very poor and the other very rich, both are blessed with salvation (18:42; 19:9, 10). The reader is also reminded of an earlier encounter between Jesus and a rich man (18:18–30), that one, however, ending sadly. Perhaps more precisely, Luke 19:1–10 recalls and almost repeats the account of Jesus and Levi (5:27–32). In both stories Jesus is dealing with a tax collector, is a guest in the publican's home, is criticized for his association with such a person, and in conclusion offers a pronouncement. A review of the comments at 5:27–32 or of the article "publican" in *Harper's Bible Dictionary* will refresh one's memory about the radicality of Jesus' act toward a tax collector. That Zacchaeus was a "chief tax collector" (v. 2; the term appears nowhere else in Greek literature) implicates him more deeply in the corrupt tax system of the Roman government. In a corrupt system the loftier one's position, the greater one's complicity in that system. While nothing of the private life of Zacchaeus is revealed in the story, this much we know on principle: no one can be privately righteous while participating in and profiting from a program that robs and crushes other persons. Such dichotomous thinking has been

218

a blight on the church throughout its history, especially in those times and places in which individualism has dominated over community and the sense of being members of one another.

This is not to say that Zacchaeus is without qualities on which a disciple's life can be built. His intense desire to see Jesus, overcoming the risk of ridicule and embarrassment, is fundamental to the happy conclusion of the story. Apparently he has heard and believes that Jesus really is "a friend of tax collectors and sinners" (7:34). Whether or not he had found the personal, social, and religious price of his wealth too high, we do not know. What we do know is that he extended hospitality to Jesus, and as a result of their meeting he goes beyond the law's requirement for restitution. Voluntary restitution called for a return of the original amount plus 20 per cent (Lev. 6:5; Num. 5:7); compulsory restitution called for doubling the original amount and, in some cases, repaying fourfold or fivefold (Ex. 22:1, 3–4; II Sam. 12:6). Some scholars, thinking that Zacchaeus' offer of restitution dulls the edge of radical grace and gives the impression of trying to earn forgiveness, have suggested that verse 8 may be a later addition as instruction to Christians about the meaning of the fruits of repentance. Such speculation is properly motivated theologically, but the story can be read another way. Zacchaeus' offer of half his possessions to the poor and a generous restitution to anyone he may have cheated can be seen as itself evidence of the radicality of grace and the power of Jesus' good news to him. After all, Luke's gospel of grace is joined to repentance, and repentance is not solely a transaction of the heart. Repentance bears fruit: this was made clear as early as the preaching of John the Baptist when crowds and soldiers and tax collectors came to him and asked, "What shall we do?" (3:10–14).

Luke 19:1–10 is therefore a story of the salvation of a man who was rich (all things are possible with God, 18:27) and a tax collector. His life-style and the resultant treatment by community and synagogue had not moved him beyond the reach of God's seeking love. He was as much a son of Abraham (v. 9) as the woman possessed of a spirit of infirmity for eighteen years was a daughter of Abraham (13:16). And if he is a child of Abraham, so are they all, including those who murmured against Jesus; and as children of Abraham they need the grace of God as much as Zacchaeus does. The words of John the Baptist return and speak as appropriately as ever: "Bear fruits

219

that befit repentance, and do not begin to say to yourselves, 'We have Abraham as our father'; for I tell you, God is able from these stones to raise up children to Abraham" (3:8). That salvation came to "this house" is probably a reference to the family and servants; the concept of household salvation is an important one for Luke (Acts 10:2; 11:14; 16:15–31; 18:8). Interestingly enough, the expression "to save the lost" became widely used in the church, although "the lost" is a very rare term. It occurs here and in the parables of the sheep, the coin, and the father (15:6, 24, 32). However, the popular use of the phrase "to save the lost" has been much more narrow than in Luke. One hears it almost exclusively in terms of a conversion and often in an even more restricted sense of "preserving a soul for heaven." Here in the case of Zacchaeus, his "being saved" refers to a conversion, to be sure, but not in any private sense. Not only is his household involved but also the poor who will be beneficiaries of his conversion as well as all those people whom he may have defrauded. His salvation, therefore, has personal, domestic, social, and economic dimensions. In addition, we should not forget that in other stories "saved" is translated "made well," "healed," and "made whole." Luke would object to confining the word to a condition of the soul. The whole of life is affected by Jesus' ministry, a foretaste of the complete reign of God. The closing pronouncement (v. 10) makes it clear: Jesus' visit in Zacchaeus' house was not a delay or a detour on his journey to Jerusalem; this was and is the very purpose of the journey. "The Son of man came to seek and to save the lost."

The Parable of the Pounds (19:11–28)
(Matthew 25:14–30)

In a manner typical of Luke, the parable is prefaced with an interpretive introduction (v. 11). According to verse 11, Jesus tells this parable to correct two misunderstandings. First, some in his following thought that the kingdom would appear immediately, that all the benefits, the freedom, the joy, the peace which they associated with the phrase "the kingdom of God" was about to be theirs. In fact, however, what they are soon to experience is Jesus "going away," and not until his return would the reign of God be complete. Second, some thought that somehow Jerusalem is the key to the kingdom's arrival. As we shall see, Jerusalem is central for Luke in the unfolding of God's purpose for Israel and the nations. It will *begin* in Jerusalem,

220

but what Jesus is about will not *end* in Jerusalem. Therefore his followers are not to take what will soon transpire in the city as final; a chapter will end, but not the story. The story will continue: "Stay in the city, until you are clothed with power from on high," and then the good news will be preached to the nations, "beginning from Jerusalem" (24:49, 47). Luke is probably also saying to the church of his time that they should not associate events in Jerusalem (the fall of the city and destruction of the temple in 70 C.E.) with the coming of the Son of man and the end of all things. As Jesus will say at 21:5–36, the end will not come until the time of witnessing to the nations is complete. Jerusalem was so vital in the memory and the hope of these people that it was natural for them to give eschatological interpretations to all major and critical events that occurred there. Again and again some Jews and some Christians were to observe the state of the Holy City and say, "Lo, here!" and "Lo, there!"

The parable of the pounds is not as familiar to the church as its "similar but different" parallel, the parable of the talents (Matt. 25:14–30). The reasons are not difficult to find; one has only to read this parable. There are two story lines: in the one, a nobleman goes away to receive the title and crown of king. However, some citizens hated him and sent delegates to prevent the coronation. When the new king returned, he had those citizens destroyed. That is a story complete in itself, although many would question that it is a parable, since it echoes contemporary history in Palestine. Archelaus, a son of Herod the Great, upon his father's death went to Rome to be crowned his father's successor. So despised was Archelaus that a Jewish embassy of fifty persons went to Rome to protest. Archelaus was not made king but ruled only over Judea, and only for a brief time (the story is told by the Jewish historian Josephus. Cf. Talbert, *Reading Luke*, p. 178). The second story line is about a nobleman going away, entrusting to ten servants ten pounds (a pound was a mina, in the Greek-Syrian monetary system worth about 100 drachmas or about three months' wages for a laborer) to be traded in profitable ways. Those who did so were richly rewarded; the one who did not was relieved of the one pound, but no other punishment is mentioned (unlike Matt. 25:30).

Some scholars are of the opinion that we have here not one parable but two, or at least fragments of two now combined awkwardly into one. Whether there were at one time two para-

221

bles combined by Luke or already joined in his source, we do not know for certain. What we do know is that in a passage that Luke calls a parable (v. 11) are two stories so joined as to be like two small trees that are so intertwined in their growth as to appear from a distance to be a single tree. But why two stories in one? A reasonable theory might be found in the nature of the audience. Luke says, "As they heard these things" (v. 11), the "they" being ambiguous. We know the Twelve are with Jesus, as is a crowd excited by but not committed to Jesus. Perhaps Jesus tells a double parable, within it a message to each group. Every preacher knows the situation: before the pulpit sit the faithful as well as those who visit now and then but without knowledge of or investment in the mission of the congregation. With the hope that no violence to the text will be done, we will look twice at the parable with its message to two audiences.

To the larger not-yet-disciple audience Jesus gives a corrective and a warning. The corrective is that he is not going up to the city to claim the throne; rather, he is going away but will return in kingly power. The warning is that for those who refuse his lordship, who reject the reign of God begun in the ministry but finalized at the parousia, the coming of the Son of man will be judgment and not joy, death and not life. This stern message will be repeated, both in lament (19:41–44) and in parable (20:9–18). The word is a harsh one, to be sure, but who is being rejected, what offer is being refused? It is God who is being rejected, God's favor which is being refused. This is not being said from a christological view which equates Jesus and God and, therefore, to reject Jesus is to reject God. Rather, it is to say that the ministry of Jesus, from his first announcement in Nazareth (4:16–30) and in every encounter with sinners, tax collectors, Pharisees, the poor, the rich, lepers, children, demoniacs, Gentiles, and women, reveals and demonstrates the mind and will of God for the world and what life is under the reign of God. And soon his death will confirm that God's seeking love does not stop short or quit but continues through suffering all the way to death. The resurrection of Jesus will confirm and vindicate not only Jesus but this presentation of God's way toward the world. To refuse this in favor of power plays, prosperity, vengeance against enemies, positions of authority, and a swelling spirit of dominance in the world is, to repeat, to reject God. What else remains?

222

The word to the disciples in the parable (allegory?) is a call for faithfulness and accountability in the interim between the departure and the return of the Lord. Disciples are not charged with keeping safe what was entrusted to them; they are to multiply it. Doubtless this refers to the spread of the word, or in Luke's own language, "The word of God grew and multiplied" (Acts 12:24). Risks were involved, to be sure; no one makes ten pounds from one, or five pounds from one, without some risk. It takes courage to witness in the world, for the gospel has its enemies. Even the third servant (called "another," v. 20; a principle of good storytelling dictates against reciting the reports of all ten servants), cautious and fearful, could have made some gains through safe steps, but silence and inactivity are inexcusable when the business is so urgent and the commission so clear (v. 13). The aphorism that closes this part of the parable (v. 26) may originally have been a cynical observation about the inequities of life ("Them that has, gets"), but its frequent appearance in Jesus' teachings (8:18; Matt. 13: 12; 25:29; Mark 4:24–25) implies that it is an operative principle in the reign of God. Experience confirms the truth of it.

Reference to Jerusalem concludes this unit (v. 28), just as it began it (v. 11). In fact, verse 28, "And when he had said this, he went on ahead, going up to Jerusalem," concludes the major section of Luke we refer to as the travel narrative, a section that began at 9:51: "When the days drew near for him to be received up, he set his face to go to Jerusalem." Behind Jesus and the Twelve are Galilee and its synagogues, its table talk and sermons in open country, its seaside audiences, and its desperately poor and ill pressing upon him at Sabbath sunset. Now they have reached Jerusalem with its temple, with its chief priests and elders, and with Pontius Pilate who comes on major feast days from his permanent quarters in Caesarea, with ample military support, in case national fervor and religious fanaticism threaten the Roman peace.

PART FIVE

The Ministry in Jerusalem

LUKE 19:29—21:38

This block of material begins with Jesus' entry into Jerusalem and concludes with the summary statement about Jesus' public ministry in the temple area (21:37-38). The next section opens with Jesus observing Passover with his disciples, the opening event of the passion narrative. Luke 19:29—21:38 will generally follow Mark 11:1—13:37, with such modifications as we have come now to expect from Luke. One major difference between Luke and the other Synoptics which will unfold clearly from this point through the end of the Gospel is the central importance of Jerusalem and the temple for Luke's understanding of the fulfillment of prophecy, the completion of Jesus' ministry, and the mission of the church (24:44-53; Acts 1:1-14). In Mark and Matthew one senses that had Jesus not been killed in Jerusalem, he would have returned to Galilee. In fact, the risen Christ tells his disciples to meet him in Galilee (Mark 14:28; 16:7; Matt. 26:32; 28:7). However, in Luke, Jerusalem is his destination and the disciples are to remain there until they receive the Holy Spirit. As to how long Jesus ministered in Jerusalem, we do not know. The church has compressed the ministry, the passion, and the resurrection into a period of eight days, Palm or Passion Sunday to Easter. There are indications, however, of a longer period (19:47; 22:53). Some scholars have considered the celebration at the time of Jesus' entry, as described by the other Evangelists but not Luke, to belong to the Jewish Feast of Tabernacles which occurs in the autumn. Such a chronology would have Jesus in Jerusalem from Tabernacles

to Passover, or roughly November until April. Again the brevity
of our Gospel records leaves us without answers to many questions that grow out of our historical curiosity.

Luke 19:29–48
The Entry Into Jerusalem

Jesus' arrival at Jerusalem and his entrance into the city are
related by Luke in three units: the entry itself (vv. 29–40), the
lament over the city (vv. 41–44), and the cleansing of the temple (vv. 45–46). The first and third units are paralleled in all the
other Gospels and are vivid in the church's ministry. What the
church remembers, however, are composites of the entry and
the cleansing, made up of details drawn without distinction
from the four Evangelists. The reader of Luke therefore should
be prepared for the difficulty of attending to Luke's account
without details which the memory wants to bring from the
other sources.

The Entry (19:29–40)
(Matthew 21:1–9; Mark 11:1–10; John 12:12–16)

The scene opens at the Mount called Olivet, near the villages of Bethany and Bethphage, less than two miles east of the
city. The Mount of Olives had strong eschatological associations
(Zech. 14:4–5), but most likely Luke is not tapping that resource
here; after all, he has just said that the end is not yet (v. 11).
Sending two disciples ahead to make preparation recalls the
beginning of the journey to Jerusalem (9:51–52). Luke would
probably have us understand that the colt was owned by a
disciple of Jesus and that Jesus is operating, not according to a
prearranged plan, but according to divine knowledge. For sacred purposes animals were used that had not previously been
employed in other service (I Sam. 6:7).

Several features in Luke's account of this event call for close
attention. First, notice that the entry involves Jesus and his
disciples. Disciples secure the colt, disciples place Jesus on the
colt, disciples called him the King who comes in the name of the
Lord (Luke only echoes Zech. 9:9; Matthew and John both
quote the prophecy). There is no ovation by the general crowds

226

that are in the city for the festival (Matt. 21:9) or by those who had gathered because of reports about the raising of Lazarus (John 12:12); Jesus is honored and praised by his followers. This is not the group which turns cold and later calls for Jesus' crucifixion. His disciples did not fully understand his messiahship, to be sure, but neither are they persons who sing praise and scream death the same week. The portrait of such a fickle crowd must come from some account other than Luke's. The story as Luke tells it is less crowded and more subdued, but it is an event of and for believers, and its meaning lies in Jesus and in their faith in him, meaning that is in no way related to public favor or disfavor, participation or nonparticipation. This is not to say Jesus' followers have come to clarity and maturity; the events soon to transpire will test them, and some will fail. But at this moment, descending the Mount of Olives, they are right.

Second, Luke's account contains no mention of hosannas, of palms, or of branches cut from trees. Those belonged to parades and festivals with nationalistic overtones, and Luke apparently wants this event to carry no such implication. Perhaps this is also the reason the bursts of praise contain no references to David or to the Davidic throne. The word "King" is used (v. 38), but it seems to be without political force. In fact, the expressions of praise to the King join Ps. 118:26 and the words of the heavenly host at the birth of Jesus (2:14). "King" is placed beside "Peace"; there is nothing here to support the charge against him before Pilate (23:2).

Finally, a feature of the episode peculiar to Luke's account is the objection by some Pharisees to the activity of the disciples (v. 39). We cannot, of course, know in what tone of voice or with what motivation the Pharisees asked Jesus to rebuke his disciples. Perhaps they feared that calling Jesus King would be misinterpreted and create political repercussions. If so, their reason might have been from self-interest; that is, let us not upset the Romans and lose what few benefits we now have. Or their reason might have been concern for Jesus' safety. After all, they had warned Jesus earlier about the threat of Herod (13:31). Of course, the Pharisees could simply be registering their own disagreement or disbelief. But whatever their problem with the activity, Jesus simply responds in a vivid image to affirm the rightness and appropriateness of his disciples' praise. "If these were silent, the very stones would cry out" (v. 40). In other words, some things simply must be said; the disciples are ex-

227

pressing what is ultimately and finally true; God will provide a witness though every mouth be stopped; opposition to Christian witness cannot succeed; and the truth will come out, it cannot long be silenced. That stones would shout is, of course, a figure of speech, but the expression does remind us that in biblical understanding, the creation is involved in events that we tend to think affect humans alone. Genesis says that the sin of Adam and Eve caused the earth to produce thorns and thistles; Isaiah sings of a reign of peace on earth when cows and bears will graze together and the lion and the lamb will lie down side by side; Matthew says a special star appeared to announce Jesus' birth, and that the earth shuddered, cracking rocks, when he died; and all the Synoptists agree that when Jesus was put on the cross, for three hours there was an eclipse of the sun. All this dramatic language reminds us of that which we sometimes forget: all life is from God, the whole universe shares together bane and blessing, life and death, and in the final reign of God "the creation itself will be set free from its bondage to decay and obtain the glorious liberty of the children of God" (Rom. 8:21). Of course, if we are silent, the stones will cry out.

Jesus Laments Over the City (19:41–44)

The disciples have hardly finished their song, "Peace in heaven and glory in the highest!" when Jesus looks up, sees the city before him, and weeps, "Would that even today you knew the things that make for peace!" (v. 42). The city is blind to its own need for repentance and forgiveness of sin (the substance of the gospel in Luke-Acts, 24:47) and to the fact that in Jesus God has visited the city with an offer of peace (v. 44). The offer was rejected and Israel chose to take up arms against Rome. Outbreaks of violence occurred intermittently until the open war which brought about the fall of the city and the destruction of the temple in the year 70 C.E. By the time Luke wrote, that war was history, and Luke draws upon that history in the description of how the Romans took Jerusalem (vv. 43–44). The lament also draws upon Isa. 29:3 specifically and the tragic scenes in Jeremiah 6 which portray the end of Jerusalem as the punishment of God. It is evident here that Luke interprets the fall of Jerusalem as directly related to its rejection of Jesus.

228

Verses 42–44 are called a lament, and so they are. The Bible is no stranger to laments: the psalmist laments, prophets lament, God laments. They are not so frequent in the New Testament, although the painful beauty of Revelation 18 is hardly surpassed anywhere in Scripture. That Jesus laments over Jerusalem is a clear revelation of his character, for a lament is complex in its nature, and it may be that not everyone is capable of such expression. A lament is a voice of love and profound caring, of vision of what could have been and of grief over its loss, of tough hope painfully releasing the object of its hope, of personal responsibility and frustration, of sorrow and anger mixed, of accepted loss but with energy enough to go on. The preacher or the teacher when dealing with this text may have to reach back of our overused "to cry" and return to the old English "to weep" in the effort to communicate the depth of passion present in Jesus.

Jesus in the Temple (19:45–48)
(Matthew 21:10–17; Mark 11:11, 15–17; John 2:13–22)

We have reflected often on the importance of the temple for Luke, the only New Testament writer to view positively this institution. Luke begins his Gospel with Zechariah in the temple, concludes it with the disciples in the temple, opens Acts with Christians attending the temple together every day, and presents Paul, so much viewed as the rebel, praying in the temple and there receiving a revelation that he preach to the Gentiles. It is no surprise, then, that Luke's account of the cleansing is the briefest of the four, for in Luke there is no hint that what Jesus did was a blow announcing the end of the temple and its services. He purifies it in order that it can be the place of his own ministry of teaching (v. 47). The sequence of cleansing and then ministering comes from Mal. 3:1–4:

> And the Lord whom you seek will suddenly come to his temple; the messenger of the covenant in whom you delight, behold, he is coming, says the LORD of hosts. But who can endure the day of his coming, and who can stand when he appears?
> For he is like a refiner's fire and like fullers' soap . . . and he will purify the sons of Levi. . . . Then the offering of Judah and Jerusalem will be pleasing to the LORD.

Therefore excesses in the system and not the system itself come under Jesus' attack. What those excesses were we can only surmise. "To drive out those who sold" can mean that the corruption lay in the exchange of Roman coins for coins acceptable in the sacred precincts. Or perhaps exorbitant prices were asked

229

for the birds and animals available and priest-approved for sacrifice. In either case, or in both, pilgrims in the city for worship were an easy mark for the greedy. Worshipers had no recourse; there was only one temple. As for the temple being a house of prayer and not a den of thieves, see Isa. 56:7 and Jer. 7:11.

The reader of Luke 19:45–46 cannot move on as though having read what is simply a historical note: Jesus purged the temple in Jerusalem. That is true enough, but what is also true is that Jesus is acting in the name of God toward an institution of his own people, an institution dedicated to the worship of God. What has happened to the temple? What happens to all institutions of lofty, even divine purpose? The temple itself is both a necessity and a danger: a necessity in that people need a place and a means for coming before God appropriately; a danger in that no institution can claim to house God. Solomon said as much at the dedication of the first temple, almost apologizing to the God whom neither heaven nor earth can contain. In the course of time, people give to the ministers at the temple more authority than they have the character to handle and tend to confuse the place with the God of this and every place. There is no regular procedure for self-criticism and so servants become officials, ministers become religious authorities, self-interests call for perpetuation, and the costs of maintenance demand new fiscal policies. Gradually a beautiful place and its witness to the sovereignty of God loses its way, until someone comes along who loves both God and the temple enough to purify it.

By saying at verse 47 that Jesus was teaching every day in the temple prior to the statement of opposition to him, Luke seems to be softening, if not removing, a direct connection between the cleansing of the temple and any plot on Jesus' life (as Mark does, 11:15–19). More likely, the total act of purification and then making the temple the seat of his ministry is the ground for hostility. The opposition to the point of seeking Jesus' death is led by the chief clergy of the temple in league with certain scribes and "principal men of the people" (v. 47; perhaps these are elders who belong to the Sanhedrin, the supreme council). For the time being, however, Jesus is safe, cushioned from their threats by his popularity with the large crowds.

Luke 20:1—21:4
Controversies in Jerusalem

Having stated at 19:47 that chief priests, scribes, and principal men of the people (elders at 20:1) sought to destroy Jesus, Luke now proceeds to fill in the substance of their opposition. In doing so, he follows closely one of his sources, Mark 11:27—12:44. There is no reason to consider these controversies as being related in chronological order. For example, Luke opens with the rather general "one day" (v. 1), that is, during his time in Jerusalem. To attempt to arrange on specific days of "Holy Week" the events that follow (prior to Thursday evening, the time of the Passover meal) is both futile and unimportant. The appropriate uses of these texts during this season of the church year is a liturgical matter and not one of historical reconstruction. What is important is that the reader be careful to discern what the issues are and who is asking the questions. A generalized and undiscriminating feeling of "Jews against Jesus," found rather widely in the churches, is to be avoided as unfair to Judaism, to Christianity, to Jesus, to Luke, and to ourselves.

The Question of Authority (20:1-8)
(Matthew 21:23-27; Mark 11:27-33)

The place of Jesus' ministry in Jerusalem is now established: the temple. Much more than Mark or Matthew, Luke will locate the activity of Jesus here. The nature of Jesus' ministry has long been established: he is teaching and preaching good news to the people. Jesus has not shifted into a different mode, as though he had a Jerusalem strategy. The audience for Jesus' ministry has changed in only one respect: he has a new group of opponents, and the opposition has a new intensity. With Pharisees, Jesus argued matters of law, tradition, and propriety; with the chief priests and their associates he is faced not only with those issues but also with the question of "turf." Priests were of the family of Levi and hence were genealogically established, chosen by God as a tribe to minister at the altar. The temple was their appointed place of religious exercise and authority. The temple is not a synagogue with its lay participation and invitation for

231

persons in attendance to speak to the assembly. The temple is totally in the hands of the clergy and the clergy-appointed. Jesus is now in their territory, not functioning as a priest, to be sure, but teaching and preaching in their precinct.

"By what authority?" is a proper question. By "these things you are doing" the interrogators are probably referring to the act of cleansing the temple as well as the teaching and preaching. The question is a larger one than simply, What right have you to be on our turf? It is a central question in religion, more so than in the practices of law and medicine, because prophets and preachers claim authority which is in some ways difficult to check out. We often applaud the appearance of a prophetic figure whose authority seems to be directly from God and not mediated through the usual academic and ecclesiastical channels. Such persons bring not only refreshment but sometimes reformation. But we also know how dangerous such persons can be. To whom does a prophet answer? Not everyone who claims to be sent of God or to be speaking by the Holy Spirit proves to be genuine. For this reason the church has sought in its various traditions to join divine call with examination and ordination by the faith community as a way not only of giving authority but of protecting the flock and maintaining continuity in the faith. Let us not, then, be too early or too easily disposed against those who ask the question or disregard the question itself. It is one that any of us, even though followers of Jesus, might have asked had we been there. That Jesus ministered with authority was early recognized in Galilee (4:31). We have before us the authoritative tradition about him, that he was filled with the Holy Spirit (4:1) and that he "returned in the power of the Spirit into Galilee" (4:14). But his contemporaries need to know, "By what authority you do these things" (20:2).

Jesus' response to the question with a question is not an attempt to be clever or evasive; he surely welcomes the possibility of their coming to faith. Rather, his question is designed to see whether his inquirers are open to an answer. If they are not open to an answer, then no answer will satisfy. The question about John's ministry gives an opportunity to give honestly their assessment of another person who recently had come preaching the word of God's coming reign. Their response to John would indicate their response to Jesus, for both had come in the name of God and had been treated similarly (7:29–35). It is immediately apparent, however, that Jesus is not going to receive an honest answer; rather, he is going to receive an expedient answer. The chief priests and their associates do not huddle over the question, "Was John a prophet of God?" but "How shall we handle this in front of these people?" Their "We do not know" thinly veiled their "We will not say." Jesus responds in kind to their real, not their spoken, answer: "Then neither will I." Nothing is resolved; the reader knows there will be another encounter.

The Parable of the Tenants (20:9-19)
(Matthew 21:33-46; Mark 12:1-12)

Luke's handling of this parable, related by all three Synoptists, is a fascinating study in communication in a setting that has already proven to be full of obstacles to hearing. Luke has already told us that Jesus has two audiences, in itself a major hurdle for a speaker: the chief priests and associates and the people (19:47-48). Jesus had been teaching the people (20:1) when the priests, scribes, and elders interrupted to raise the question of Jesus' authority (vv. 2-8). In that exchange it is evident that these religious leaders are not open to what Jesus is saying. How does one get such persons to listen? Jesus turns to the people and addresses them, but in the presence of the leaders who are no longer confronted directly but who are made overhearers. The parable is not *to* them but it is *about* them, a fact that becomes evident at the close of the parable: "They perceived that he had told this parable against them" (v. 19). Thinking themselves not involved, they listened in as Jesus spoke to the people, only to discover that Jesus was addressing them, but indirectly. In fact, Jesus teaches by double indirection, since he uses a parable, a literary means of indirect communication, drawing in the listener to active participation. For the people to whom Jesus speaks, the communication is also doubly indirect, being both a parable and on a subject not specifically pertinent to them but to the priests nearby. For the people the parable is a warning about position- and power-hungry leaders.

The parable itself, in the form in which we receive it, is really a parable interpreted allegorically to reflect events that did, in fact, occur (as in 19:11-27). The vineyard was a familiar image of God's heavy investment of time, work, care, and patience, with the anticipation of fruitful return (Isa. 5:1-7; Ezek. 15:1-6; 19:10-14). The vineyard was in the hands of tenants for

233

a long time (v. 9), perhaps referring to the period prior to John. The servants who came with God's demand for a return on the investment are the prophets, including John; and the beloved son (v. 13) is, of course, Jesus. The tenants are the religious leaders who not only forget they are God's tenants but swell with the notion that they can actually take over as owners of the enterprise, especially when they take the son outside (Jerusalem, Heb. 13:12–13) and kill him. The word of final punishment on the tenants (leaders) stuns the people (v. 16), for they sense that they too will fall with the nation as God gives it over to others.

The story that is unfolded in the parable brings to mind first the fall of Jerusalem and its subsequent control by the Roman military. The interpretation of the destruction of Jerusalem as God's punishment for the religious establishment's treatment of the prophets (Acts 7:52) and rejection of Jesus was apparently not uncommon among early Christians. Beyond the fall of the city, however, the parable anticipates the movement of the gospel from Jews to Gentiles. We must not understand the move to Gentiles as either arbitrary or complete. Throughout Luke-Acts, even with repeated stories of rejection in the synagogues, there continued to be followers of Jesus among the Jews. But the parable has meaning beyond both the destruction of Jerusalem and the giving over of the vineyard to others (Gentile Christians). If history carried no lesson, it is a question whether Luke would have recorded this allegorized parable. If in Luke's time, or ours, tenants of God's vineyard deceive themselves with grand thoughts of place and power, there are always others to whom God can give over the trust. In fact, one thinks of those places in the world that were once the missionary fields for Europe and America, places where now the church is lively and strong, in painful contrast to the established and endowed but dead churches of the Western world.

In verses 17–18 Luke joins the quotation of Ps. 118:22 and an allusion to Isa. 8:14–15, both of which point to the critical role of Jesus in the story of salvation history. Because Luke believes that the law, the prophets, and the psalms all speak of Christ (24:44), the promise/fulfillment pattern is frequent in both the Gospel and Acts. Jesus is the rejected but exalted stone that completes God's building, or as the early preachers put it, "God has made him both Lord and Christ, this Jesus whom you crucified" (Acts 2:36). The stone image in verse 18 is quite

234

different from that of verse 17, but in its own way it also affirms Jesus as the "head of the corner." Jesus is the centerpiece of God's work, says Luke, and therefore how Jesus is treated determines one's life ultimately. This determination may be present (v. 18*a*) or future (v. 18*b*), but certain and final in either case. This view of Jesus as the critical factor in the lives of people is not new here; Luke had stated it in the words of Simeon when the infant Jesus was presented at the temple: "Behold, this child is set for the fall and rising of many in Israel, and for a sign that is spoken against . . . , that thoughts out of many hearts may be revealed" (2:34–35).

The Question of Tribute to Caesar (20:20–26)
(Matthew 22:15–22; Mark 12:13–17)

Luke keeps before us the double audience, the priests and the people, with the people, responding favorably to Jesus, providing the cushion of support which served to protect Jesus from his hostile opponents (vv. 19, 26). Having felt the stinging judgment of the parable of the vineyard, the chief priests and the scribes are now ready to seize Jesus, but they cannot openly. Any hope of success in removing Jesus lies in entrapment. However, at this point in their planning, trapping Jesus in religious heresy would not be enough; he must be trapped in remarks that would constitute political treason, giving his accusers ground to bring him before the governor, Pontius Pilate (v. 20). The scribes and the priests cannot themselves set the trap, because Jesus is on the alert, having already faced their question about his authority (vv. 1–8). Their needs, then, are two: questioners with a chance of success and the question to be put to Jesus.

As for the questioners, Luke identifies them simply as "spies," pretending to be sincere ("honest men," NEB; literally, "righteous"). Mark and Matthew identify the interrogators as a coalition of Pharisees and Herodians, but Luke consistently places the temple clergy before Jesus as opponents in Jerusalem and the spies are undoubtedly from their circle. With flattering lips and hostile intent the spies approach Jesus, but their anonymity and verbal disguises are ineffective; Jesus perceives their "craftiness" (Mark has "hypocrisy"; Matthew, "malice").

As for the question, it is a volatile one and so polarizing that the interrogators are convinced that whatever Jesus' answer, he will alienate half his audience. Their hope, of course, is that he

235

will incriminate himself. The matter of taxes paid to Rome was especially incendiary among Galileans. The Jewish historian Josephus reported that in the year 6 C.E. Judas the Galilean had declared it to be treason against God to pay taxes to Rome. It is in an atmosphere of anti-Roman revolts, both in fact and in plotting, that Jesus is asked, "Is it lawful [proper; permitted] for us to give tribute to Caesar, or not?" (v. 22). Jesus' response makes it clear that he will not be lured into a political power struggle. If he wishes to state or to act out a position in relation to the Roman government, it would not be done in the context of insincere and hypocritical word games. What, then, did Jesus say in the pronouncement, "Then render to Caesar the things that are Caesar's, and to God the things that are God's" (v. 25)?

On one level, one can say, of course, that Jesus was very insightful into the political implications of his answer; that Jesus outwitted his opponents and beat them at their own game; and that his answer was sufficiently unclear as to draw no fire from either the priests or the people. But to leave it there is unsatisfactory. The church from Luke's time until the present has had to deal with Caesar and the claims of Caesar on the lives of those in his realm, and the church needs more than clever wit and debating skills. Good answers to crafty opponents are one thing, but at issue are decisions, priorities, and loyalties. As in other matters, the church looks to Jesus for guidance. While Christians struggle with the confession "Jesus is Lord" in Caesar's world, the taxes continue to come due.

Several statements can be made about Jesus' response, "Render to Caesar . . . ." First, the issues are too complex to be laid out in two lists, duties to God and duties to Caesar. Second, every situation calls for discernment as to what really is at stake. For Luke, all rulers come under the sovereignty of God, and to try to rule outside that sovereignty is to come under God's wrath (Acts 12:20–23). On the other hand, the Roman government at times gave favorable protection to Christians and as a result received from Luke very good marks (Acts 13:7, 12; 16:35–39; 18:12–17; 19:35–41; 22:25–26; and elsewhere). For those who call Caesar "Lord" the matter is simply handled. For those who call Caesar "Satan" the matter is just as simply handled. But if the church can at times support the state and at other times must resist the state, then answers are neither simple nor final. The struggle resumes anew in every situation. Third, for Jesus personally the question put to him was a real test. In the desert, prior to his public ministry, Jesus had wrestled with this very issue (4:5–8). In fact, both Mark 12:15 and Matt. 22:18 report that Jesus says to his questioners, "Why put me to the test?" In other words, Jesus is facing not simply a tough theological question but a difficult personal question. In the final analysis, he found himself opposed by both the political and the religious authorities; church and state conspired against him. One can hardly imagine a heavier demand on a person: called to obey God, not simply in the face of political wrath but without the support of the community of faith. It still happens. Finally, Jesus' words about Caesar and God meant that the church would have to continue in every time and place to interpret in specific ways the meaning of those words. The range of those interpretations is reflected in the New Testament (Rom. 13:1–7; I Tim. 2:2; Titus 3:1; I Peter 2:13–17; Rev. 13; 18).

**The Question Concerning
the Resurrection of the Dead (20:27–40)
(Matthew 22:23–33; Mark 12:18–27)**

This is the third and final question (Matthew and Mark have four questions, but the fourth Luke dealt with earlier, 10:25–28) put to Jesus by opponents during his Jerusalem ministry. It is a question which under other circumstances would have elicited a pastoral response, for the question of the resurrection is vital not only to the Christian faith but to all people who reflect on life and death. Paul dealt with the subject when it arose among Christians as a confusing doctrine (I Cor. 15) and when the deaths of friends and relatives had created for one church a mood of unrelieved bereavement (I Thess. 4:13–18). Here the question comes to Jesus with no personal investment on the part of the interrogators; their aim is to argue, to embarrass, to force Jesus into one particular school of thought, or perhaps just to divide the audience. There is among them no spirit of inquiry or desire to learn. They are simply baiting Jesus with one of their classic "what if" questions, a question on which their minds had been settled long ago: there is no resurrection of the dead (v. 27; Acts 23:8). The Sadducees (the name may have derived from Zadok, high priest under Solomon) were one of several parties within Judaism. Judaism has never been mono-lithic, and to say "the Jews believed" is to be misinformed and to misinform. Sadducees were of the priestly class, many of

237

them aristocratic and wealthy, they were theologically conservative, and Scripture for them consisted of only the five books of Moses. No teaching was authoritative if it was not found in the Pentateuch, and they found no doctrine of the resurrection in the books of Moses (cf. the article on Sadducees in *Harper's Bible Dictionary*). The Pharisees, on the other hand, not only included the prophets and the writings in their Scripture but also believed in the authority of the oral tradition from Moses. In that oral tradition was the basis for belief in the resurrection. The subject was heatedly debated between the two parties, a fact that Paul made use of to draw attention away from himself during his trial before the Jewish council (Acts 23:6–10).

Unlike many of us who give vent to frustration when grilled by persons who have no intention of being influenced by our responses, Jesus answers the question rather than the attitude prompting it. His answer is twofold. The first part (vv. 34–36) simply points out the inappropriateness of the question, given the difference between life in this age and the age to come. In this age, the fact of death makes marriage and perpetuation of life essential. However, in the age to come there is no death, but those who attain to the resurrection are equal to the angels, they are children of God. Notice how far this is from the notion of the immortal soul, an idea that has intruded itself into Christian doctrine. Immortality is based on a doctrine of human nature that denies death; resurrection is based on a doctrine of God which says that even though we die, God gives life to the dead.

In the second part of his answer Jesus draws on the Sadducees' own Bible, the books of Moses (vv. 37–40). Their question is based on the levirate law of marriage (Deut. 25:5–10) which details the duty of a man toward a deceased brother. Jesus answers them with Ex. 3:6: God is a God of the living and not of the dead. It follows then, says Jesus, that Abraham, Isaac, and Jacob are living, not dead. There is nothing here to initiate or support doctrines of intermediate states of being between death and resurrection.

The two parts of Jesus' answer to the Sadducees constitute an argument from reason (conditions of this life do not constitute proof of conditions in the next) and Scripture (Ex. 3:6) for the belief in the resurrection of the dead. In this belief Jesus was in agreement with the Pharisees. To what extent these two lines of argumentation were used by early Christians is not known.

238

Since its documents are addressed to Christians, there is little attempt to *prove* the resurrection in the New Testament. Matthew gives briefly an argument for the resurrection of Jesus (Matt. 27:62—28:15), at Pentecost Simon Peter made a case for the resurrection of Jesus from Ps. 16:8–11 (Acts 2:24–31), and Paul argued both Christ's resurrection and ours with a church in which this was an issue among believers (I Cor. 15:12–58). Apparently some in Corinth (as was the case in other churches) interpreted resurrection experientially (we have been raised to new life in Christ) but not eschatologically. Paul argued for the truth of both interpretations. Since Luke believed that the Old Testament testified to Jesus' passion and resurrection (24:44–46), we may assume that arguments from Scripture such as we have in Acts 2:24–31 were common in early Christian preaching as Luke's research recovered it. But in all these cases the argumentation has to do with the resurrection of Jesus, not with a doctrine of resurrection in general. Resurrection was first of all a matter of Christology: God has vindicated Jesus by raising him from the dead. From that proclamation came the belief in the resurrection of believers. Therefore, while Jesus' words to the Sadducees may have been used in and by the church to counter doubts about resurrection, apparently the primary attention was not on resurrection as such but on the resurrection of Jesus. On that belief depended the understanding of both the present and the future life of his followers. Remove from the discussion the resurrection of Jesus and talk about life after death remains interesting but for Jesus' followers ceases to be very important.

Some scribes who overheard Jesus' response to the Sadducees speak to him approvingly of his answer. While it is possible that they are admiring of his logic, more likely they were scribes of the Pharisees and therefore agreed with Jesus concerning resurrection. According to Luke (v. 40), the interrogation of Jesus by critics and opponents ends. He continues to teach the people in the temple (v. 45). We may be sure, however, that the end of questioning does not mean the end of plotting, for some minds are fixed: Jesus must be delivered to the governor (20:20).

The Question of Jesus About the Son of David (20:41–44)
(Matthew 22:41–46; Mark 12:35–37*a*)

The question-answer period of Jesus' public ministry in Jerusalem ends with Jesus asking the question. To whom the question is addressed is in Luke left unclear ("them") as is the group to whom he refers, "How can *they* say . . . ?" (v. 41). At issue is the identity and characterization of the Messiah; "they" say he is the son of David. One would think, since points of agreement between Jesus and the religious leaders are precious few, that Jesus would not have raised this as a question. After all, has not Jesus already been identified in this Gospel as son of David (1:32, 69; 3:31), and has not Luke already made much of Jesus' birth being in David's city (2:1–20)? In fact, as recently as Jericho, Jesus received and responded favorably to the praise of a blind beggar: "Jesus, Son of David, have mercy on me!" (18: 35–43). What, then, is the problem? Apparently it is not the term but the interpretation of it which is at odds with Jesus' understanding of the Messiah (cf. the comments at 18:35–43). The expression "son of David" is both genealogical and qualitative, meaning "David-like," just as "son of exhortation" means "having the quality or capacity to exhort." The "David-like" dimensions of the expression had apparently taken on such military and political meanings that Jesus cannot embrace the title. For Jews to say "Jesus is Messiah [Christ]" meant that they had to modify their understanding of Messiah in view of their understanding of Jesus. Terms and titles do not modify Jesus; Jesus modifies the terms and titles. The problem with messianic expectations is that they can blind one to the Messiah whom God sends. For example, some Christians have poured into the expectation of the second coming of the Messiah ideas and images that seem quite foreign to the New Testament's portrait of Jesus as Messiah.

Is Jesus the son of David? Yes and no. Much depends on who says it and what is in mind. Apparently Jesus found what "they" said about the Christ as David's son inappropriate or inadequate or incorrect. He offers a corrective in the quotation of Psalm 110. Jesus' use of this psalm presupposes that it is a psalm of David and that it already had been interpreted messianically. On the basis of Psalm 110, Jesus declares the Messiah David's Lord, not David's son. This enthronement psalm served the early church well in its presentation of Jesus as exalted to God's right hand as both king and priest. No other Old Testament text is used more frequently or more widely in New Testament christological affirmations. Even so, it is but one of many supportive texts, just as "son of David" is but one among many titles for the Christ. In fact, not even the title "Christ"—that is, "Mes-

240

siah"—was appropriate and meaningful in every situation. As an apostle to Gentiles, Paul used, at least in the letter to the Romans, "Jesus is Lord" as the essential Christian confession (Rom. 10:9, 10). Perhaps Luke's point in our text, therefore, is that no single title or descriptive term should be the sole normative designation for Jesus. He was son of David, but not that alone. He was David's Lord, but not that alone. We have already seen in Luke that Jesus was also Elijah-like and Jonah-like. Perhaps Luke can teach us to think in analogies in our Christologies, but not to insist on closure in an impatience to locate and label the heretics.

A Warning and an Example (20:45—21:4)
(Matthew 23:1-36; Mark 12:37*b*-40)

Luke follows Mark in joining this warning about scribes and the example of a poor widow. One can account for the word about scribes because they were characters in the preceding episode. However, we should note that in that encounter with Jesus they appear in a positive light. In a Torah-centered culture, the keeper and interpreter of the law was a person of importance and honor. There is no reason to assume that all of them had corrupted the office, but some of them had, and Jesus warns against such leadership. But how does the episode involving the widow become joined to that of corrupt scribes? Two possibilities offer themselves. One, the devouring of widows' houses (v. 47) is a charge against the scribes, thereby introducing the subject of widows. A second possibility is that the scribes and the widow present to the disciples contrasting models of behavior: the one ambitious and greedy, the other humble and generous to the point of sacrifice.

The communication dynamics are fascinating. The place is the temple, the ones being addressed by Jesus are the disciples, the ones overhearing are the people, and the lessons draw upon two observations: on the one hand proud and ambitious scribes and on the other a poor widow offering her gift among the rich. The people hear Jesus; they need to know the kind of leadership to be expected from Jesus' disciples. The disciples know the people are listening; accountability and expectations are clear to everyone.

As for the warning about the scribes (vv. 45-47), Luke has already presented the core of this message in the woes on scribes and Pharisees (11:37-54). However, the history of the

241

church has proven the need repeatedly for Jesus' warning about ambition and greed, twin vices to plague the leadership of the church from the beginning (Acts 4:32—5:11; 20:33–35; Rom. 16:18; Phil. 3:19; I Peter 5:2–3; II Peter 2:3). Given the general tendency of the faithful to trust spiritual leaders, the door to greed and self-promotion is opened wide to the fraudulent and the insincere. Many believers act out their relation to God in their relationship with their minister; regrettably some clergy do not have the character to handle that level of trust. The warning was and is appropriate, especially in the matter of taking over widows' houses as administrators in the faith community (Acts 4:34–37).

In sharp contrast to the poor model offered by the scribes stands that of the poor widow whose lavish generosity consisted of giving two lepta, coins of the very least value and the sum of her possessions. The presence of the rich putting in large gifts would have even further diminished what she gave had it not been for Jesus. He did not romanticize the small gift or strike out against the large. He weighed all the gifts not by sentiment but by a standard that was the same for all: How much does one have remaining after the offering is made? Thus measured, the widow's gift was by far the greatest, because she had nothing left. The offering of everything, whatever the amount, is the unexcelled gift.

The disciples had already revealed their appetite for greatness (9:46). Jesus points to the act of the poor widow and says, "So you are interested in greatness? Then here is your example; hers is the greatness which belongs in the reign of God."

Luke 21:5–38
The Apocalyptic Discourse of Jesus

The word "apocalyptic" comes from "apocalypse" which means "revelation," perhaps most familiar to the church as the name of the last book of the New Testament, the Apocalypse or Revelation to John. Although there are apocalyptic sections in other writings (e.g., Isa. 24—27) the book of Daniel is the best Old Testament representative of this genre of literature. Quite a few late Jewish and early Christian writings outside the canon are of this type. In fact, apocalyptic writing was popular in Christian circles for a millennium. Not all uses of the word "apocalypse," however, have to do with a special kind of literature. Paul insisted that he received his gospel not from human sources but "by revelation" (Gal. 1:12) and that he went to Jerusalem to meet with other Christian leaders "by revelation" (Gal. 2:2). But as a kind of literature, apocalyptic deals with a revelation, or series of revelations, usually by means of an angel, which discloses the supernatural world beyond the world of historical events. The focus is on eschatology, the end of the world as we now experience it and the beginning of a new world. Usually the transition is described in terms of transformations cosmic in scope and nature, along with judgment of failed persons and institutions and the vindication of God's saints. Although some apocalypses involve ascensions into another world, both the Apocalypse to John and the apocalyptic discourse of Jesus in Luke 21 (Mark 13; Matt. 24:1–38) join historical events with descriptions of what is going on behind and beyond history. Major historical crises triggered apocalyptic thinking. For example, the destruction of Jerusalem is the historical event that prompted the apocalyptic speech of Jesus in the text before us as well as the apocalypses we know as Fourth Ezra and Second Baruch. In other words, in an apocalypse of this type, what is going on is mixed with what is *really* going on, history being set in the larger context of God's purpose, the whole being an extraordinary writing with historical descriptions laced with symbols, signs, and mysterious figures of speech. As strange as this literature may seem to us, it is a dramatic witness to the tenacity of faith and hope among the people of God. Amid painful and prolonged suffering, when there can be seen on the horizon of predictable history no relief from disaster, faith turns its face toward heaven not only for a revelation of God's will but also for a vision of the end of the present misery and the beginning of the age to come. It is hope's response to the cynic who mocks the faithful, saying, "Where is the promise of his coming? For ever since the fathers fell asleep, all things have continued as they were from the beginning of creation" (II Peter 3:4).

Luke obviously has Mark 13 before him, but again Luke is a writer and not a copier, so modifications are to be expected.

243

The discourse is prompted by the remarks of "some" (v. 5) and not specifically of disciples. Jesus speaks in the temple and not away from the temple on the Mount of Olives (vv. 5–7, 37–38). The Mount of Olives was the place of lodging at night (v. 37). The audience for the discourse is "all the people" and not the disciples in private (Matt. 24:3) or the original four disciples (Mark 13:3). Among the differences in the speech itself, most noticeable are Luke's verse 28 and his own ending (vv. 34–36). We need also to keep in mind that Luke has already discussed the parousia at 17:20–37 and therefore extracts from this discourse some comments already before the reader. The apocalyptic discourse proper (vv. 8–36) is prompted by Jesus' prediction of the fall of the temple and the two questions which "they" (v. 7) asked in response: When? and What will be the sign? What follows falls into seven parts:

8–11	Signs of the end
12–19	The time of testimony preceding the end
20–24	The fall of Jerusalem
25–28	The coming of the Son of man
29–31	The parable of the fig tree
32–33	The time of the coming of the Son of man
34–36	The ending to the discourse

The signs of the end are threefold: the appearance of false messiahs and false calculators of time and place (v. 8); wars, tumults, and international conflicts (vv. 9–10); and natural disasters with cosmic terror (v. 11). The coming to conclusion of God's purpose will affect not just Israel but all nations, not just the nations but the entire cosmos. There is no area of God's creation so remote as to be unaffected by God's fulfillment of the divine intention (cf. comments at 17:20–37). However, disciples are not to be so preoccupied with these events as to be terrified or led astray by those who claim to have probed the divine mysteries and ascertained the time and place. The important thing to keep in mind is that before the end there is to be a time of witnessing (vv. 12–19). Those claiming "The time [kairos, opportune time] is at hand!" (v. 8) fail to understand that calculations of time (chronos, calendar time) do not lead one to know the fulfillment of God's time (kairos). The present (for Luke's church and for us) is a time for bearing testimony (v. 13). Notice that Luke first states the signs of the end and then

244

describes what precedes it. The chronology is reversed in the service of the writer's point. In writing and in speaking, the principle of end stress says to state last that which is of first importance. In this case it is the call to faithful witness under unusual stress and pain. Because of their witness, disciples will be brought before synagogues (fulfilled in Acts 4—5) and before governors and kings (fulfilled in Acts 24—26). Hatred, betrayal by relatives and friends, and death await them. In those crises, however, they will be given "a mouth and wisdom" (v. 15, a Semitism for an appropriate message; cf. 12:11–12). In Luke-Acts, one of the functions of the Holy Spirit is to inspire speech.

Verses 16–17 make verse 18 difficult, creating what seems to be a contradiction. Verse 18, "But not a hair of your head will perish," is not fulfilled in Acts; in fact, disciples did suffer death (Acts 22:4), including the Jerusalem leader Stephen (Acts 7:54–60) and the apostle James (Acts 12:2). Perhaps verse 18 is a misplaced saying (12:7; Matt. 10:30), or it may mean that the persecutors can kill in a physical sense but in a far more important way disciples will be kept safe. In any case, faithfulness and endurance under threat, under arrest, and under penalty of death are the qualities of disciples during this time of witnessing. Disciples are not exempt from suffering. There is nothing here of the arrogance one sometimes sees and hears in modern apocalyptists, an arrogance born of a doctrine of a rapture in which believers are lifted above the conditions of persecution and hardship. There are no scenes here of planes falling from the sky because believing pilots have been raptured or cars crashing on the highway because their drivers were believers and hence have been lifted to an indifferent bliss. According to our text, we are in a time of witnessing in the face of suffering and death, but "by your endurance you will gain your lives" (v. 19). If anyone doubts that this period of testimony is still present, that doubt will be removed by attendance at an All Saints service in which can be heard a roll call of the imprisoned and murdered faithful who are our contemporaries.

In verses 20–24 Luke describes the destruction of Jerusalem, an event that had occurred ten to twenty years prior to Luke's writing. Mark had set the fall of the city in an eschatological context, alluding to a prophecy of Daniel (Mark 13:14–20), but Luke removes the fate of Jerusalem from the eschaton. What Luke relates is what happened in 66–70 C.E. when the

Roman armies destroyed Jerusalem and the temple. Luke's point seems to be that believers were not to interpret the end of Jerusalem as the clear sign of the end of the world. What remains is "the times of the Gentiles" (v. 24). This may be a reference to the Gentile mission which went out from Jerusalem, the record of which is provided in Acts. Luke understood that Paul, while witnessing in synagogues in every city, was increasingly engaged in bringing to fulfillment the time of the Gentiles. "Let it be known to you then that this salvation of God has been sent to the Gentiles; they will listen" (Acts 28:28). According to Paul's own words, he accelerated his work among Gentiles in order to provoke the Jews (Rom. 11:13–24). Paul's conclusion to his extraordinary probing of the purpose of God was that God's desire was to have mercy on all (Rom. 11:32), "for from God and through God and to God are all things. To God be glory for ever. Amen" (Rom. 11:36). Luke would agree, for nowhere in Luke-Acts, for all its repeated accounts of the rejection of Jesus and his missionaries by the Jews, does Luke declare that God has abandoned Israel. The reader should not, therefore, interpret a door opened to Gentiles as a door closed to Jews. "A certain man had *two* sons."

The remainder of the discourse up to the hortatory conclusion (vv. 34–36) sketches what is to be after "the times of the Gentiles are fulfilled" (v. 24). The entire cosmos will be disturbed, radically affecting human life everywhere (vv. 25–27). As we reminded ourselves at 17:22–37, both Testaments not only mark significant events in the drama of God's way in the world with radical changes in creation but also insist that redemption has a cosmic dimension. Recall, for example, Rom. 8:18–25. In fact, it was Paul who developed a Christology adequate to embrace all creation in the act of the cross and the resurrection (Phil. 2:6–11; Col. 1:15–20). But both Matthew and Luke tell us that heaven and earth signaled in unusual ways the birth and the death of Jesus. Yet even earlier, prophets had spoken of the day of the Lord as shaking and altering heaven and earth. Luke himself cites one such prophet in the sermon of Simon Peter at Pentecost. So much attention has been given to the outpouring of the Holy Spirit on that day and the fulfillment of the prophecy of Joel 2:28–32 concerning the gift of the Spirit that the latter part of Joel's prophecy quoted in the sermon gets overlooked. Listen to Joel through Simon Peter:

And I will show wonders in the heaven above
and signs on the earth beneath,
blood, and fire, and vapor of smoke;
the sun shall be turned into darkness
and the moon into blood,
before the day of the Lord comes,
the great and manifest day.
And it shall be that whoever calls on the name of
    the Lord shall be saved.

                    Joel 2:30–32 as quoted
                        in Acts 2:19–21

As the gift of God's Spirit at Pentecost was not a private experience within the individual heart, so the coming of the Son of
man at the last cannot be properly described in terms of private
experience. The human heart is too small a screen on which to
cast that grand scene. For all that Christian faith means to each
individual who embraces it, the church cannot continue to permit, much less endorse, a subjective captivity of the gospel. Not
even the community of faith is adequate as the arena of Christ's
saving work. The whole creation stands at the window eagerly
awaiting the arrival of the day of redemption for the children
of God (Rom. 8:19). The final changes in heaven and earth are
not, therefore, to usher in a time of terror for the faithful;
rather, they are to realize that these are signs of the time of
their redemption (v. 28).

At this point Jesus relieves an audience awed, bedazzled,
and perplexed, if not frightened, by images of cosmic convulsions accompanying the Son of man by bringing his message
within the range of their present experience. In a parable (here
parable has the sense of analogy or comparison) he says these
signs announce the arrival of the kingdom, just as the leafing of
a tree signals the approach of summer. And when might this be?
Jesus' answer is not intended to support those who thought that
his arrival in Jerusalem would be the arrival of the kingdom
(19:11), nor is Jesus himself entering into that chronological
calculating which he so recently rejected (v. 8). Then when? In
this generation (v. 32). This answer is as specific and as nonspe-
cific as the word "generation." The word can refer to a period
of approximately thirty years or to a period of an indefinite
number of years but characterized by a particular quality such
as suffering or waiting or witnessing. At least we know that

247

Luke is here locating his audience between the time of God's punishing Jerusalem and God's judgment of all nations in the coming of the Son of man whose arrival will mean the redemption of the faithful. The answer to the question When? gives hope and encouragement but does not remove the audience from the time of testimony in the face of hostility (vv. 12–19).

Having moved the listeners from the realms of cosmic signs to their experienced world of nature, Jesus now moves them finally to themselves. The life of disciples, after all is said and done, is not one of speculation or of observation but of behavior and relationships (vv. 34–36). After such a discourse as this, how are the hearers to leave the presence of Jesus? Overwhelmed? Terrified? Despairing? Shall they shake off its effects in order to return to the routine they knew before? No; eschatological thinking is vital to faithful conduct and to hope which resists cynicism. There will be an end to life as it now is, an end that comes as both judgment and redemption. Whether we go or he comes, personal theological preferences do not alter eschatology, and contemplation of that fact should have some sanctifying influence. Such thinking should keep our souls athletically trim, free of the weight of the excessive and useless. Such thinking should aid us in keeping gains and losses in proper perspective. Such thinking should chase away the demons of dulling dissipation and cheer us with the news not only that today is a gift of God but also that tomorrow we stand in the presence of the Son of man.

With verses 37–38 Luke gives a summary statement of the rhythm of Jesus' life in Jerusalem. During the day he taught the people in the temple; at night he lodged on the mount called Olivet. His days began early, meeting the people at the temple for full days of teaching. We have had few occasions to relate Luke to the Gospel of John, but these verses provide one. In a remarkably similar passage, John says: "They went each to his own house, but Jesus went to the Mount of Olives. Early in the morning he came again to the temple; all the people came to him, and he sat down and taught them" (John 7:53—8:2). Some manuscripts then follow with the story of Jesus and the woman taken in adultery. However, a few manuscripts locate the story after Luke 21:38. One can see by the similarity between Luke 21:37–38 and John 7:53—8:2 how scribes would find Luke a comfortable setting for the story. In fact, one could easily argue

248

that the encounter between Jesus and the woman is more congenial to Luke than to John. But this is to speculate; in the text of Luke that we have received, chapter 21 concludes with verse 38. With this summary, Luke provides the reader with the closing scene of Jesus' public ministry.

PART SIX

The Passion Narrative

LUKE 22:1—23:56

   The Gospels of the New Testament are strikingly, and one might even say painfully, brief, even the longest of them. And given the fact that three of them often, and all four sometimes, tell the same stories, the sum total of recorded events and saying hardly approaches a biography. It is no wonder that disciples of Jesus have welcomed discoveries such as those at Qumran and Nag Hammadi in the hope that they might add to our knowledge of Jesus. Of the records we have in the canonical Gospels, the largest body of materials deals with the passion and the resurrection. The Synoptists each devote three full chapters to the events of less than four days, while John gives nine of his twenty-one chapters to that same period. However, this proportion is not surprising, since the gospel preached in the early church centered in the death and resurrection of Jesus. Paul said the tradition he received and preached dealt with the death, resurrection, and appearances of Christ (I Cor. 15:3–8). Of the ten christological affirmations in the Apostles' Creed, five have to do with the passion and resurrection. Some scholars believe this to have been the first material shaped into a narrative, and so regarded as the inner sanctum of the faith that it early became almost standardized, thus protected from major alterations. Some few scholars have even suggested that the passion and resurrection narratives were memorized and passed along as the tradition. There are some variations among the four tellers of the story, but the similarities are remarkable. We shall call attention to such variations as may help us to hear Luke more clearly. We will no doubt see the church's fingerprints on the narratives, since they were and are so central to the church's self-understanding, its preaching, its liturgy, and its initiation of new members.

As for the passion narrative proper, it begins with Jesus' observance of the Passover meal with his disciples and concludes with his burial.

Luke 22:1–38
Jesus' Last Meal with His Disciples

This section consists of four units: the conspiracy against Jesus (vv. 1–6); preparation for the Passover meal (vv. 7–13); institution of the Lord's Supper (vv. 14–20); and farewell instructions (vv. 21–38).

The Conspiracy Against Jesus (22:1–6)
(Matthew 26:1–5, 14–16; Mark 14:1–2, 10–11)

The death of Jesus is at hand. The place says so: his death was to be in Jerusalem (9:31). The time says so: the Passover is near (Luke does not distinguish between Passover and the seven-day Feast of Unleavened Bread which followed, Ex. 12:6, 15; Lev. 23:5–8), the festival commemorating the exodus from Egypt (Ex. 12). On the Mount of Transfiguration, Moses and Elijah had spoken with Jesus about his approaching exodus (departure) in Jerusalem (9:31). The characters say so: the chief priests and the scribes have for some time been seeking to destroy Jesus, but he is so popular with the people that they have been a barrier to plots against Jesus (19:47–48; 20:19). An earlier effort to entrap Jesus in treasonous speech had failed (20:20). Now the people who had been but a buffer between them and Jesus pose a threat to the vested interests and positions of the chief priests and the scribes. There could be a riot or a revolt, and who knows what response the Roman military would make. Their scheming hardens. And the opportunity for Jesus' death says the time is at hand. Satan, last seen at 4:13, left off tempting Jesus until an opportune time. That opportunity (v. 6) comes through one of the Twelve (Luke's way of placing Judas among the Twelve seems a reluctant acknowledgment, v. 3). Whether the unusual word "Iscariot" identifies Judas geographically, genealogically, or ideologically is not clear, but it

252

does distinguish him from the other apostle of the same name (6:16). Judas agrees to find the opportunity to hand Jesus over (betray) to the chief priests and officers (leaders among the Levites and therefore temple-based, Acts 4:1; 5:24) when the crowds favorable to Jesus are absent.

The church has never been fully persuaded by its own efforts to explain Judas Iscariot. "Satan entered into Judas," but Judas had to let him in, "for the Son of man goes as it has been determined; but woe to that man by whom he is betrayed!" (v. 22). Judas has been called a thief, a money lover, a devil from the beginning. His betrayal has been called the act of a greedy man, a disappointed man, a man chosen for an ugly task, a man trying to force Jesus to act by precipitating a crisis. Here is one who was chosen after a night of prayer to be in the inner circle of Jesus. He was taught and then sent to minister with apostolic authority. He enjoyed the same success as the others on those missions to preach, to heal, and to cast out demons. He was in every sense of the word an apostle. What happened? There would be no value in attempting a new theory to explain Judas. The church is at its best when it stops asking, "Why did Judas do it?" and instead examines its own record of discipleship.

Preparation for the Passover Meal (22:7–13)
(Matthew 26:17–19; Mark 14:12–16)

Although Luke speaks of the Feast of Unleavened Bread (v. 1) and the day of Unleavened Bread (v. 7), there is no doubt in Luke that it was the Passover meal that began the Feast of Unleavened Bread which Jesus observed with his disciples (vv. 8, 13, 15). This is no unimportant detail, for the Jewish Passover not only serves as background for the Christian Table of Remembrance but the celebration of liberation from slavery in Egypt provides directly and indirectly meanings for the Lord's Supper. Sending two disciples ahead to make preparation recalls 19:28–34 and the preparation for Jesus' entry into the city. Here, however, the two are named, anticipating Acts, in which Peter and John appear repeatedly as a team (Acts 3:1—4:22; 8:14–25). In fact, in Luke's second listing of the apostles in Acts 1:13, Peter and John are the first two names. If John is the beloved disciple unnamed in the Fourth Gospel, then in that Gospel also Peter and John are repeatedly linked from the farewell meal through the resurrection.

That Jesus will now appear in the city and therefore break

253

his routine of moving between the temple where a friendly crowd surrounds him and his night lodging on the Mount of Olives poses for him a real danger. In view of that, one could easily read Jesus' instructions to Peter and John as intriguing prearrangements, as shadowy moves in a mystery novel. "A man carrying a jar of water [unusual; women carried the water] will meet you; follow him" (v. 10). And there is no reason not to think in terms of Jesus' having made plans for observing the Passover. However, both here and at 19:28–34 Luke probably wants the reader to think in terms of Jesus' prophetic knowledge. Since the room was already furnished, preparation consisted of purchasing bread, wine, herbs, and a lamb that had been approved by a priest as unblemished and properly slain (no bones broken and drained of blood, some of which was smeared on the facing of the door, Ex. 12). The bread unleavened, the lamb roasted whole and to be fully consumed, and the bitter herbs all carried messages of harsh slavery and the flight to freedom.

Institution of the Lord's Supper (22:14–20)
(Matthew 26:26–29; Mark 14:22–25)

The New Testament carries four accounts of the institution of the Lord's Supper, the three Synoptics and I Cor. 11:23–26 which is the earliest form of the tradition coming to us. John records Jesus' last meal with the disciples, but its centerpiece is the washing of feet (John 13:1–20). In John's Gospel, the account most akin to the Lord's Supper is that of Jesus feeding the multitudes at Passover time (ch. 6). The meal is variously referred to in the New Testament and in subsequent traditions: the Last Supper, the Lord's Supper (I Cor. 11:20), the Mass ("meal"), the Communion ("participation" or "fellowship," I Cor. 10:16), and the Eucharist ("to give thanks," Luke 22:17). While observed with varying frequency in different traditions, it has been historically set on Thursday evening of Holy Week, called Maundy Thursday, "maundy" being a form of the word *mande* from which we get "mandate" or "command." That particular night is thus the Night of the Commandment, the commandment referring to the memorial meal and/or the washing of feet.

254 Luke has shaped the tradition so as to present the evening as a classical occasion of farewell by a leader to his followers: first

the meal (vv. 14–20) and then words of warning, instruction, and encouragement for the days that lie ahead (vv. 21–38). In this arrangement the indication of a betrayer at the table is delayed until after the institution of the Lord's Supper, unlike Matthew and Mark who place it earlier. By so doing, Luke not only clarifies any uncertainty as to whether Judas received the bread and the wine, a very important consideration in a gospel that extends forgiveness to a prodigal, tax collectors, a dying thief, and crucifiers, but also puts in sharper focus the betrayal by Judas. Not only does he deliver Jesus to the enemy but he violates a covenant in the body and blood of Jesus.

It is evident that the practices of early Christian communities have affected all the traditions of the last meal. In fact, Christian observance and reflection on this meal have influenced the way the believing community remembered other meals at which Jesus was host. At the feeding of the five thousand, Luke says Jesus took, blessed, broke, and gave (9:16), clearly eucharistic language. At table with the two disciples at Emmaus, the risen Christ took, blessed, broke, and gave (24:30). It is as though, because of this last supper, no meal among disciples is just a meal, because no loaf is just bread, no cup is just wine.

Luke's record of the meal itself consists of two parts: verses 14–18 and 19–20. The problems for the reader are several and have to be dealt with at the outset if the passage is to be free to have its effect. The most apparent difficulty is the sequence of cup, bread, and cup. The order of cup and then bread is not unique here: both I Cor. 10:16 and the early Christian writing called the *Didache* have the cup before the bread, but here alone is there a second cup. However, the second cup appears in verse 20 which is absent from some manuscripts of Luke. These manuscripts end verse 19 at "This is my body," omit 19*b*–20, and resume at verse 21. The editors of the RSV (1971 ed.) chose to include the longer reading, while the NEB uses the shorter. Most of the manuscripts have verses 19*b*–20, but they have been regarded as a problem for three reasons: shorter readings generally are regarded as more likely to be original than longer ones; verses 19*b*–20 are remarkably like I Cor. 11:24–25; and these verses add a second cup. Clearly, traditions have influenced each other, just as traditions about Jesus' post-resurrection appearances tended to blend into one another, as

255

we shall see at chapter 24 (for details concerning the textual variants, cf. Fitzmyer, *The Gospel According to Luke*, 2:1387–1389).

By following the longer reading, we have a way to understand verses 14–20. Luke seems to have combined two traditions about the meal, each consisting of a set of parallel sayings. In verses 15–18, the two sayings are associated with the Passover in two ways: its fulfillment ("for I tell you I shall not eat it until it is fulfilled in the kingdom of God") and its eschatological orientation ("for I tell you that from now on I shall not drink of the fruit of the vine until the kingdom of God comes"). The Passover meal was very forward-looking, the food to be eaten after the family had packed their belongings for the journey to the promised land. So here the words of Jesus probably point forward to the messianic banquet, although his words have an interim fulfillment in the postresurrection meals with the disciples (24:30–31, 41–42; Acts 1:4; 10:41). Verses 15–18, therefore, emphasize the meal as historically linked to the Passover, as eschatological in its orientation, and as providing fellowship by means of a shared cup.

The second unit (vv. 19–20) preserves a tradition centering on two other sayings: "This is my body which is given for you" and "This cup which is poured out for you is the new covenant in my blood." In time this language came to be interpreted in sacrificial terms as atonement for sin. However, Luke's account is governed by the Passover, and the Passover lamb was not a sin offering. The lamb sacrificed for sin was another ritual; the Passover lamb was the seal of a covenant, and the Passover meal commemorated that covenant offered to the faith community by a God who sets free. Jesus' blood seals a new covenant offered to the faith community by a God who sets free. Jesus' blood seals a new covenant offering a new kind of freedom, a release from captivity to sin and death, a new covenant extended by the liberating God to all who believe, both Jew and Gentile. Those who share in this covenant are joined to one another, life to life, as signified and sealed in the cup divided among themselves. This last meaning of the tradition, the binding of disciples to one another, became extremely important to Paul as he sought to create congregations in which Christians were members of one another (I Cor. 11:23–34). But both traditions preserved by Luke, if that indeed is what he has done, are rich with meanings for the community of faith, none of them having lost their appropriateness or their vitality in the passing of time or the changing of place.

Farewell Instructions (22:21–38)

Although not nearly as extensive as in John 13—17, the narrative of the Last Supper in Luke is a farewell occasion in that the leader takes leave of his followers, warning, exhorting, and encouraging them for the days ahead. Some of this material is peculiar to Luke, but two units are found earlier in Mark and Matthew. As mentioned earlier, both Mark and Matthew place the indication of the betrayer prior to the institution of the Lord's Supper. In addition, Luke places at the supper the dispute about greatness, found in the other Synoptists prior to Jesus' arrival in Jerusalem (Mark 10:42–45; Matt. 20:25–28). By thus locating these two episodes after the supper, Luke has spoken two very strong words to the church. First, betrayal of Christ has occurred and can again occur among those who partake of the Lord's Supper. The finger of indictment points at that first table, to be sure, but, for Luke, betrayal lies not prior to the covenant meal, hence becoming an item of history, but within the circle of the covenant, and hence a continuing warning. Second, by placing the dispute about greatness at the Lord's table, Luke again changes an ugly moment in the history of the Twelve into a very real and present exhortation to those who share the table. Love of place and power was a problem for the first followers of Jesus, to be sure, but it continues to be so. The remainder of the New Testament, church history, and today's ecclesiastical journals concur in their witness to this infectious disease among so many who lead Christ's church. Luke will not allow us simply to scold the ambitious apostles; every time we sit at the Lord's table, these words (vv. 24–27) on humility and service return as a reminder and a warning.

Before we leave these first two units (vv. 21–23, 24–27), two notes are in order. First, in verse 23 the disciples "began to question one another, which of them it was that would do this." This would seem at first to be quite different from Mark's report which has them saying to Jesus, one after another, "Is it I?" (Mark 14:19). However, in Mark the disciples' question is framed with a negative particle which, in the Greek language, means that the question expects a negative answer. In other words, "It is not I, is it?" Therefore both Mark and Luke present disciples who do not have self-doubt but rather doubts about

257

the others. Not surprisingly, such followers dispute about greatness (v. 24). Second, verse 22 is a very succinct affirmation of both God's purpose ("The Son of man goes as it has been determined") and human responsibility ("but woe to that man by whom he is betrayed!"). In other words, God's purpose will be fulfilled even if it means using human failure and sin, but human failure and sin are not excused, because God uses them in the fulfillment of divine purpose.

The third unit (vv. 28–30) is directly related to the second, being the positive reversal of the negative scene in verses 24–27. The disciples in their dispute about greatness must have argued over their places at the table, since seating indicated importance. Having warned them that pursuit of greatness was totally foreign to the reign of God, Jesus makes a promise that says, in effect, that place is a gift of God. God grants places at the messianic banquet and honored places of leadership in the kingdom. Sitting on thrones judging the twelve tribes of Israel is not to be taken as a promise that Gentiles will judge Jews or that the church will judge the synagogue. The expression belongs to eschatological speech in which crowns, thrones, reigning, and judging fill the descriptions of the final future of the faithful, the exact opposite of their state on earth. For example, "If we have died with him, we shall also live with him; if we endure, we shall also reign with him" (II Tim. 2:11–12). Or, "Be faithful unto death, and I will give you the crown of life" (Rev. 2:10). Or again, "He who conquers, I will grant him to sit with me on my throne, as I myself conquered and sat down with my Father on his throne" (Rev. 3:21). True exaltation is, therefore, God's gift to those who faithfully endure the hardships of Christ, who share his suffering, and who have entered into the "covenanted" (v. 29; "assigned," RSV; "vested," NEB) relation with Jesus which Jesus had with God.

The fourth unit in the farewell instructions (vv. 31–34) is peculiar to Luke. Jesus predicts accelerated and enlarged activity on the part of Satan, the adversary, the accuser, the tempter (Zech. 3:1–3). Satan had been rebuffed by Jesus in the desert (4:1–12) but not dealt a fatal blow. He would return at an opportune time (4:13), that opportunity coming in the weakness and deceit of Judas (22:3–6). With the treachery of Judas and the arrest of Jesus, all the others (the "you" of v. 31 is plural) will be put to a severe test ("sifted," Amos 9:9). With the death of Jesus and the failure of the apostles, thinks Satan, the threat to

258

his reign by the reign of God will be ended. Those uncomfortable with the image of a Satan must not allow themselves to miss the tension and critical nature of this moment between Jesus and his followers. It might be helpful to speak of opponents and adversaries. If that does not seem true to reality, then a life of full engagement in those ministries which Jesus extended to the poor, the social outcasts, political traitors, the morally and physically diseased, and religious rejects will do it. Either opponents will appear in overt and covert forms and from surprising quarters or Satan is dead. Since all of them will be put to the test and for a time fear will overpower faith, how can they be restored? The need is for leadership in the absence of the leader, but who can do it if all are wounded? Jesus turns to Simon Peter (and here the "you" is singular, v. 32) who will falter, but through Jesus' intercession he will repent (turn again), regain his courage, and be a source of strength for the others. Peter insists he is ready now, without prayer or repentance, but Jesus tells him that before tomorrow morning he will have demonstrated in unthinkable ways that he is not. The prophecy of Jesus concerning Peter is a detailed recital of what, in fact, did occur: denial (vv. 54–61), repentance (v. 62), experience of the risen Christ (24:34), leadership (Acts 1:15; 2:14), prison (Acts 4:3; 12:3–5), and, according to John 21:18–19, a martyr's death. Christian leaders are not those exempt from fear, doubt, discouragement, and repeated testing but those who are supported by prayer and who, through repentance and forgiveness, find grace and strength to continue.

The fifth and final unit in the farewell instructions (vv. 35–38) is also found in Luke alone. The prediction of the testing that all disciples were to face and of the denial of Peter has moved the words of the departing leader to its deepest level of seriousness. The gravity of the situation has begun to make its impression on them; Simon Peter himself mentions prison and death. His loyalty is commendable, but a vow made at a distance from danger, however sincere, is sometimes abandoned under fire, with no excuse except "I never realized it would be like this." Jesus wants to impress upon them how it will be. He does so by contrasting this time when they are to be on their own with the previous time they were without his presence. On those earlier missions they were totally vulnerable but depended on the hospitality of their hosts (v. 35) to meet their needs. Now, says Jesus, there will be no hospitality but rather

259

threat and danger, and the disciples will have to depend on their own resources. In fact, Jesus will be treated as a criminal among criminals (Isa. 53:12), and the charges against him will spread to them (and they did, Acts 4:1–22). This will be the kind of night, says Jesus, on which one will sell one's own clothes to buy a sword. Jesus is speaking symbolically, but they hear him literally and reveal that they already have two swords. Give the disciples credit: they know this is not Galilee with its success stories and pressing crowds of people favorably impressed; this is Jerusalem, danger is moving in on them, and they are in a life-and-death situation. And give the disciples some sympathy: they respond to danger by instinct, sword for sword, weapon for weapon, blow for blow; that is, prepare for danger by becoming dangerous. This is not, of course, the way of Jesus; this contradicts the very nature of the reign of God. But we should not be overly critical of them when, after twenty centuries, many who name Jesus as Lord not only endorse the way of the sword but also personally subscribe to the view that violence ends violence. If Caesar must carry a sword, let Christians pray and work for its eventual removal; let disciples of Jesus lament, not celebrate. In the battles facing the Twelve, swords will be useless: a sword would not help Judas, a sword would not help Simon, a sword would not help frightened and fleeing disciples. But they thought so. Jesus knew they did not now understand, and so he said, "Enough of this talk; drop the subject."

Luke 22:39–53
The Arrest of Jesus

At the Mount of Olives (22:39–46)
(Matthew 26:30–46; Mark 14:26–42)

As we have repeatedly reminded ourselves, the first duty of the interpreter is to read the text carefully. This is especially important when a text deals with an event or a saying that is vivid in the memory of the church, but a memory that has usually been formed into a picture harmonized from all the sources, in this case, the four Gospels. Let us then attend to Luke's account. First one notices the brevity of the story, in length lying between the rather elaborate narrative of Mark and Matthew and the total omission of the prayer scene by John (John 18:1–2). Luke locates the event on the Mount of Olives at "the place" where Jesus had been lodging at night (21:37). Mark and Matthew call the place Gethsemane; John simply calls it "a garden" (John 18:1). Luke does not have three of the disciples join Jesus as an inner circle of prayer; all are asked to pray lest they enter into temptation. Jesus comes to the sleeping disciples once, not three times, and Luke explains their sleep as due to sorrow (v. 45), a condition that does prompt excessive sleeping, as we know. The reprimand is therefore softened and not repeated. Finally, notice that Jesus kneels in prayer rather than falling to the ground, as the other Synoptists have it. As we shall see, these differences in details are not unimportant.

A brief word needs to be said about verses 43–44 which the RSV (1971 ed.) places in the footnotes. Very important early manuscripts of Luke on which translators depend do not have these two sentences, although there is sufficient evidence for the NEB editors to feel justified in including them. When the problem is approached logically, it is easier to argue for their having been added by some early scribes than for their having been omitted by others. Without these verses, Luke does not portray Jesus in anguish, wrestling for hours with the will of God. The scene is more like the other occasions of Jesus in prayer. With verses 43–44, Jesus experiences the intense anguish that Mark and Matthew describe. In addition, the ministering angel (Dan. 3:25, 28) recalls Jesus' temptation as Mark presents it (Mark 1:13). In a word, then, verses 43–44 transform the scene to correspond in nature, if not in language, to that presented by the other Synoptists and join Luke's witness to theirs in testifying to the humanity of Jesus, an important consideration in view of the spiritualizing tendencies afoot in the early church. However, the following remarks will assume the absence of verses 43–44 from the text, but not in order to protect an image of a Jesus who does not agonize or sweat. On the contrary, Luke's Jesus even without these verses is very much the model for all his followers in his prayer life and in the manner of his facing crises.

As we have repeatedly observed, Jesus is presented by Luke as a man of prayer (3:21; 5:16; 6:12; 9:18; 9:28; 11:1) and as a teacher of prayer (11:1; 22:40, 46). As one who prayed regularly, sometimes all night, and especially at significant times in his life (baptism, choosing the Twelve, prior to asking the disciples for

261

a confession of faith, at the transfiguration, etc.), Jesus on that night at the Mount of Olives is portrayed consistently by Luke. Arrest and death are near, to be sure, but the one who has a disciplined life of prayer need not writhe and fall on the ground before that final hour. Sure, he wanted the cup to pass; of course, the pain and the shame of the next day were dreaded prospects, but from the day of his baptism Jesus has through prayer lived in the will of God. The Jesus whom Luke describes on that night of prayer is not one who does not know death; rather, he is the one who knows God. Jesus the man of prayer is therefore the model of the Christian life, from baptism to death, and especially in the sense that a lifetime of prayer can be a source of strength on those occasions when one is not only seeking God's will for oneself but also called upon to help others who seek desperately for guidance and strength.

Jesus Taken Captive (22:47–53)
(Matthew 26:47–56; Mark 14:43–52)

The crowd that comes to take Jesus consists of chief priests, temple officers, and elders, the very ones who have conspired to destroy Jesus since his arrival in Jerusalem (19:47). The presence of crowds favorable to Jesus had hindered all their ploys during the day. Their opportunity would have to be at night, but that would require knowledge of his lodging place. Judas has provided that knowledge. How appropriate, says Jesus, that they work at night, for they act in the power of darkness. Daylight is not congenial to their deeds (v. 53). Jesus has not sought death; his movements in Jerusalem and his prayer this very night (v. 42) establish that. But neither does he resist or fight his captors. One of the disciples does fight to defend Jesus (John 18:10 says it was Peter), wounding a slave of the high priest, but Jesus restores the slave's right ear and calls a halt to the altercation (vv. 50–51). Violence as a means of avoiding death is rejected.

The scene that night at "the place" (v. 40) is, of course, abhorrent to all followers of Jesus, but feelings for Jesus and against his captors should not blind us to the ironies in the event. Jesus is seized by the clergy. The clergy, until now, have been frustrated in their designs by the people who listened gladly to Jesus. In fact, the clergy have been afraid of the people (22:2), but now they are able to advance their plan through the services of a defector and traitor among Jesus' followers. Judas'

262

act of treason is made even more offensive by his attempt to disguise betrayal with a kiss, a sign of affection (Mark and Matthew say Judas actually did kiss Jesus). A disciple with genuine affection draws a sword in defense of Jesus. So an enemy comes with a kiss and a friend with a sword; things are not always what they seem. But Jesus sees through it all, stops both the kiss and the sword, and confronts his captors with the truth. However, when treachery, fear, and hatred are galvanized into a course of action, regardless of how unjust or violent, the truth must wait; no one has ears for it now. And so the peaceful one who forgives robbers is seized as though he were one.

Luke 22:54–71
The Jewish Trial

To speak of Jesus' appearance before Jewish authorities as a "trial" is to use the term quite unofficially; perhaps "hearing" would be more appropriate. The language becomes important if one is seeking to locate and define responsibilities for the death of Jesus, a task difficult to fulfill, for several reasons. First, the accounts are not court records but reports more concerned about results than process. Second, the Gospel records of the entire trial proceedings are very brief. And finally, the four Evangelists differ with one another in some important details (Matt. 26:57–75; Mark 14:53–72; John 18:12–27). Readers interested in an attempt at historical reconstruction will probably find Raymond E. Brown's arrangement of the four accounts with major positions argued to be of help (*The Gospel According to John*, 2:791–802). Our purpose here is to notice Luke's report of what happened between the arrest and the appearance before Pilate.

Since Jesus was taken captive by priests, temple officers, and elders, it is natural that disposition of him begin with the religious authorities. Jesus is taken to the house of the high priest the night of the arrest and there held in custody until the next morning (vv. 54, 66). There is no trial before the council that night, as in Mark's report (Mark 14:54–64). Luke tells of Jesus suffering physical and verbal abuse at the hands of his guards (vv. 63–65), but this occurs while he is in custody and not,

263

as Mark 14:65 and Matt. 26:67–68 have it, during or at the close of his trial. One notices also that Luke has Peter's denials taking place prior to the trial, while the other Evangelists interweave Jesus' trial inside with Peter's "trial" outside. Strikingly, of the eighteen verses in Luke's account, only six deal with the trial of Jesus before the council, while nine are devoted to Peter's denials. Luke's report of the evening's events following Jesus' arrest falls into three distinct units: Peter's denials (vv. 54–62), the mistreatment of Jesus (vv. 63–65), and the trial before the council (vv. 66–71). We will attend briefly to each unit in the order of Luke's presentation.

So sharply is the camera focused on Simon Peter in the courtyard that none of the other disciples are mentioned. Mark says they all abandoned Jesus (Mark 14:50), but here we can only speculate as to their behavior on the night Jesus said they would be sifted like wheat (v. 31). In the prediction at the table earlier, it was Simon Peter who received the primary attention: he would be tested, he would fail, he would repent, and he would subsequently be a source of strength to the others (vv. 31–34). The story before us tells of the fulfillment of three of those four prophesies. The fourth would have its fulfillment after the resurrection (Acts 1—5). Peter's presence in the courtyard of the house of the high priest lies somewhere between courage and cowardice. He follows the arrested Jesus and by entering the courtyard could possibly make good on his pledge, "I am ready to go with you to prison and to death" (v. 33). Yet he follows at a distance (v. 54), a fact that, along with the darkness of night, separated him from Jesus and any harm that might follow from association with a felon. However, Peter had been seen daily in the temple area with the other disciples in the company of Jesus, and the fire in the courtyard gives off sufficient light to make recognition of him possible. Three witnesses, a woman and two men, say as much: "with him," "one of them," and "with him; for he is a Galilean." How Peter was identified as a Galilean is not stated; Matthew says it was his speech (Matt. 26:73). Three times Peter denies knowledge of or association with Jesus. Luke reports no invoking a curse upon himself or denial with an oath (Mark 14:71), but Peter's defection from the group and his abandoning Jesus is no less clear and complete. He has been tested, and he failed. However, at verse 61 Luke inserts a moving scene not found in the other accounts: "And the Lord turned and looked at Peter." That look triggered

264

Peter's recollection of the conversation earlier that evening and he is immediately overcome by remorse. The first step on the path to repentance and restoration has been taken. We can only guess the processes of healing that must have taken place among the disciples prior to Pentecost when Peter stood with the eleven and preached (Acts 2:14).

Abandoned now by the only disciple who had entered the courtyard, Jesus is alone, his loneliness now exaggerated by the darkness both of the night and of the blindfold. That Jesus has been called a prophet seems especially to draw the ridicule and abuse by those holding him in custody, although they verbally attacked Jesus in many ways. Interestingly, in Luke Jesus is not accused of blasphemy by the council; rather, the word is used to describe the treatment of Jesus: they reviled (blasphemed) him (v. 65). Jesus had predicted that such treatment would be a part of his humiliation in Jerusalem (18:32), but even so, the silent acceptance of this mistreatment is remarkable. Luke is very likely offering the church a model of behavior when one is delivered to authorities because of one's faith (21:12–19). Certainly this scene was recalled later to instruct and encourage persecuted disciples: "Christ also suffered for you, leaving you an example, that you should follow in his steps. He committed no sin; no guile was found on his lips. When he was reviled, he did not revile in return; when he suffered, he did not threaten" (I Peter 2:21–23). John's Christ did not, however, take this abuse so quietly (John 18:19–23).

At sunrise Jesus was taken before the Jerusalem Sanhedrin, a Jewish judicial council. The word "sanhedrin" is used so variously in biblical and nonbiblical literature that it is difficult to know for certain whether there was only one or several, whether it had clearly defined powers and personnel, and its relationship to local Roman authorities (see the article in *Harper's Bible Dictionary*). Here in 22:66–71, "their council [sanhedrin]" consists of chief priests, scribes, and elders. Later, Luke will say that there were both Sadducees and Pharisees in the membership of the council (Acts 23:1–7), but from the outset Jesus' opposition in Jerusalem has come from these three groups and they now have him officially in their custody and subject to their interrogation. Luke's record is quite brief: the high priest is not mentioned as presiding, no witnesses are called, there is no charge about destroying the temple, and the charge of blasphemy is not stated, although it may be implied.

265

The questioning is entirely christological, the two questions put to Jesus serving as indirect testimony to who he is: Are you the Messiah? and, Are you the son of God? Although in question form, from the lips of the highest authorities in Judaism come the affirmations central to Luke's presentation of Jesus. The response of Jesus to the interrogation has three parts. First, he tells them that they are not really interested in his answers as the basis for faith. Their minds are set; they will not accept his answers or answer his questions. Second, Jesus alludes to Dan. 7:13 and Ps. 110:1 to declare his future place of power in the presence of God. And finally, by responding "You say that I am," Jesus makes the council responsible for its own interpretation of who he is and, hence, the council's actions toward him. Jesus has protected himself legally but to no avail. The reader knows that the council has through its interrogation declared who Jesus is, that the council does not believe that declaration, and that the council considers Jesus' performance before it as self-incriminating. The council feels he has testified against himself with sufficient clarity to give it grounds to accuse him before the Roman governor. The council knows, however, that a christological debate will not play well before a Roman governor. Therefore Jesus' testimony about his relation to God must be translated into political terms or the council has no case. What that political interpretation will be has not yet surfaced, although the question to Jesus about tribute to Caesar (20:20–26) was asked in the search for a case worthy of the governor's attention (20:20). We can assume that issue will reemerge.

Luke 23:1–25
The Roman Trial and Sentencing

Jesus had prophesied that in his suffering and death he would be handed over to Gentiles (18:32). That time has now come. However, Luke does not permit the reader the move from a Jewish phase to a Gentile phase of the proceedings against Jesus. The Jewish involvement continues to the end, and it is important to notice how Luke portrays that involvement and to speculate as to why he does so. All the Evangelists relate the examination of Jesus by Pilate and the pressure put on the governor by the Jews (Mark 15:1–15; Matt. 27:1–26; John 18: 28—19:16), the record in the Fourth Gospel being the most extensive. However, in the case of Luke, we have the sermonic recitals of these events in the early chapters of Acts which will help us to understand Luke's narration of the passion of Jesus. It might be helpful at the outset to relieve ourselves of the task of ascertaining degrees of responsibility and guilt for the death of Jesus. Who killed Jesus? The answer is, the Roman soldiers under the authority of the prefect of Judea, Pontius Pilate. However, students of Luke have long recognized Luke's less than ugly portrayal of Pilate's role in the matter, the details of which we will examine shortly. Pilate, says Luke, found Jesus innocent and wanted to release him. Some scholars understand this presentation of Pilate to have been prompted in part by Luke's desire to demonstrate to Roman officials that there is not, nor has there been, fundamental incompatibility between the church and Rome. One recalls in this regard the opening address to Theophilus (1:1–4), perhaps a Roman official, and the numerous occasions recited in Acts on which Paul the Roman citizen was rescued, given protective custody, and given rights of appeal from Jerusalem to Caesarea to Rome. The tendency to defend Christianity before Roman authority is probably present. However, theological tendencies do not fully prevail over history, and the historical record is there in Luke: Pilate acquiesced to pressure and "Jesus he delivered up to their will" (v. 25). That Pilate declared Jesus innocent does not lessen but rather increases his burden in the matter.

However, Luke will not accept the above paragraph as the full answer to the question, Who killed Jesus? Israel in assembly in Jerusalem insisted on the death of Jesus. Jerusalem, "killing the prophets and stoning those who are sent to you" (13:34), now kills another prophet. The early Christian preachers in Jerusalem would say to "all the people" (Acts 3:11) that they had delivered up and denied Jesus "in the presence of Pilate, when he had decided to release him. But you denied the Holy and Righteous One, and asked for a murderer to be granted to you, and killed the Author of life" (Acts 3:13–15). Does this mean that Luke is not only pro-Roman but also anti-Jewish? Hardly. We have had repeated occasions to notice Luke's insistence on the continuity between Judaism and Christianity, on the adequacy of the Hebrew Scriptures to move their readers to faith in Jesus as Messiah, on the favorable view of Jerusalem and the

267

temple, on the pious Jewish family from which Jesus came, and on the portrayal of Jesus as a true Israelite in worship and in obedience to the law of Moses. How, then, are we to understand Luke's presentation of the involvement of the Jews in the death of Jesus? It is time to turn to the details of the text before us for at least a partial answer.

Luke does not focus on the high priest or any specific group in the Jewish delivery of Jesus to Pilate. Throughout verses 1–25 Luke uses expressions such as "the whole company" (v. 1), "the chief priests and the rulers and the people" (v. 13), and "they all" (v. 18). But the whole of this Gospel up to this point argues against this being a broadside anti-Jewish portrayal. Rather, it is the basis for Luke's call to Israel to repent. Israel will be called to repentance just as Germany was, or as the United States has been. To pinpoint blame, to isolate a few as culprits might satisfy the law, but the problem is broader and deeper. Israel's Scriptures, said Luke, bear witness to the Messiah (24:44; Acts 3:21), but Israel rejected the Messiah. That fact does not end the story, however, for repentance and forgiveness are to be preached, *beginning* in *Jerusalem* (24:47). Hence after the resurrection, the disciples declared to Jerusalem, "And now, brethren, I know that you acted in ignorance, as did also your rulers. But what God foretold by the mouth of all the prophets, that his Christ should suffer, he thus fulfilled. Repent therefore, and turn again, that your sins may be blotted out, that times of refreshing may come from the presence of the Lord, and that he may send the Christ appointed for you, Jesus" (Acts 3:17–20). Indictment, call to repentance, and the offer of repentance is no more anti-Jewish than Paul's indictment of Athens for idolatry (which he said was also done in ignorance), his call to repentance, and offer of forgiveness (Acts 17:22–31) is anti-Gentile.

The particular act that the early Christian preachers summarized as delivering up and denying in the presence of Pilate (Acts 3:13) consisted of three parts: turning Jesus over to Pilate, bringing charges against Jesus, and insisting that the charges constituted grounds for execution. The charges were three: that Jesus was a revolutionary, that he forbade taxes to Caesar (recall 20:25), and that he claimed to be Christ a king (23:2). These charges reflect neither the findings of the earlier interrogation by the Sanhedrin (22:66–71) nor the nature of Jesus' ministry. Jesus had been called Christ (9:20; 18:38) and king (19:38), but he had not made those claims to thrust himself into the role of leader of the people. As for the charge, "He stirs up the people" (v. 5), it had a ring of truth in it but not in the way the accusers wanted Pilate to perceive it. Jesus did stir up the people: preaching the reign of God and giving people a foretaste of that reign through healing, exorcising demons, and releasing them from hopelessness and despair did arouse the crowds. While not directly political, the ministry of Jesus did have political implications in the sense that politics has to do with the life and welfare of a community. No one who ministers in the manner and tradition of Jesus can claim to be innocent of political influence. On the whole, institutions are conservative and depend on the stability of the status quo for continuity. A community in ferment because many have had a new taste of health and hope and freedom poses a threat to all whose positions and privileges are predicated on everything remaining as is. Those in authority can argue reasonably that change will be costly and painful and that it is to everyone's advantage to remove those who stir the people. Of course, institutions can change by their own initiative, or they may welcome agents of change, but such self-evaluation and self-criticism are rare. No one enjoys feeling the ground shifting beneath the feet; if a crucifixion promises stability, then some will find reasons for the crucifixion. And they need not be evil people; they may be good people who have in the course of time gradually turned from the originating purpose to political expedients, which now protect them from those who remind them of that purpose.

Pilate knows his responsibility: to keep peace in an area known for its revolutionary activity. In his mind all the charges center in one question and he asks it directly: "Are you the King of the Jews?" (v. 3). Jesus' answer, "You have said so," is taken by Pilate as a denial; the same answer to an earlier question by the Sanhedrin was taken as an admission (22:70). Different people can hear opposite messages in the same words, a fact that should keep the pulpit and the classroom draped in humility. Pilate makes the first of three declarations of Jesus' innocence (vv. 4, 14, 22) but without persuasion. His learning that Jesus was a Galilean seemed to offer a way out, since conveniently Herod Antipas, tetrarch of Galilee, was in town.

Herod welcomes the opportunity to see Jesus (vv. 6–12). For some time Herod had sought to see Jesus (9:9) and reportedly wanted to kill him (13:31–33), but here he seems satisfied to interrogate Jesus, toy with him, try to get Jesus to perform a

269

sign, treat him with contempt, make fun of him, and, as a final touch, dress Jesus as a royal figure, returning him to Pilate as if to say, "Here's the king!" The accusers of Jesus among the Jews were not about to let Jesus be released through some slippage or carelessness between these two rulers. Hence they accompany Jesus to Herod's residence and return with him again to Pilate. Jesus does not leave their surveillance. The agreement between Pilate and Herod that Jesus did not deserve death (v. 15) and their cooperation in this unusual trial cemented a new relationship between them. Psalm 2:2 is fulfilled: "The rulers take counsel together, against the LORD and his anointed" (Acts 4:25–28). What a basis for a friendship!

Luke's position on the trial of Jesus is summarized in verses 13–16: all Israel is assembled against Jesus; Pilate tells them that an examination of Jesus proves their charges wrong; Rome (Pilate and Herod) is unanimous in its judgment of Jesus' innocence; Pilate is willing to chastise Jesus and release him. Yet the chain of events that was begun when Satan entered Judas (22:3), who led the chief priests to arrest Jesus (22:47), the chief priests who now lead the people to deny Jesus, seems unstoppable on its way to engineer the death of Jesus. Pilate repeats his position a third time, to no avail. The irony of it is that the multitude, for all their shouted concern about the dangerous Jesus the revolutionary who stirs up the people, requests the release of Barabbas, an insurrectionist and a murderer. The contradiction in such behavior is lost on them; when minds are made up, there is no room for reason. One cannot avoid recalling the countless champions of freedom who have acted violently to deny freedom in the name of freedom. Some ancient manuscripts add verse 17 (cf. footnote, RSV), a borrowing from Mark 15:6, to explain about the prisoner release, an episode not clear to the reader as Luke so briefly presents it. And so Pilate gave the sentence, but the voice of the crowd prevailed (v. 23); it was their demand which was granted (v. 24); it was to their will that Jesus was delivered (v. 25). Notice that Pilate's soldiers do not mock Jesus (Matt. 27:27–31; Mark 15:16–20).

Luke 23:26–56
The Crucifixion of Jesus

On the Way to the Crucifixion (23:26–32)
(Matthew 27:32; Mark 15:21)

Luke alone describes the way to the place called The Skull, Matthew and Mark remarking only about Simon of Cyrene. "And as *they* led him away" (v. 26): one has to believe that Luke leaves "they" ambiguous so as to include those to whom Pilate delivered Jesus. The soldiers will appear later (v. 36), but Luke will not allow them alone to bear the responsibility for what will now take place. Roman law permitted pressing persons such as Simon of Cyrene (in northern Africa) into service (Matt. 5:41), but in Luke's account he is the symbol of true discipleship, carrying the cross "behind Jesus" (v. 26). John says Jesus carried his own cross (John 19:17), compelling commentators who insist on harmonizing accounts to picture Jesus beginning on the way carrying the cross, falling beneath it, and then being relieved of it by Simon of Cyrene. Apparently the following crowd represents the reappearance of those common people who daily listened to Jesus in the temple. Once again Luke finds in the women an unmatched sympathy and grief, for they alone weep over what is happening. The background is Zech. 12:10. Jesus tells them that the greater cause for tears is unbelieving Jerusalem. So terrible will be its fate that the fortunate women will be those without children. In that day, Hosea's prophecy of cries for shelter going unheeded will be fulfilled (Hos. 10:8). Jesus recites a proverb (v. 31) to the effect that if such a tragedy as his death can occur in a time relatively noninflammatory, imagine the holocaust when Jerusalem is a tinderbox. Then in a brief note Luke introduces the fact that two others were being crucified with Jesus (v. 32). This introduction prepares the reader for their participation in the story later, but it also fulfills Isa. 53:12, cited earlier at 22:37: "And he was reckoned with transgressors." As we have seen repeatedly, it is important to Luke that the Hebrew Scriptures testify to Jesus and that in him they are fulfilled. Jerusalem's blindness to the time of God's visitation and ignorance of who Jesus is (23:34) are, therefore,

271

inexcusable and justify the call to the city to repent and receive forgiveness. There is an ignorance that is due to lack of opportunity, but this is an ignorance due to a closing of the eyes.

The Crucifixion (23:33–43)
(Matthew 27:33–44; Mark 15:22–32)

The reader has to be impressed by the brevity of the record of the event that has, more than any other, stirred the mind, heart, and soul of the church. The simple, straightforward report contrasts sharply with the flood of feeling-filled poetry, music, and homilies that has flowed since. The very nature of the biblical account reminds us that for all the anger, sorrow, and pain generated in the followers of Jesus by this scene, its significance lies first of all in the historical fact of the crucifixion. "Suffered under Pontius Pilate, was crucified, dead, and buried": the church confesses this, even on Easter, and with the fact that Jesus Christ was executed as a criminal among criminals all serious Christian reflection must deal.

Luke gives us the place: The Skull. He does not use the Aramaic "Golgotha" (Latin: Calvary). Tradition has placed it on a hill, but none of the Evangelists say so. Perhaps it was because crucifixions were usually placed in highly visible locations that the idea of a hill arose. Luke assumes that the reader knows what a crucifixion involved and therefore provides almost no details. A cross is literally an impaling stick or an upright stake and did not necessarily include a second piece of wood, as the word "cross" implies. As early as the Persians, bodies of criminals, dead or living, were thus put on public display as a deterrent to crime. The Romans made it a widely used form of execution for common criminals because it not only warned the public about crimes against Rome but also added shame, pain, and slow death to the executed. Apparently the Romans added the crossbeam, although crosses continued to have a variety of shapes. It was usually this crossbeam which the criminal carried to the place of execution, and the body was affixed by ropes or nails. Luke tells us who attended the execution. The soldiers assigned to crucifixion detail are there, of course. They make sport of Jesus, mocking him with the title "King of the Jews," saying that surely a king can save himself (vv. 36–37). What motivated the offer of vinegar, a sharp wine drunk by soldiers, is not stated. Luke omits the wine mixed with myrrh, an anesthetic (Mark 15:23). The offer of vinegar recalls Ps. 69:21.

Whether it is the soldiers who cast lots for Jesus' clothing (v. 34; Ps. 22:18) is not clear; the identities of those who did it are concealed and revealed in Luke's "they." The rulers of the Jews are there, mocking Jesus with two titles, Messiah and Chosen One (recall 9:35), saying that surely such a one, having saved others, could save himself (v. 35). Together with the soldiers, these rulers revive the voice of temptation first heard in the desert, "If you are the Son of God" (4:1–13). Jesus again refuses to call upon the power of God for his own comfort or security. If he is, in a larger sense, to save others, he cannot save himself. And Luke says the crowd is there, the crowd that hung on Jesus' words daily in the temple, but before this spectacle they only watch in silence (v. 35). Had they entertained any thought of action, they probably felt powerless before the forces of religion and government joined in the execution of Jesus.

Luke turns our attention twice to the ones on the crosses. The first time is to hear a word from Jesus: "Father, forgive them; for they know not what they do" (v. 34). Some early and important manuscripts omit this saying, and some scholars argue against it, pointing out that it is awkwardly located, that the "they" is unclear in its reference, that the ignorance motif occurs in Acts (Acts 3:17; 13:27; 17:30) but not in the Gospel, and that the prayer sounds very much like Stephen's in Acts 7:60. The manuscript evidence is worthy of consideration, but the other arguments are not convincing. The location of the saying and the indefinite "they" relate to each other; at this point in his narrative Luke uses "they" apparently in a deliberate way to involve both Jews and Romans in the crucifixion. If "they" are so implicated, then "they" are the beneficiaries of the prayer for forgiveness. The statement is as Lukan and as appropriate on Jesus' lips as his instructions to forgive (17:4) and to love one's enemies (6:35). As for the use of Acts to interpret the Gospel, this is quite in order. In writing the Gospel, Luke anticipated Acts, so that much in the Gospel has its fulfillment and clarity in Acts. To try to understand either without the other is a fruitless exercise in excessive rigidity.

The second time Luke turns our attention to the crucified ones (vv. 39–43), it is to hear the three communicate with each other. One of the criminals adds a third to the two taunts (rulers, soldiers) already heard: he says, in effect, if you are the Messiah, get us down from here. The other criminal rebukes him, distinguishes between their own justly deserved punishment and

273

that of the innocent Jesus, and expresses faith in Jesus by asking to be remembered when Jesus comes into his kingly power. Jesus assures him a place in Paradise (the abode of the righteous dead, II Cor. 12:3; Rev. 2:7). In this exchange between Jesus and the penitent criminal, recorded only in Luke, the Evangelist is able not only to witness, however sketchily, to the exaltation of Christ into his glory (24:26; Acts 2:32–36) but also to record an act of salvation in a situation in which the word "save" has been used in taunts and ridicule. Three times he has been mocked with "Save yourself," the one criminal adding "and us." Here Jesus does save someone, and that the one saved is a dying criminal is totally congenial to the types of persons blessed by Jesus throughout his ministry. In his own dying hour, Jesus continues his ministry: "For the Son of man came to seek and to save the lost" (19:10).

The Death of Jesus (23:44–49)
(Matthew 27:45–56; Mark 15:33–41)

In six verses, a single paragraph, Luke reports Jesus' death. The report consists of three parts: the unusual signs preceding the death, the death itself, and the responses of the persons who are present. Luke joins Mark and Matthew in remarking on the darkness over the land from noon until three. This phenomenon can be interpreted in a number of ways. The darkness could be a symbol of the powers of evil at work. Jesus had said at the time of his arrest, "This is your hour, and the power of darkness" (22:53). His death and resurrection will scatter this darkness. Or one might consider the darkening of the whole land as a prophecy or portent of the tragic days ahead for a land that had rejected God's Christ. Early Christians, including Luke, related the fateful war of 66–70 C.E. to the denial of Jesus by Jerusalem and its leaders. Or again, the darkness could be nature's participation in the event taking place. The Scriptures frequently witness to the whole creation's involvement in those affairs which affect human history. We have had several occasions to note creation's witness to God's activity among us (cf. comments at 17:22–37 and 21:25–28). If stones cry out when disciples are silent (19:40), why would not the sky darken when the Son of God hangs dying? The tearing of the temple curtain (v. 45) is not recorded in Mark and Matthew until after the death, which could give it different symbolic meaning. Here again, interpreters differ. The temple veil divided the Holy of

274

Holies from the Holy Place. Some scholars take Luke's meaning to be that God has left the temple (the glory of God has departed), the Holy of Holies no longer being the secret dwelling place of God. Others understand the tearing of the veil to mean that Jesus is entering God's presence. The most common interpretation, however, and the one developed at length in the epistle to the Hebrews, is that the open curtain means that the way of access to God through Jesus' act is now available. In combination the two signs speak of the effect of the death of Jesus upon the whole earth and upon the central institution of religion in particular.

As for the death itself, there is no conversation about Elijah or the cry of dereliction which some took to be a call to Elijah (Mark 15:34–35). Rather, the cry of Jesus in Luke is a prayer of trust in God and the committing of his spirit into God's care. There is nothing here of anger or doubt or thrashing about in the throes of death. Rather, Luke writes of serenity, acceptance, and trust. Jesus died sometime in the afternoon of the day before the Sabbath, which was Passover. His last words were a quotation of Ps. 31:5: "Father, into thy hands I commit my spirit!"

Following the death, Luke records three responses: in the person of the centurion Rome again declares Jesus innocent (v. 47); the crowds go home deeply sorrowful and penitent (beating the breast, v. 48; cf. 18:13); and Jesus' acquaintances and the women who had followed from Galilee witness his death (v. 49). Witnessing his death is necessary in order that they be qualified witnesses to his resurrection. We would ask Luke who these women are, but he has already told us (8:1–3), and the way they are mentioned here alerts the reader to expect their reappearance later in the story. That these Galileans stood "at a distance" may prompt the interpreter to recall Luke's earlier uses of the expression (16:23; 18:13; 22:54) in order to determine if the distance is that of humility, fear, non-involvement, or separation.

In the brief accounts of Jesus' crucifixion and death, Luke has managed to weave into the narrative more theological reflection than may at first be apparent. From the lips of his deniers and detractors he is called God's Christ, the Chosen One, and King of the Jews. Both a Roman officer and a criminal dying with him acknowledge his innocence. The rulers, the soldiers, and one of the criminals speak of him, in derision to be

275

sure, as one who saves, and in his dying hour he does save a sinner. From the cross Jesus announces forgiveness, for Luke the very heart of the gospel (24:47; Acts 2:38), and in that word of forgiveness is stated the fundamental problem plaguing both Jews and Gentiles (Acts 3:17; 13:27; 17:30): they act out of ignorance even though the sources of knowing (Moses and the prophets in the one case, creation and conscience in the other) were available to them. Paul and others will develop more fully other interpretations of the death of Jesus, but already here in Luke's account of the crucifixion, the reader has been given a cup quite full.

The Burial of Jesus (23:50–56)
(Matthew 27:57–61; Mark 15:42–47)

Jesus died away from home, and on Friday afternoon, with the Sabbath fast approaching. The proper care of the body with spices and ointments could wait; the pressing need is to remove the body from the cross and place it somewhere, at least temporarily. According to the law of Moses, if a man were punished by death and his body hanged on a tree, the body was to be removed and buried the same day (Deut. 21:22–23). Apparently under the Roman occupation this law was applied to crucifixions (Fitzmyer, *The Gospel According to Luke*, 2:1524). Although Jesus was executed as a common criminal, his body was not tossed in a common grave; on the contrary, that in death he was accorded great respect is affirmed by Luke in three ways. First, the body of Jesus was claimed and cared for by a member of the Sanhedrin. Joseph is identified by address, position, character, and attitude toward Jesus and his message. That he "was looking for the kingdom of God" (v. 51) places him among the pious such as Simeon and Anna (2:25–38). That he had not consented to the Sanhedrin's action against Jesus does not tell us whether he abstained when the vote was taken or took the floor in defense of Jesus. In either case, his going to Pilate to claim the body and his burying it are acts of courage, as Mark points out (Mark 15:43), and won for him a place alongside Simon of Cyrene in the church's memory of the crucifixion.

Second, the respect shown Jesus in death is noted in the description of the tomb as one "where no one had ever yet been laid" (v. 53). Only Luke and John (John 19:41) contain this reference to the tomb as being one worthy of such a person, recalling the entry into the city on a colt "on which no one has ever yet sat" (19:30).

Finally, respect for Jesus' body is shown in the actions of the women of Galilee. They observe where and how the body is laid; just as they had given financial support to Jesus during his life (8:1–3), so now they prepare the spices and ointments for a full and proper burial, once the Sabbath has passed (v. 56).

Among the Evangelists only Luke adds the observation, "On the sabbath they ·[the women] rested according to the commandment" (v. 56). Their behavior is both surprising and not surprising. It is not surprising in that Luke has been careful all along to place the career of Jesus and his followers within the piety which respected the law and customs of Judaism. In death as at birth (2:21–39), the law of Moses has been kept. However, the behavior is a bit surprising in that observing the Sabbath as usual seems not to recognize and mark the unusual event that has occurred. Jesus is dead. For three hours darkness covered the whole land, and the temple veil was torn in two. In other words, heaven is dramatically interrupting the course of nature and breaking with the religious past as a way of announcing the unique significance of that which has transpired, and yet the women of Galilee keep to their routine schedule and observe the Sabbath. One could defend their behavior by pointing out that at the time of a death, there really is little anyone can do. Nobody goes to work, nobody goes to school, nobody is hungry, nobody has anything to say, nobody feels very helpful. But on a deeper level, their keeping the Sabbath makes all kind of sense. When the ground gives way beneath the feet, when heaven and earth are shaken, when life's reason has been removed by death, something has to be the same, dependable and certain. What, at such a time, could be more nourishing and stabilizing than the same house of worship, the same pew, the same Scriptures, the same faces, the same prayers, the same voices, the same order of service? Luke is not reporting a case of mindless legalism but how a group of women found a place to stand when everything seemed to be shaken out of order.

Long before Luke wrote his narrative, the burial of Jesus had become part of the Christian proclamation. Luke's report in Acts of early Christian preaching contains reference to the burial of Jesus (Acts 13:29). But in a much earlier record, Paul says that the gospel tradition he received included the clause

277

"he was buried" (I Cor. 15:3–4). Simple logic would call for a statement of the burial as an essential preface to the proclamation of the resurrection of Jesus from the dead ("from among the dead ones"), but in theological debate the reference to burial became even more important. There were unbelievers to be persuaded that the gospel was not a pleasant word centered in a vague doctrine of immortality; rather, Jesus died, was buried, and was raised from the dead. There were also those Christians who could find no way to embrace in their Christologies the actual death of Jesus. Some preferred to believe that Simon of Cyrene, since he carried the cross, was crucified by mistake. Others entertained theories of a plot according to which Jesus was given a drug while on the cross which so arrested his life signs as to convince his crucifiers he was dead. Of course, the followers of Jesus found it extremely difficult to pronounce the words, "Jesus is dead"; the church always has. To this day, some churches withhold nothing in the celebration of Easter, while not marking at all Good Friday, as though there could be a resurrection without a corpse. Such well-meaning but clearly erroneous thinking about Jesus Christ had become sufficiently pervasive in the early church that the framers of the Apostles' Creed felt it important to counter it in a fourfold affirmation: "Suffered under Pontius Pilate, was crucified, dead, and buried."

A final word about Luke's record of Jesus' burial. While Jesus was on the cross, both Jews and Gentiles acknowledge, in tones of derision to be sure, who he is. Now in death, Jesus is honored, symbolically speaking, by the entire country. Not only were the women of Galilee present and attentive to Jesus but Luke points out that Joseph is a Judean ("from the Jewish town"; v. 50 means, literally, "from a town of the Judeans"). Galilee and Judea, north and south Palestine, male and female join to tell the reader that for all that has occurred Jesus has not been totally abandoned. With that positive note, Luke makes a place for expectation, for some small hope that the story has not yet ended.

PART SEVEN

The Resurrection Narrative

LUKE 24:1–53

Luke opened his Gospel with infancy narratives that were uniquely his own in the sense that they were not told by the other Evangelists. Luke now closes his Gospel with a resurrection narrative that is almost uniquely his own, the empty tomb account (24:1–12) clearly drawing on Mark 16:1–8, a version of which is found in Matthew, with John's empty tomb story being quite different. But even in the units of the resurrection narrative peculiar to Luke we will have occasion to notice repeated instances of influences from the other Gospels. For example, the RSV (1971 ed.) will carry notes at 24:5, 12, 36, 40, 51, and 52 saying "Other ancient authorities add" or "Other ancient authorities omit." This simply means that scribes who copied the manuscripts quite early permitted, consciously or unconsciously, the resurrection stories in the other Gospels to influence what they were writing. In some cases they probably were remembering Mark or John while writing Luke; in others, they may have been intentionally harmonizing. There was certainly no attempt to deceive or to reduce the faith in any way. On the contrary, the general tendency was to enlarge the story. This cross-fertilization of texts is to be taken as evidence that the early church treated the resurrection stories as one story, and the blending occurred as it does with us: two, three, or four accounts of one event, even though each has its own accent and purpose, tend to become one account in the church's memory. The church has, however, in its more reflective moments, frowned on such harmonizing, not only because it tends to blur

279

what each Evangelist is saying but also because the harmonized story becomes, in effect, a fifth Gospel. We will try here to listen to Luke and urge the preacher or the teacher not only to do so but also to use the notes about variations in the text to help the congregations better understand what a Bible is and how it is transmitted. Small attention to such matters now and again in sermons and lessons will help immensely to give believers their Bible while removing superstitious views of it.

Luke's resurrection narrative consists of four units: the empty tomb (vv. 1–12), appearance on the road to Emmaus (vv. 13–35), appearance in Jerusalem (vv. 36–49), and blessing and departure (vv. 50–53). In Luke, all the appearances of the risen Christ are in or near Jerusalem, and they are told as occurrences on one day, the first day of the week. Perhaps they had been so framed for the church's observation of Easter, a possibility strongly supported by the content itself. Before moving to the individual units, the reader would do well to ponder the whole of chapter 24 as a worship experience. Notice that first there is the announcement that Christ is risen, but with little immediate effect. Then comes a period of instruction from Scripture followed by an experience of the living Christ in the breaking of bread. This experience is communicated, and in a setting filled with fear, belief, disbelief, and joy the experience occurs again. With further instruction from Scripture, the disciples receive Christ's promise of the Spirit and are commissioned. Christ gives them his benediction and leaves them to a life of joy and praise. We had occasion to observe in Luke's opening chapters the number of songs, prayers, doxologies, and benedictions, suggesting liturgical use. Now at the close of the Gospel the reader senses being returned to the sanctuary, perhaps the place where the story we are about to read is most at home.

Luke 24:1–12
The Empty Tomb

280

The earliest form of the gospel tradition that has come to us is recalled by Paul as that which he had received (I Cor. 15:3–7). Strikingly, that tradition, which focuses heavily on the resurrection and the appearances of the risen Christ, mentions neither the empty tomb nor the role of women. Both are important to all the Evangelists (Matt. 28:1–10; Mark 16:1–8; John 20:1–10), and to none more than Luke. The discovery of the tomb opened and the body gone not only opens Luke's resurrection narrative but the discovery by the women is repeated in the witness of the two on the road to Emmaus (vv. 22–23) and their story confirmed by others who went to the tomb and found it just as the women said (v. 24). Of course, an empty tomb in and of itself does not present a persuasive argument for the resurrection; an empty tomb means the body is not there. The burden of the Christian proclamation was on the experience of the risen Christ by his followers, as Luke was to say later: Jesus' life and death all of you know, but that God raised him from the dead, "of that we all are witnesses" (Acts 2:32; cf. 3:15). But the empty tomb story joined to the witness of those who saw the risen Christ strengthened and heightened the impact of the church's proclamation. Not only that, but the empty tomb supported the very important point that the one raised was the crucified and buried Jesus. The church from the beginning has refused to allow resurrection to be interpreted in terms totally subjective. Matters of faith are never finally *proven,* nor faith generated by an incontrovertible argument. Faith is communicated by witness, but that witness is not reduced to how believers have felt about their experiences of Jesus Christ. The one raised from the dead said to his followers, "See my hands and my feet, that it is I myself; handle me, and see" (v. 39). This, says Luke (all the Evangelists agree), means the tomb was empty.

As for the women, they are so prominent in the narrative that Luke is comfortable identifying them as "they," delaying their names until the end of the episode (v. 10). The women of Galilee do not make their first appearance only at the tomb; they had already witnessed the crucifixion (23:49) and the burial (23:55) as well as now the empty tomb. In fact, it is only after they enter the tomb and discover the body missing that Luke introduces the two messengers in dazzling apparel (v. 4). The women of Galilee are thoroughly qualified witnesses, lacking only the experience of the risen Christ. Luke's reference to the two men (later referred to as a vision of angels, v. 23) joins this episode to the transfiguration (9:30) and the ascension (Acts 1:10) and may indicate how Luke wants the reader to classify and understand this story. This is to say that transfiguration, resurrection, and ascension may be understood as one general category of experience.

Close attention to the experience of the women in the tomb will tell us a great deal not only about them but about Luke's Gospel and about Luke's anticipation of the continued account in Acts. The women (three are named, along with other women, v. 10) are mildly reprimanded for seeking the living among the dead (some scribes borrowed a line from Matt. 28:6 and added it to v. 5). They should have known better, say the messengers, because Christ had told them in Galilee that he would be betrayed, crucified, and on the third day raised (vv. 6–7). This brief creedal formula, repeated essentially in verses 26 and 46, lies at the center of the proclamation that was to produce repentance and forgiveness of sins (v. 47). It is important to notice that the men said "he told you" (v. 6) and that the women "remembered his words" (v. 8). Four matters of significance are conveyed in verses 6–8. First, Galilee belongs to the preparatory past. Luke has "he told you, while he was still in Galilee," while Matt. 28:7 and Mark 16:7 have "he is going before you to Galilee." Mark anticipates and Matthew describes (Matt. 28:16) a meeting of the risen Christ with his followers in Galilee, but it is not so in Luke's account. For him, Jerusalem is now the center for Christ's appearances (vv. 13–43), for the commissioning and empowering of the disciples (vv. 44–53), and for the mission of the church to the world (Acts), "For out of Zion shall go forth the law, and the word of the LORD from Jerusalem" (Micah 4:2).

Second, the text assumes that Christ had told the women that he would be betrayed, crucified, and raised. This information places the women in the inner circle of disciples with whom such a prediction had been shared. One can here see Luke enlarging the circle of disciples to anticipate Acts in which the group gathered in prayer and awaiting the Holy Spirit includes the eleven, Mary the mother of Jesus, his brothers, and the women, in all about 120 persons (Acts 1:12–15). In fact, here in verse 8 the women tell their experience to the eleven and "to all the rest," and again at verse 33 the eleven are gathered "and those who were with them." While Luke regards the apostles as a special group, he does not limit the special experiences with Christ and the Holy Spirit to them alone. The reader of such accounts, although removed by time and place, is made to feel that he or she is not merely an observer but a participant in the story of the church made up of believers, both men and women.

Third, and this is already implied in the preceding comments, in Luke the women are not commanded to go and tell the disciples, as both Mark and Matthew have it. The women are not errand runners for disciples; they are disciples. While it is true they relate their experience to the eleven and others, such reporting was congenial to the excitement of the event and no different from other exchanges of witness.

Finally, the faith and the witness of the women consisted of three elements: the discovery of the empty tomb, the word of the two messengers, and their remembrance of the words of Jesus. Often the third factor is overlooked, but it is very important in the Gospel and is confirmed in our experience. After the resurrection, disciples remembered and understood. The two at Emmaus experienced Christ in the breaking of bread and then remembered what Jesus had said on the road (v. 32). Faith does not usually move from promise to fulfillment but from fulfillment to promise. Remembering is often the activating of the power of recognition. For this reason alone it is most important that the teacher and the preacher share with the listeners the story of Jesus and of the church. Such recitals may not strike fire at the time or be heard as matters of burning relevance; however, the times will come when the congregation will remember and it will make all the difference. But one cannot remember what one has not heard.

That the apostles did not believe the report should not be explained by saying it was because the report was given by women (v. 11). There has been too much of such flippancy; no doubt men bringing the same report would have met the same unbelief. Their faith waits on a confirming experience of the risen Christ, an experience that was not without its own element of unbelief (v. 41). In the meantime, verse 11 reminds all of us who celebrate Easter so easily what a burden the resurrection of the dead places on faith, even among those close to Jesus.

In the RSV (1971 ed.), the NEB, and some other translations, verse 12 is placed in the footnotes. This is not because there is a lack of strong support for the verse in the ancient manuscripts; in fact, the weight of evidence seems to support including it in the text. The questionable status of verse 12 is due rather to the belief that it is a direct borrowing from John 20:3–10 and that

283

its presence in the text would create a contradiction with verse 34. That the various resurrection traditions influenced each other is evident in a number of places. However, verse 12 would not be as uncomfortable in the text as some have supposed. Peter going to the tomb could be an instance of what verse 24 reports: "Some of those who were with us went to the tomb, and found it just as the women had said; but him they did not see." Verse 34, rather than standing in contradiction, could refer to a subsequent experience of Peter. But whether or not the preacher and the teacher include verse 12 in the narrative, Luke has communicated the atmosphere of confusion, disturbance, and doubt, the followers of Jesus awaiting some confirmation of the reports that Jesus has indeed been raised from the dead.

Luke 24:13–35
Appearance on the Road to Emmaus

Persons with an interest in the narrative form for preaching and for doing theology need look no farther for a model than the story before us. This account ranks with the parable of the loving father and Paul's voyage to Rome as a display of Luke's literary skills. The narrative is peculiar to Luke, intersecting other resurrection narratives only at verse 34, which confirms an earlier tradition about an appearance of Jesus to Simon Peter (I Cor. 15:5). The story is typically Lukan in that it echoes an Old Testament story, the Lord's appearance to Abraham and Sarah at Mamre (Gen. 18:1–15). Also typically Lukan is the journey as the frame for the story. The time is Easter evening (vv. 13, 29), making this passage a natural choice for Easter evening worship services. In fact, the story may have been composed with worship in mind: notice the focus on word and sacrament, with a summary of the gospel, and movement from the table to witnessing to others. The characters are three, two disciples and Jesus incognito, but in conversation the three function as two, Jesus and Cleopas or Jesus and "they." A listener can follow it easily. The plot is carried in a comfortable and interesting balance between the narrator and the conversation of the characters. The movement is by walking, slowly and hopelessly from

Jerusalem to Emmaus, and then hastily and hopefully from Emmaus to Jerusalem. It is not important that Emmaus has never been identified with certainty, that one of the two disciples is totally unknown to us, and that Cleopas is encountered nowhere else. These uncertainties, natural questions for the historically curious, recede before the memorable impact of the story.

Anyone whose interest in the narrative form for preaching and for doing theology has been curbed by a suspicion that the story is a form too frail to carry the freight of biblical and theological content may find that suspicion at least partially removed by the text before us. Even though beautiful and complete stories do not invite interrupting comments, let us walk through this passage marking the major theological themes Luke has woven into this narrative.

1. Christ is known by revelation. Luke says of the two disciples, "But their eyes were kept from recognizing him" (v. 16), and at verse 31, "And their eyes were opened and they recognized him." Clearly, more is involved than their blindness due to shock or an inability to recognize Jesus due to some transformation of his appearance. We have had occasion earlier in this Gospel to note Luke's way of mixing divine action and human freedom. Following a prediction of the passion, the meaning of what Jesus was saying was concealed from the disciples (9:45). They were not ready or able to receive such a message at that time, but later in remembrance it would be understood. For Luke, neither God nor Christ can be known except by revelation (10:22), a viewpoint shared by Matthew (Matt. 16:17) and Paul (I Cor. 2:6–16). Faith is not coerced or overwhelmed by revelations to the unprepared. Notice that in the Gospels the risen Christ appears to disciples, not to unbelievers on the street and in synagogues to frighten them into an acquiescing faith. After instruction in Scripture and the Lord's Supper, the two disciples recognize Jesus.

2. Summary of the gospel recited. On the lips of Cleopas, Luke gives a summary of the gospel (vv. 18–24) beginning with the ministry of Jesus and concluding with the report but not the experience of the risen Christ. The summary is thus incomplete until Christ adds the word of resurrection (v. 26) and then makes himself known to them (v. 31). Concise statements about Jesus, his mighty works, suffering, death, and resurrection are the content of Christian preaching according to Luke and are

285

found repeatedly in Acts (Acts 2:22–36; 3:12–15; 5:29–32; 13: 16–39).

3. Old Testament Scriptures witness to Jesus. The two disciples are reprimanded for their unbelief on the grounds that the suffering, death, and resurrection of Jesus are set forth in Scripture, and they should have known (vv. 25–27). Throughout this Gospel we have observed Luke's insistence not only that Jesus and his followers properly obeyed the Scriptures but that Jesus fulfilled the prophecies of the Scriptures. These prophecies pointed both to his ministry (4:16–30) and to his suffering, death, and resurrection (vv. 26–27, 44–47). For this reason, Luke regards the Scriptures as sufficient for the generation of faith (16:31). That portion of Israel which rejected Jesus as Messiah did so because of their failure to understand their own Bible. This ignorance (Acts 3:17) God will forgive, but now that the risen Christ (vv. 25–27, 44–47) and the Holy Spirit (Acts) have opened the true meaning of the Old Testament texts, repentance is in order (v. 47; Acts 2:38; 3:19). For Luke, then, the gospel of Jesus Christ continues and brings to fulfillment the law, the prophets, and the writings.

4. Christ is revealed in the sacramental meal. That this meal in Emmaus is the Eucharist, the Lord's Supper, is quite evident in the language: "took . . . blessed . . . broke . . . gave . . ." (v. 30; 22:19; 9:16), but other details as well confirm the judgment. The meal begins with an act of hospitality, an invitation to a stranger by those who prepared the table (v. 29). It is the presence of Christ at a table opened to a stranger which transforms an ordinary supper into the sacrament. Christ is in a sense the guest ("Come, Lord Jesus"), and yet he is the host who breaks the bread, blesses God, and shares with those at table. It is in this act that the disciples recognize the stranger as Christ (vv. 31, 35). The disciples have now experienced Christ in word (interpreting the Scriptures) and sacrament (the breaking of bread). There is no doubt that Luke is writing not only the story of Jesus but also that of the church which knows him in these ways. The importance of experiencing the living Christ in word and sacrament cannot be overemphasized. There were, says Luke, special appearances of the resurrected Christ to a number of his followers. In fact, Luke says that such appearances continued for forty days before he was received up into glory (Acts 1:1–11). Yet were that the whole of the story, all believers except those select few would experience only the absence of

Jesus, fated to try to keep faith alive on the thin diet of these reports of his having once been seen by others. Thus all subsequent generations would have been secondhand Christians, removed by time and place from the Camelot of Luke-Acts. But Luke here tells us that the living Christ is both the key to our understanding the Scriptures and the very present Lord who is revealed to us in the breaking of bread. His presence at the table makes all believers first-generation Christians and every meeting place Emmaus.

5. *Disciples understand by remembrance.* "Did not our hearts burn within us while he talked to us on the road, while he opened to us the scriptures?" (v. 32). There is no word about any response of the disciples at the time Christ is interpreting the Scriptures (v. 27), but now, having experienced him at the table, they recall the extraordinary nature of the time with him on the road. In comments at verses 6–8 we have recalled the central role of memory in faith and understanding and need not repeat those comments here. We would do well, however, to pause for reflection both upon the many occasions in which Scripture reminds us that "after the resurrection the disciples remembered his words" and upon our own confirming experiences. There are three times in which to know an event: in rehearsal, at the time of the event, and in remembrance. In rehearsal, understanding is hindered by an inability to believe that the event will really occur or that it will be so important. At the time of the event, understanding is hindered by the clutter and confusion of so much so fast. But in remembrance, the nonseriousness of rehearsal and the busyness of the event give way to recognition, realization, and understanding. This is a time of understanding an important trip, a wedding, a gathering of friends, or a conversation with a stranger turned Christ at table.

6. *Disciples witness to what they have seen and heard.* The return of the two disciples from Emmaus to Jerusalem (vv. 33–35) serves three functions in Luke's narrative. First, they must share their good news. Having been turned from sadness and despair by having been at table with Christ they now recognized, their excitement moves them naturally toward their brothers and sisters who have been trapped in the same hopelessness. Their witness is to other disciples, not to the world; that task must wait until they are empowered from on high. But witness and proclamation have their place among believers as

287

well as unbelievers. The message that creates a believing community needs to be heard again and again by that community. To do so is to confirm, strengthen, encourage, and deepen faith.

Second, the return to Jerusalem joins the experience of these two disciples to that of Simon Peter (v. 34) and that of the eleven in the company of others (vv. 36–43). Their different encounters with the risen Christ are thus understood as one experience. This fact will be very important in the opening of Acts, for the church after Jesus will begin with all the disciples together and making a common witness (2:14).

Finally, returning to Jerusalem to report is vital in Luke's understanding of the church. Jerusalem is the center of the Christian mission and the apostles are in positions of authority in the Christian fellowship. Preachers scatter to Judea, Samaria, and to the ends of the earth, but they return with reports to Jerusalem. This was true of Simon Peter after a preaching tour of Palestine (Acts 9—11) and of Paul after each of his missionary journeys (Acts 13—21). The whole of Luke-Acts testifies to this focus on Jerusalem: Jesus moves toward Jerusalem, the gospel moves out from Jerusalem. Paul, who in his letters reports looking quite differently on Jerusalem, nevertheless had to deal with the Jerusalem church and its leadership, as tense as those negotiations were (Gal. 1—2). It is not surprising, then, that the women at the tomb report to the apostles (vv. 9–11), as do the two disciples who, having walked from Jerusalem to Emmaus, return to the city that same evening.

Luke 24:36–49
Appearance in Jerusalem

This unit is in two parts: the account of the appearance to the eleven and company (vv. 36–43) and the final instruction, commission, and promise (vv. 44–49). As for the appearance itself, two characteristics of form need to be noted. First, the similarity between verses 36–43 and John 20:19–21 is striking, whether or not that similarity is due to literary kinship. As the footnotes in the RSV (1971 ed.) point out, some manuscripts of this passage contain inserts from John: at the close of verse 36 (John 20:19), and verse 40 (John 20:20). Some parishioners will need help with such textual variants lest the mood of uncertainty about the text become erosive of faith. The preacher and the teacher want always to give the Bible to the listeners, not take it away. Whether one follows the judgment of the editors of the RSV and the NEB in the omissions at verses 36 and 40 or favors the inclusion of the material in question, as many manuscripts do, it needs most of all to be clear that no one is playing fast and loose with the text but rather that all are seriously seeking to know what Luke wrote. While this commentary has not sought to tarry long over textual variants, it has seemed important to remind the reader that such occasions of differences in texts and in English translations provide important teachable moments. For a discussion of these variants, Joseph Fitzmyer's commentary (he favors including both texts in question) is helpful *(The Gospel According to Luke,* 2:1575–1576). The second formal quality of verses 36–43 to be noted is the pattern of narration. Although much briefer than the Emmaus story, verses 36–43 have essentially the same form: the risen Christ appears, the disciples do not recognize him, they are scolded for doubting, food is shared, they respond in wonder and joy. Here, however, Jesus' instructing of the disciples in Scriptures is delayed (vv. 44–47) to become part of the commissioning.

The similarity of form notwithstanding, verses 36–43 introduce a theme quite different from that of the Emmaus story: the corporeality of the risen Christ. In spite of the reports from the women, the two disciples who came from Emmaus, and Simon Peter, the apostles and others present are frightened, thinking they are seeing a spirit, that is, an apparition or ghost (cf. Matt. 14:26). Ignatius, a second-century bishop of Antioch, paraphrased the expression, "See that I am not a bodiless ghost" *(Epistle to Smyrneans* 3:2). In our language, we might say that the disciples thought they were encountering the dead, not the living. Jesus offering his body for examination and eating fish in their presence constitute a dramatic double insistence. First, the Christian faith does not embrace the Greek notion of the immortality of the soul, that is to say, that there is an indestructible element of human life, a soul or spirit, which comes into the body at birth and returns to God at death. Rather, the gospel teaches that Jesus died and God raised him from the dead, and the hope of believers takes its shape from that central affirmation. Of course, Jesus' very palpable presence after he had died creates special questions for faith. Paul, for example, heard and tried to answer such questions as "How are the dead raised? With what kind of body do they come?" (I Cor. 15:35). Luke is not addressing the issue of the resurrection of believers, but the matter is pertinent here in that some persons reason from a general idea of the immortal soul which all possess to an explanation of Jesus' resurrection. Luke wants to say with his accent on the physicality of Jesus' presence that the resurrection of Christ will not fit the old notion of immortality. God has acted in a unique way in raising Jesus.

The second insistence in Jesus' unusual presentation of himself to the disciples is that the risen Christ is the Jesus who died. This identification is critical, not just for theology but also for defining the nature of the Christian life. If the Jesus who died belongs to the historical past but the one disciples now follow is the eternal Christ, then the Christian life can take on forms of spirituality that are without suffering for others, without a cross, without any engagement of issues of life in this world, all the while expressing devotion to a living, spiritual Christ. The Gospels say no to such a definition of discipleship. Even Paul, whose letters make few references to the life of the historical Jesus, insisted on joining crucifixion with resurrection. He proclaimed Christ crucified (I Cor. 1:23; Gal. 3:1); the risen Lord of the church had nail scars in his hands. This is Luke's point here: "See my hands and my feet" (v. 39) is Christ's word to the church. Easter is forever joined to Good Friday, and to follow the risen Christ is to follow the one who bore the cross. Perhaps some small realization of this truth was beginning to dawn on the disciples whom Luke describes with a phrase both beautiful and realistic: they "disbelieved for joy" (v. 41).

As stated above, verses 44–49 contain instruction, commission, and promise. The instruction is not new but rather stresses continuity between the words of the risen Christ and the historical Jesus ("These are my words which I spoke to you, while I was still with you," v. 44) and between the historical Jesus and the Old Testament Scriptures ("that everything written about me in the law of Moses and the prophets and the psalms must be fulfilled," v. 44). More is involved here than simply prophecy and fulfillment; that the gospel is in continuity with what God has been doing and planning in the Jewish Scriptures is repeatedly underscored by Luke. From the beginning when Mary and Joseph did all things according to the law of Moses (2:21–40)

290

until the Christian preachers drew their messages from the Old Testament (Acts 2:16–36), Luke has reminded the reader of the consistent faithfulness of God. That Jerusalem was to be the center from which the gospel was to go to the nations (v. 47) was dictated by Scripture (Isa. 2:3). But this understanding of Scripture was not already in the disciples' minds; the risen Christ opened their minds to understand them (v. 45; cf. comments at vv. 25–27). It was this understanding of the Jewish Scriptures, that they bore witness to Christ, which constituted the heart of the earliest Christian preaching, according to Acts.

The commission of the disciples, like their instruction, was rooted in the Jewish Scriptures ("Thus it is written," v. 46). To say that "it is written" is the equivalent of saying, "It has been God's plan all along." In other words, the new is not new but is the old properly interpreted. The plan of God already set forth in Scripture contains a message and an offer that constitute the charter of the Christian mission. The message is that the Christ (Messiah) should suffer and on the third day rise from the dead (v. 46). The offer is the gift of repentance and forgiveness of sins (v. 47; Acts 2:38; 3:19; 5:31; 11:18; 17:30). For a fleshing out of this message, see Peter's sermon on the day of Pentecost: Acts 2:14–36 is the message; verses 37–41 extend the offer. That this message and offer should go to all nations was not a later development of the Christian mission only after Israel (though not all) rejected the gospel. On the contrary, says Luke, the mission to the world was God's plan from the beginning: "It is written . . . that repentance and forgiveness of sins should be preached in his name to all nations" (vv. 46–47). To be sure, the disciples did not so understand and so behave from the beginning. It took repeated revelations and proddings by the Holy Spirit for even the apostles to realize that God accepts from every nation those who turn to God. In fact, in the message and the offer are couched the first two major problems with which the church had to struggle: coming to terms with the idea of a suffering and dying Messiah and accepting non-Jews into the fellowship without distinction. After twenty centuries, preaching a crucified Christ and accepting all people equally continue as problems haunting the corners of the church, awaiting full and free resolution.

Jesus knew that neither the message nor the universal offer would fit the natural inclinations of his followers. They are not ready to preach a crucified and risen Messiah and they are not

291

ready to look favorably on an audience from all nations. They must wait, then, for the promise, the promise of power from God, the Holy Spirit (v. 49). God will empower them for the task, but they are not yet ready even to receive that power. As Luke continues the story in Acts, their waiting was for fifty days, from Easter to Pentecost, a period filled with further experiences with the risen Christ, worship, and prayer (Acts 1:1-14). We will not here continue the story beyond the Gospel, except to note the term describing the Holy Spirit: power. The three New Testament writers who speak most about the Holy Spirit are John, Paul, and Luke. For John, the Spirit is the continuation of Christ's presence in the church, leading, reminding, teaching, comforting. For Paul, the Spirit creates in us the Christian life and equips us with gifts for ministry. For Luke, the Spirit empowers the church for its mission in the world. Of the three accents, oversimply stated, to be sure, Luke's has been for the church the most unsettling, for, according to Luke, the Holy Spirit has moved the church into areas in which it otherwise would not have gone and into activities in which it otherwise would not have engaged. Power disturbs, and yet it is not usually until afterward in reflection that we relate disturbances to the Holy Spirit.

Luke 24:50-53
The Blessing and Departure

Luke is the only Evangelist to describe the final departure of Jesus as a specific event with time and place. His departure is implied in Matt. 28:16-20 in the commissioning scene on a mountain in Galilee. Mark has no departure, unless one accepts the questionable longer ending (Mark 16:9-20) which has, at verse 19, "was taken up into heaven, and sat down at the right hand of God." The Fourth Gospel contains a lengthy farewell section (John 13—17) which actually precedes the account of the death and resurrection. In that farewell, especially in the prayer, Jesus is perceived as being with his disciples and yet already glorified and with God (John 17:9-19). The strikingly different way Luke handles the narrative of Jesus beginning with the crucifixion is that he treats as separate episodes the

292

crucifixion, the resurrection, the forty days of appearances to his disciples (Acts 1:3), and the ascension (Acts 1:9). Other writers not only do not chronicle the forty days of appearances but they join resurrection to exaltation to God's right hand, without an ascension story. In fact, in the Gospel of John, being "lifted up" refers both to the crucifixion and to resurrection-exaltation. In other words, crucifixion, resurrection, and exaltation are viewed as one movement, most often referred to as the glorification of the Son. In noticeable contrast, Luke separates these elements into distinct episodes described as different historical moments. Many church traditions follow Luke by observing Ascension Day forty days into the Easter season and ten days before Pentecost.

Perhaps a word needs to be said about differences between the close of Luke and the beginning of Acts. According to Luke 24, the appearances of the risen Christ occur on Easter Day, with the ascension taking place on the night of that same day. In Acts 1:1-11, appearances occur for forty days prior to the ascension. Why the difference when the author is the same? We would expect an overlap in the two volumes, the second reviewing the ending of the first before continuing the story. This was and still is a common literary practice. As for Luke 24 presenting the narrative as a single-day series of events, perhaps a comment earlier is the best explanation. The whole of Luke 24 seems to be contoured for an Easter worship service, and if so, this would explain the condensation into one-day events which in Acts are related with a broader chronology. Some scribes, however, were sensitive about the difference and so omitted from verse 51 the words "and was carried up into heaven." By eliminating the ascension from Luke 24, the appearances could continue for forty days, as Acts says. A number of manuscripts omit verse 51*b*, and it does provide a more comfortable alternative (the NEB takes this course), but the weight of evidence supports the inclusion of these words. As for the difference in the place of the ascension, Luke 24:50 has Bethany, while Acts 1:12 says the disciples, following the ascension, returned from the Mount of Olives. Since Bethany is a village on the upper ridge at the edge of the Mount of Olives, there is no reason to let the difference in wording hinder the reader's progress through the narrative.

293

The departure (vv. 50-51) consists of the blessing and the ascension. The blessing is a priestly act in which Jesus places his disciples in the care and favor of God. Even before the promised Holy Spirit comes (v. 49), the disciples are assured of God's kind attention. In the language of the Fourth Gospel, Jesus has not left them orphans (John 14:18). As for the ascension, time would be better spent dealing with it as a theological image than with theories of levitation. What does Luke say when he speaks of an ascended Christ? A number of interpretations come to mind. At an elementary level, the ascension means that the period of his appearances to his followers has ended. Henceforth, the disciples are to be in a posture of anticipation, looking toward his return (Acts 1:11; 3:20–21) but in the meantime awaiting the promised power from God (v. 49). The period of the church between Jesus' departure and his return is not a desert in which believers alternate between memory and hope in an effort to sustain themselves. Both are vital for faith, to be sure, but in the meantime there is Pentecost. Pentecost completes Easter just as Easter completes Good Friday. A church without Pentecost cannot shout "He is risen" loudly enough to sustain Easter week after week. Inevitably there will come to such churches the post-Easter slump, the special efforts, some of them almost carnival, to keep attendance and participation up, and the growing cynicism of ministers who lash out at those who attend services only at Easter and Christmas. Perhaps most of all ascension means that Christ has entered into his glory (v. 26), exalted and enthroned at God's right hand. As Peter and the other apostles were soon to declare at Pentecost,

> Being therefore exalted at the right hand of God, and having received from the Father the promise of the Holy Spirit, he has poured out this which you see and hear. For David did not ascend into the heavens; but he himself says, "The Lord said to my Lord, Sit at my right hand, till I make thy enemies a stool for thy feet." Let all the house of Israel therefore know assuredly that God has made him both Lord and Christ, this Jesus whom you crucified.
>
> Acts 2:33–36

The disciples are not dejected and downcast by the departure of Christ, nor do they look longingly back to Galilee and the life they knew before he called them to follow him. Instead, they look for the power from on high, and in this hope they return to Jerusalem and to the temple, full of joy and blessing God.

With these words, Luke has come full circle. He began his

294

Gospel with a scene in Jerusalem, in the temple, at the hour of worship. Events in that opening scene generated anticipation in the reader: God is at work and something marvelous is about to happen. The reader is again in Jerusalem, in the temple, at the hour of worship. Events in this closing scene again generate anticipation: God is at work and something marvelous is about to happen.

SELECTED BIBLIOGRAPHY

BROWN, RAYMOND E. *The Birth of the Messiah: A Commentary on the Infancy Narratives in Matthew and Luke.* Garden City, N.Y.: Doubleday & Co., 1977.
————. *The Gospel According to John,* vol. 2. Anchor Bible. Garden City, N.Y.: Doubleday & Co., 1970.
BURKE, KENNETH. *Counter-Statement.* Berkeley and Los Angeles: University of California Press, 1968.
CADBURY, HENRY J. *The Making of Luke-Acts.* New York: Macmillan Co., 1927.
CAIRD, GEORGE B. *The Gospel of St. Luke.* Baltimore: Penguin Books, 1963.
CONZELMANN, HANS. *The Theology of St. Luke.* Translated by Geoffrey Buswell. New York: Harper & Brothers, 1960.
CROSSAN, JOHN D. *In Parables: The Challenge of the Historical Jesus.* New York: Harper & Row, 1973.
DANKER, FREDERICK W. *Jesus and the New Age: A Commentary on St. Luke's Gospel.* Philadelphia: Fortress Press, 1987.
DODD, C. H. *The Parables of the Kingdom.* Rev. ed. New York: Charles Scribner's Sons, 1961.
DONAHUE, JOHN R. *The Gospel in Parable: Metaphor, Narrative, and Theology in the Synoptic Gospels.* Philadelphia: Fortress Press, 1988.
DRURY, JOHN. *Luke.* New York: Macmillan Co., 1973.
————. *Tradition and Design in Luke's Gospel.* New ed. Atlanta: John Knox Press, 1977.
ELLIS, E. EARLE. *The Gospel of Luke.* Rev. ed. Greenwood, S.C.: Attic Press, 1974.
FITZMYER, JOSEPH A. *The Gospel According to Luke,* 2 vols. Anchor Bible. Garden City, N.Y.: Doubleday & Co., 1981, 1985.
FORD, J. MASSYNGBERDE. *My Enemy Is My Guest: Jesus and Violence in Luke.* Maryknoll, N.Y.: Orbis Books, 1984.
Gospel Parallels. 4th edition. Nashville: Thomas Nelson, Publishers, 1979.
Harper's Bible Dictionary. San Francisco: Harper & Row, 1985.
JERVELL, JACOB. *Luke and the People of God: A New Look at Luke-Acts.* Minneapolis: Augsburg Publishing House, 1972.
JUEL, DONALD. *Luke-Acts: The Promise of History.* Atlanta: John Knox Press, 1983.
KRIEGER, MURRAY. *A Window to Criticism: Shakespeare's Sonnets and Modern Poetics.* Princeton: Princeton University Press, 1964.
MARSHALL, I. HOWARD. *The Gospel of Luke.* Grand Rapids: Wm. B. Eerdmans Publishing Co., 1978.
MORRIS, LEON. *The Gospel According to St. Luke.* Grand Rapids: Wm. B. Eerdmans Publishing Co., 1974.
PERKINS, PHEME. *Hearing the Parables of Jesus.* New York: Paulist Press, 1981.

SCHWEITZER, ALBERT. *The Quest of the Historical Jesus.* Translated by W. Montgomery. New York: Macmillan Co., 1961.

SCHWEIZER, EDUARD. *The Good News According to Luke.* Translated by David E. Green. Atlanta: John Knox Press, 1984.

———. *Luke: A Challenge to Present Theology.* Atlanta: John Knox Press, 1982.

STEIN, ROBERT H. *An Introduction to the Parables of Jesus.* Philadelphia: Westminster Press, 1981.

TALBERT, CHARLES H. *Reading Luke: A Literary and Theological Commentary on the Third Gospel.* New York: Crossroad Publishing Co., 1982.

WILDER, AMOS N. *The Language of the Gospel: Early Christian Rhetoric.* New York: Harper & Row, 1964.

WILDER, THORNTON. *The Bridge of San Luis Rey.* New York: Harcourt, Brace & Co., 1959.